School Violence:
Fears Versus Facts

School Violence:
Fears Versus Facts

Dewey G. Cornell
Curry School of Education
University of Virginia

LAWRENCE ERLBAUM ASSOCIATES, PUBLISHERS
2006 Mahwah, New Jersey   London

Senior Acquisitions Editor: Lane Akers
Editorial Assistant: Karin Wittig-Bates
Cover Design: Tomai Maridou
Full-Service Compositor: MidAtlantic Books & Journals, Inc.

This book was typeset in 10.5/12 pt Goudy Old Style, Italic, Bold, and Bold Italic. Headings were typeset in Nueva
Bold Extended and Nueva Roman Bold.

Lawrence Erlbaum Associates, Inc., Publishers
10 Industrial Avenue
Mahwah, NJ 07430
www.erlbaum.com

Library of Congress Cataloging-in-Publication Data

Cornell, Dewey G.
  School violence : fears versus facts / Dewey G. Cornell.
    p. cm.
  Includes bibliographical references and index.
  ISBN 0-8058-5423-1 (alk. paper)—ISBN 0-8058-5424-X (alk. paper)
  1. School violence. 2. Bullying in schools—Prevention. 3. Aggressiveness in children.
  4. School shootings. I. Title.
  LB3013.3.C68 2006
  371.7'82—dc22

                                                                                  2006011754

Books published by Lawrence Erlbaum Associates are printed on acid-free paper, and their bindings
are chosen for strengh and durability.

Printed in the United States of America
10 9 8 7 6 5 4 3 2 1

Contents

Figures and Tables

Preface

My studies of youth violence began unexpectedly in 1983, when I was working as a forensic clinical psychologist for a state psychiatric hospital in Michigan. I was assigned the evaluation of a 16-year-old boy who had bludgeoned a 14-year-old girl to death in her home one day after school. The case was especially troubling because the boy had no history of violence, delinquency, or even misbehavior at school. He told me that he had never been in a fight, did not use drugs, and was not a gang member. On the contrary, he was a soft-spoken boy whose main ambition in life had been to play on his high school baseball team. An extensive battery of neurological and psychological tests administered over a period of weeks found nothing abnormal. Asked why he had so brutally murdered this girl, he simply replied, "She called me pizza-face."

With great reluctance, he explained that she had been calling him "pizza-face" for more than a month, and that other students had joined in the teasing. As the taunting went on, he became increasingly angry and clinically depressed, and began having nightmares. No one—his teachers, the school counselor, or even his baseball coach—realized what was happening, and his classmates had little understanding of the effect they were having on him. He was too ashamed to seek help; his parents were divorced, and his troubled relationships with them compounded his feelings of rejection and abandonment. In the end, he became so distraught that avenging this wrong became an obsession, even though he understood what the legal consequences would be. As more than one teenaged homicide defendant has said to me over the years, "Nothing seemed worse than what I was going through, so prison didn't seem so bad."

This case was a lesson for me in the unexpectedly powerful effects of teasing and bullying on adolescents, and the profound importance of being respected by one's peers. The girl's cruel remark was more damaging to his self-esteem than a physical beating. I found that the academic literature in psychology had a lot to say about the devastating effects of mental illness, substance abuse, and traumatic violence—but practically nothing about ordinary teasing.

After this boy was given the maximum sentence (life in prison without possibility of parole), I began a study of 72 juvenile homicide cases and puzzled over the variety of motives and circumstances that defied simple explanation. By 1986, when I joined the faculty of the Curry School of Education at the University of Virginia, crime statistics were showing that youth violence was a growing problem. I continued my research and clinical consultation in this area and, in 1993, the Virginia Youth Violence Project, which I direct, began to provide training and consultation to schools in violence prevention and safety issues.

The highly publicized school shootings of the late 1990s convinced the American public that schools were increasingly dangerous places, and schools began to tighten security and institute draconian zero tolerance policies. The specter of Columbine radically altered the social climate in schools, and all over the country students were subject to harsh disciplinary consequences for seemingly minor infractions: Kindergarten students who played cops-and-robbers during recess, a Boy Scout who accidentally left his pocket knife in his pocket, and a girl who brought a butter knife in her lunchbox were subject to suspension or expulsion from school.

The purpose of this book is to examine widespread misconceptions about the nature of youth violence and the safety of schools that have fostered a fear-based reaction to school violence. Objective studies have shown repeatedly that schools are safe places, and the level of violence in schools is actually much lower than suggested by both news reporters and academic researchers, both of whom have exaggerated the severity and pervasiveness of the problem. To be sure, there are some dangerous schools in America, but they are the exceptions; they are dangerous because they serve dangerous communities and are underfunded and understaffed.

This book addresses problems that plague all schools, no matter their demographics, such as bullying and fighting. I describe the variety of school programs that have been demonstrated in scientific studies to prevent violence and promote healthy student development, and contrast them with some popular—but ineffective—programs that continue to drain the limited resources allocated to education.

I wrote this book with several audiences in mind. First, I thought of educators—teachers, administrators, counselors, psychologists, and other staff members—who work in our nation's schools. I also thought of my students at the University of Virginia and other students in psychology, education, sociology, social work, law enforcement, and public policy. In writing each chapter, however, I frequently found that I was thinking of parents and what I would like them to know. I have had many occasions to interview the parents of an adolescent who has been arrested for murder, and nothing is more painful to them than to contemplate what they might have done differently.

Parents must not overlook or disregard signs of depression or serious mental disorder in their children, and they must be willing to seek help when a child expresses ideas that are suicidal, homicidal, or delusional. Parents must actively supervise their children and understand the dangers posed by access to weapons and drugs. They need to be better informed about the effects of entertainment violence on their children's attitudes and values. And they must take teasing and bullying seriously.

As with any book written for multiple audiences, it is inevitable that some chapters will please some readers more than others. Scholars may want more details of scientific studies and more extensive statistical evidence, while parents and school administrators may want more emphasis on practical recommendations. I will leave it to the readers to choose what sections they want to read lightly, but in several places I felt it was necessary to provide sufficient detail to clarify important points and refute some of the prevalent misconceptions about school violence.

I hesitated to use the term "school violence" in the title of this book because it might imply that there is a certain form of violence intrinsic to schools or that violence in schools is different from violence taking place outside of schools. In fact, the focus on violence in schools is artificial, since violent acts by young people can occur in any setting. Nevertheless, public concern about violence in schools has had a tremendous impact on American educational policies and practices, and so school violence has become a new construct with social and psychological significance that must be addressed. Readers will find chapters on entertainment violence and the role of guns in violence that might seem out of place in a book concerned with school violence; on the contrary, these are critical environmental factors that influence youth violence across settings.

There are case examples in every chapter, most of which are derived from my work as a forensic clinical psychologist. Excerpts always sacrifice the complexity of the complete case, and some details have been modified or disguised; these cases, therefore, should be viewed as illustrations rather than biographical accounts.

I have more persons to thank for ideas, advice, encouragement, and assistance in writing this book than I can list here. I wish to thank my colleagues in the Curry School, my editorial assistant, Barbara Nordin, my graduate students in the Curry Programs in Clinical and School Psychology, and my wife, Nancy.

1

The Fear of School Violence: An Overview

On the 21st of March 2005, sixteen-year-old Jeff Weise murdered his grandfather, a police officer, and used his squad car to drive to Minnesota's Red Lake High School armed with his grandfather's shotgun and a handgun. Wearing a black trench coat and protected by a bulletproof vest, he killed the school security officer and then proceeded from classroom to classroom, killing a teacher and five students and wounding at least seven others. Police officers arrived approximately eight minutes after the shooting began and opened fire on Wiese, striking him three times before he turned his own weapon on himself and committed suicide.

   The Red Lake tragedy revived a complex and multifaceted debate over violence in our schools. This book examines the questions and controversies that fuel this debate, with an emphasis on distinguishing fear from fact. The unforgettable images from schools in Paducah, Jonesboro, Columbine, and Red Lake made a deep impression on the American public. The fear of school shootings has driven school authorities to adopt harsh zero tolerance policies that expel thousands of students every year, yet have no proven effect on school safety. In an attempt to prevent teen violence and drug use, schools spend hundreds of millions of dollars every year on popular prevention programs that have been proven to be ineffective—and at the same time, ignore approaches and practices that have been shown to work.

   This chapter provides an overview, showing how each subsequent chapter addresses important research and policy issues concerning school violence. Each of these issues is introduced by showing its relevance to the Red Lake shooting, which was a paradigmatic case because it demonstrated so many of the key factors that underlie the problem of school violence. Each chapter begins with a fundamental question and an illustrative case example, then presents research evidence that answers the question.

Highly publicized, extreme incidents like the Red Lake shooting understandably stimulate concern about the level of violence in our schools. The first question that these events raise is whether our schools are safe. Chapter 2 shows how the public has been misled into believing that juvenile violence has soared and that schools have become dangerous places. On the contrary, a careful review of the facts shows that juvenile violence has declined dramatically since the early 1990s and that schools are fundamentally safe.

A second, basic question raised by the Red Lake shooting is whether such tragedies can be prevented. Studies of school shooters by the FBI and the Secret Service, synthesized in Chapter 3, reveal a combination of factors in their psychological adjustment and peer relationships that makes it possible to prevent most school shootings without elaborate security or expensive programs. Chapter 3 also shows that the most extreme school shootings—which have received the greatest attention in the news media—are atypical cases and far less likely to occur than the public perceives. Furthermore, most deaths that do occur at school involve circumstances that require a different approach to school security. Efforts to prevent the highly publicized, but actually quite rare, rampage shootings divert attention and resources from more common forms of violence. This book explains how the lessons from psychological research on youth violence can be used to improve school safety.

In addition, Chapter 3 synthesizes findings from the law enforcement studies of school shootings and applies them to the shooting at Heath High School in Paducah, Kentucky. In this case, a fourteen-year-old boy opened fire on a prayer group, killed three girls and wounded five others, then abruptly laid down his handgun and exclaimed, "I can't believe I did that—please kill me now." A psychological analysis of this boy shows the "perfect storm" of factors that led to a one-in-a-million act of violence, including bullying, mental illness, violent video games, peer encouragement, and ultimately, access to guns.

GUNS

Jeff Weise would not have killed so many people at Red Lake if he had not had guns to do it. Chapter 4 examines the role of guns in school violence. Gun violence by young people soared in the 1980s, and juvenile homicide arrests tripled by the early 1990s; this generated a wave of fear and a widespread call for action. The political controversy over gun control clouded analysis of a fundamental problem: too many juveniles had illegal, unsupervised access to handguns, and when immature and impulsive youth carry guns, even ordinary disputes and arguments can escalate into killings. In fact, more than three-fourths of the murders committed by juveniles involved guns (Cornell, 1993). The fact that guns are not the *cause* of youth violence does not mean that guns do not play a critical role in escalating aggressive behavior into more violent outcomes. Psychological research discussed in this chapter shows how access to guns can influence a young person's attitudes and decision-making process.

How many youths are bringing guns to school, and how much violence takes place that never makes it to the newspapers? Public perceptions of school violence have been skewed not just by media focus on a few extreme cases, but by researchers who used, and continue to rely on, faulty surveys and polls that exaggerate the danger of violence in schools. One of the most widely cited statistics, for example, is the claim that students bring an average of 135,000 guns to school every day. A Google search of "135,000 guns" retrieved more than 130 links in 2005, almost twenty years after the national study that generated this number was conducted. Organizations ranging from the American Sociological Association to the National Crime Prevention Council to the National School Boards Association promulgated this claim to support policy recommendations on various issues such as gun control, juvenile justice, and school safety. Despite all the attention given to this statistic, its source is not accurately reported; how it was extrapolated from a questionable school survey goes unexplained by all of these organizations. Chapter 4 unravels the mystery of where "135,000 guns" came from, and why it is unreliable.

BULLYING

Classmates admitted that Weise was often picked on and teased for his appearance and odd behavior (CNN, March 25, 2005; De, 2005). Other kids punched and kicked him in middle school, but this stopped when he grew to be over six feet tall (Rave, 2005). Even so, kids continued to make fun of him, and he was taunted so often that he frequently refused to go to school. He made no secret of his anger and contempt for those who rejected him. Like many of the other victims of bullying who lashed out by going on a lethal rampage, he was alienated from his peers and his community; he sometimes wore his hair dyed red and spiked into horns. As a member of the Red Lake band of the Chippewa tribe, he was openly critical of Native Americans and went so far as to place pro-Nazi postings on the website for the National Socialist Green Party. He called himself a "Native Nazi." He even referred to himself by the German name Todesengel, which means "angel of death." In many other school shootings, the attacker, like Wiese, appeared to be a victim of relentless bullying who responded by rejecting conventional values and becoming morbidly preoccupied with violent revenge (O'Toole, 2000).

Chapter 5 addresses bullying, which in recent years has become one of the hottest topics in academic and educational circles. A widely-cited national study reported that three out of ten students are frequently involved in bullying as a victim or bully (Nansel et al., 2001). How pervasive is bullying, and what can be done about it? There is a risk that schools will over-react to the problem of bullying, defining it so broadly that they overlook truly serious forms of bullying and implement programs that ultimately prove to be ineffective. Schools are rapidly implementing bully prevention programs, most of them modeled after the Olweus program developed in Norway. Although the federal government has endorsed and supported this program, studies of its effectiveness have yielded disappointing results (Smith et al., 2004) and there is a risk that the national movement to prevent bullying will fail. Instead, schools must do a better job of defining bullying, teaching students what bullying is, and encouraging students to seek help when they are being bullied.

ENTERTAINMENT VIOLENCE

Like other students who committed school shootings, Weise spent a lot of time playing violent video games and watching violent movies. A few months before the shooting, he created an animated video in which a gunman kills four people before taking his own life (Haga, 2005). Clearly, he had been preoccupied with thoughts of killing people long before his fantasies were translated into action.

Weise was also an avid fan of rap music with violent themes, such as the album "Self-inflicted" by a band called "Project: Deadman" (Von Sternberg, 2005). Weise especially liked the so-called "Horrorcore" school of hip-hop and posted statements on the fan Web site for Mad Insanity Records. A San Francisco-based rapper named Mars defended himself against accusations that his music affected Weise, stating, "I write a lot of crazy lyrics, but there's something wrong about anyone who blurs the line between reality and entertainment. Maybe it inspired him, but no one knows what was going on in Jeff Weise's mind" (Von Sternberg, 2005). Mars went on to say, "A lot of people who post on my Web site are a bunch of crazy kids," he said. "They write about suicide, murder, guns. But to get to a place where you do something, you have to be kind of crazy, pretty warped as a person."

Congressional debate over the influence of entertainment media violence on youth is a perennial topic that dates back to the 1950s when Congress investigated the impact of television violence. Although spokespersons for the television and movie industry have repeatedly promised to impose their own voluntary restrictions in lieu of government regulation, the level of violence children watch today is far beyond what Congress could have imagined fifty years ago; no one imagined video games in which the players can maim and kill their opponents in surrealistic scenes filled with bloody, mangled bodies. One of the most popular video games rewards players for having sex with prostitutes and then killing them (*USA Today*, July 14, 2005).

The evidence that entertainment violence can cause actual violence is reviewed in Chapter 6. Literally hundreds of scientific studies conducted around the world have led to the conclusion—officially accepted by numerous medical and scientific organizations—that exposure to entertainment violence increases a child's aggressive thoughts, feelings, and behaviors and, over time, increases the risk that a child will engage in violent criminal behavior as an adult (Anderson, Berkowitz, et al., 2003). Nevertheless, news reports of these studies have consistently minimized and discounted the findings, so that the public has not been well informed (Bushman & Anderson, 2001). Chapter 6 concludes with the arguments commonly raised by the entertainment industry's defenders, and explains why they should be dismissed.

VIOLENCE PREVENTION

Weise was a troubled young man with a history of psychiatric treatment for depression (Haga, 2005; Rave, 2005). He had attempted suicide at least once by cutting his wrists and he was being seen for mental health counseling; his dose of Prozac had been increased just a week prior to the shooting. One statement he posted on the internet reflected his suicidal feelings, "Most people have never dealt with people who have faced the kind of pain that makes you physically sick at times, makes you so depressed you can't function, makes you so sad and overwhelmed with grief that eating a bullet or sticking your head in a noose seems welcoming" (Zenere, 2005). His emotional troubles are yet another factor he shared with other students who had gone on shooting rampages; depression and suicidal behavior were identified in most of the cases studied by the Secret Service (Vossekuil et al., 2002).

Schools have implemented hundreds of programs designed to address mental health problems in students, to promote positive social behavior, and to prevent aggressive and antisocial behavior. Chapter 7 will review the evidence for effective programs and describe those that can substantially reduce fighting and other misbehavior at school. Although effective programs are available, they are often overlooked in favor of less successful approaches that seem more appealing. Chapter 8 will identify four popular but highly controversial approaches—Juvenile boot camps, Drug Abuse Resistance Education

(D.A.R.E.), Scared Straight, and school uniforms—that are widely used despite clear evidence that they are ineffective.

Student Threats

Could the school shooting at Red Lake have been prevented? The attack seemed to have been carefully planned and methodically carried out. Both the FBI (O'Toole, 2000) and Secret Service (Vossekuil et al., 2002) studies of school shootings reported that nearly all of the attackers made some of their classmates aware of their intentions and engaged in weeks or months of planning that could have been recognized as a harbinger of impending violence. Several potential school shootings have been prevented because students who knew about their classmate's intentions sought help (O'Toole, 2000).

Many Red Lake students knew that Weise had threatened to commit a violent act of revenge. Dozens of students were questioned before a grand jury about their possible knowledge of Weise's intentions, and one student was arrested as a potential co-conspirator (Louwagie, Burcum, & Collins, 2005). Weise made numerous direct and indirect references to what he might do in statements to his peers and in numerous web postings. During the 2003–04 school year Weise was questioned by police after he allegedly told classmates that he was going to "shoot up the school" (Zenere, 2005). Another sign of Weise's violent intentions was his animated video of a gunman going on a suicidal rampage, which was posted on the web for all to see.

Should the school have done more to investigate Weise and determine whether he posed a threat to others? Is school suspension—the most widely used disciplinary response to violent behavior—an effective response to a dangerous student? A new approach to investigating student threats—termed "threat assessment"—is described in Chapter 9. In 1999, the FBI's National Center for the Analysis of Violent Crime convened a national conference on school shootings and subsequently issued a report (O'Toole, 2000) concluding that schools should use a threat assessment approach to identify potentially dangerous students. In 2002, a joint report of the U.S. Secret Service and Department of Education similarly recommended that schools train threat assessment teams (Fein et al., 2002).

Although two government reports recommended that schools conduct threat assessments, there was no assurance it would work. Could the threat assessment approach used in law enforcement be adapted for schools? To answer these questions, a team of researchers at the University of Virginia, headed by the author, took on the task of field-testing threat assessment in 35 public schools (Cornell, Sheras, Kaplan, Levy-Elkon, et al., 2004; Cornell, Sheras, Kaplan, McConville, et al., 2004). The results of this field-test are reported in Chapter 8.

Why Fear Matters

The fear of violence is important because fear has driven schools to make radical changes in how schools function and how students are disciplined. Anxious school administrators have responded with strict zero tolerance policies that dictate severe punishment for even accidental violations of school rules.

Stunned by testimony on the growing juvenile crime wave, in 1994 Congress passed the Gun-Free Schools Act, which required that schools expel for one calendar year any student found to be in possession of a firearm at school. Although the law permitted local school districts to modify the expulsion on a case-by-case basis, this provision was frequently overlooked in favor of less flexible policies that mandated automatic expulsion for all infractions.

In the 1996–97 school year, 6,093 students were expelled for firearms violations (Sinclair, Hamilton, Gutman, Daft, & Bolcki, 1998). The total number of expulsions for firearms violations is misleading; many of these expulsions did not involve guns, but other kinds of weapons, such as firecrackers and pellet guns. What matters is that schools felt compelled to expel students in unprecedented numbers based on the belief that a tough zero tolerance policy was necessary to prevent violence. Students were expelled for bringing BB guns, cap guns, and other toy guns to school; in several cases, students were expelled for possession of the tiny pieces of plastic that are shaped like guns and sold as accessories to G.I. Joe action figures.

The fear of violence went beyond guns to include any object that might be construed as a weapon (Skiba & Peterson, 1999):

- A five-year-old in California was expelled after he found a razor blade at his bus stop, carried it to school, and gave it to his teacher.
- A nine-year-old in Ohio was suspended for having a 1″ knife in a manicure kit.
- A seventeen-year-old in Chicago was arrested and expelled for shooting a paper clip with a rubber band.

How many boys have shot a paper clip or a spitball at someone with a rubber band or engaged in some other playful, but mildly aggressive, mischief?

In addition to the thousands of students expelled from school on the basis of the Gun-Free Schools Act, millions more were suspended for shorter periods for other disciplinary violations. A 2000 report by the Advancement Project and The Civil Rights Project of Harvard University concluded that "Zero Tolerance has become a philosophy that has permeated our schools; it employs a brutally strict disciplinary model that embraces harsh punishment over education" (p. 3).

How many students are suspended from school in the interest of school safety? Statistics are slow to be compiled and difficult to interpret. In 2005, the National Center for Education Statistics (DeVoe et al., 2004) released its 2004 report on school crime and safety, but the data on school disciplinary actions were based on the 1999–2000 school year. In that year, 54 percent of schools took "serious disciplinary action" (suspension, expulsion, or transfer) for safety-related disciplinary offenses. Of the 1.1 million disciplinary actions taken by these schools, 83 percent involved suspensions of five or more days, after which the student could return to school. Approximately 11 percent were expulsions with no school services, and 7 percent were transfers to other programs, such as alternative schools.

What had students done to merit these punishments? The most frequent disciplinary violation was for physical fights or attacks (35%), followed by threats (22%) and possession of alcohol or illegal drugs (20%). Only six percent involved a "firearm or other explosive device." It is impossible to determine how many school disciplinary actions are a reflection of the zero tolerance model, but news reports regularly document cases that seem unnecessarily harsh:

- In Longmont, Colorado, a 10-year-old student was expelled when she turned in the small cutting knife her mother had placed in her lunchbox to cut her apple (Cauchon, 1999).
- In Alexandria, Louisiana, a second-grader was expelled for bringing her grandfather's gold-plated pocket watch to school because the watch had a tiny knife attached (Lewin, 1997).
- In Newport News, Virginia, A kindergartner was suspended for bringing a beeper from home and showing it to classmates during a field trip (CNN, 1996b).
- In Fairborn, Ohio, a 13-year-old honor student was suspended from school for 10 days for accepting two Midol tablets from a classmate. (CNN, 1996a).
- In Ocala, Florida, two boys, ages 9 and 10, were arrested and taken from school in handcuffs because they had drawn stick figures depicting a classmate being stabbed and hanged (Local6.com News, 2005).

In another case that received nationwide attention because it had been videotaped by a camera in the classroom, police in St. Petersburg, Florida arrested and handcuffed a five-year-old girl who had thrown a violent tantrum at school (Ksdk.com, 2005). Asked whether police had simply gone through the motions of arresting the girl in order to teach her a lesson, the St. Petersburg police spokesperson replied, "We don't arrest people to teach them a lesson. We arrest people if a crime occurred and the victim was responsible for that crime." (One wonders if the statement that the *victim* was responsible for the crime isn't a Freudian slip). The police spokesperson insisted that the child was deserving of arrest, asserting, "There is no minimum age for criminal culpability." However, the State Attorney's office determined that the child was too young to face criminal prosecution and the charges were dropped.

The author has received numerous appeals from parents seeking help when a school has suspended or expelled their child for a seemingly trivial violation. For example, a police officer called to report that his son, a high school senior, had been expelled from school for a weapons violation. He had gone camping over the weekend and inadvertently left a knife under the seat of his car. The school conducted a search of the parking lot the next day and someone spied the handle of the knife under the seat. Although the boy had not carried the knife into the school or threatened or endangered anyone, and even though he had a reasonable explanation for why it was in his car, in a climate of fear and zero tolerance, he was deemed to be so dangerous that he had to be expelled from school. He had hoped to become a police officer like his father, but now with an expulsion on his record, that career was no longer possible.

Consider the multiple cases in which students have been suspended, and in some cases arrested, for pointing their fingers and shouting "pow-pow" while playing games such as cops and robbers on the playground (Rutherford Institute, 2003). In previous generations, students who engaged in such behaviors might have been admonished by their teachers, but certainly not placed in handcuffs and hauled off to jail.

The arrest and expulsion of students for seemingly minor acts of mischief or misbehavior appears to be excessively punitive and unreasonable, yet this happens in every part of the United States. Despite periodic public outcry and criticism of school officials, zero tolerance punishments—which have persisted for over a decade—are not a passing phenomenon. The fear that drives zero tolerance has been fed by two biasing influences: news media attention to extreme cases that do not reflect the circumstances in most schools, and errors and exaggerations in expert opinion and academic research on youth violence. A central purpose of this book, therefore, is to identify and correct some of these errors and exaggerations, and to highlight research that demonstrates more effective and reasonable ways to prevent violence and keep schools safe.

2

Are Our Schools Safe?
From Juvenile Crime to
School Violence

The perception that our schools are unsafe grew out of a broader fear of juvenile crime. School violence is intrinsically a form of youth violence (Moeller, 2001), so it is important to understand the larger problem of violent juvenile crime, which soared in the United States during the late 1980s; juvenile homicide, in particular, more than doubled (Blumstein & Wallman, 2000). This troubling increase, which was not observed in adult crime rates, led many academics to speculate that something ominous was taking place in the younger generation that would have a permanent impact on American society.

Fortunately, the rise in juvenile violence peaked in the early 1990s and had reversed by the end of that decade. Much of the temporary increase in juvenile violence was attributed to the emergence of the crack cocaine market and the associated proliferation of drug gangs and juvenile access to handguns (Blumstein & Wallman, 2000). Unfortunately, years after juvenile crime had begun its decline, the perception remained that the nation was plagued by a new generation of lawless and violent youth. A comparatively small group of adolescents of the 1980s created a reputation for youth in general that has persisted for two decades—even though today's adolescents belong to a different generation.

There is no better example of the exaggerated fear of youth violence than the myth of the superpredator. In 1995, a Princeton criminologist and Brookings Institute scholar, John J. DiIulio, Jr., wrote a provocative and influential article for *The Weekly Standard* entitled, "The Coming of the Superpredators," in which he asserted that although "the youth crime wave has reached horrific proportions from coast to coast . . . the next class of juvenile offenders will be even worse." Based on the demographic fact that the number of teenage boys would increase substantially over the next ten years, DiIulio predicted that there would necessarily be "a sharp increase in the number of super crime-prone young males." His forecast followed a similar, but less dramatic, prediction by his former mentor, Harvard criminologist James Q. Wilson (1995).

DiIulio described the upcoming generation of superpredators as "morally impoverished" and "perfectly capable of committing the most heinous acts of physical violence for the most trivial reasons." He emphasized how frightened he was by such "stone-cold" boys when he interviewed them in jails, and how much they disturbed everyone else in the criminal justice system, from tough cops to hardened adult criminals. To underscore the seriousness of the problem, DiIulio calculated there would be 270,000 *additional* superpredators by 2010.

In 1996, DiIulio introduced the term "juvenile superpredator" to the Senate Judiciary Committee, and in his testimony opined that "the kids doing the violent crimes are more impulsively violent and remorseless than ever" (DiIulio, 1996). The same year, he co-authored a book on juvenile crime, *Body Count: Moral Poverty . . . and How to Win America's War Against Crime and Drugs,* with former Education Secretary William Bennett and the director of the Council on Crime in America, John Walters. The authors confidently asserted that America was about to experience an unprecedented crime wave committed by remorseless juvenile killers:

> America is now home to thickening ranks of juvenile 'superpredators'—radically impulsive, brutally remorseless youngsters, including ever more pre-teenage boys, who murder, assault, rape, rob, burglarize, deal deadly drugs, join gun-toting gangs and create serious communal disorders. They do not fear the stigma of arrest, the pains of imprisonment or the pangs of conscience.

The idea that America was about to experience an unprecedented crime wave by hundreds of thousands of remorseless superpredators helped fuel a massive change in the juvenile justice system. Legislatures across the nation enacted laws that hastened the transfer of juvenile offenders to adult courts so that they could receive longer sentences and modified delinquency statutes to emphasize punishment over rehabilitation for those who remained in the jurisdiction of the juvenile system (Redding, Goldstein, & Heilbrun, 2005). States also lessened juvenile confidentiality laws and gave more authority to prosecutors to seek harsher sentences.

The number of delinquency cases judicially waived to criminal court surged upwards; precise figures are elusive as many jurisdictions used automatic transfers that did not require a formal hearing. As might be expected, many more juveniles were incarcerated in adult facilities (Austin, Johnson, & Gregoriou,

2000). The number of juveniles admitted to state prisons more than doubled from 3,400 in 1985 to 7,400 in 1997, while the number of juveniles in adult jails jumped over 500 percent from 1,629 in 1984 to 9,105 in 1997.

The rush to prosecute more juveniles as adults and to incarcerate them for longer periods had no discernible effect on juvenile crime: Studies that compared states before and after they changed their laws, or that compared states with different laws, found no deterrent effect and no effect on juvenile crime (Redding & Mrozoski, 2005). On the contrary, juveniles prosecuted as adults were *more* likely to commit future crimes than their peers in the juvenile system. Exposing juveniles to adult offenders seemed only to solidify their identity as criminal offenders and increased the likelihood that they would re-offend when they were released from adult institutions. Findings such as these led the Committee on Juvenile Justice (1997) of the New York City Bar Association to conclude:

> Prosecuting more youths in the adult system, and increasing the time they will spend in adult facilities, is resoundingly unwise. Extensive research demonstrates that teenagers who are prosecuted in the adult system are more often re-arrested and are re-arrested for more serious offenses than those teenagers who are prosecuted as juveniles. Treating juveniles as adults will not serve to reduce crime or increase community safety but may actually have the opposite effect (p. 451).

More difficult to measure was the impact of the change in attitude and perceptions of public officials and legislators, who shifted public policy away from prevention and rehabilitation efforts toward the politically popular "get tough" notions that DiIulio and others advocated. As discussed in Chapter 7, the widespread—but mistaken—belief that "nothing works" in preventing juvenile delinquency led to funding cuts and the withering of treatment efforts. In the past decade, hundreds of studies have demonstrated the effectiveness of mental health treatment and crime prevention approaches with children and adolescents (Evans et al., 2005; Redding, Goldstein, & Heilbrun, 2005), but this reassuring news has yet to overcome the legacy of fear and pessimism that continues to drive public policy.

After DiIulio and others made their predictions, researchers began to protest that the idea of superpredatory youth was a myth: The pattern of juvenile violence did not support the existence of a new breed of predatory youth who would commit indiscriminate crimes without remorse. In fact, property crimes such as burglaries, auto thefts, and larcenies—which are far more prevalent than violent crimes—did not increase (Cook & Laub, 1998). Homicides increased, but only those committed with guns; murders involving knives and other weapons did not go up. And while murders of strangers increased, murders of family members did not. Most of the homicides were concentrated in a few large cities, which skewed national crime rates, but did not demonstrate a change across a whole generation. By the time these contrary findings were raised, however, the frightening but unfounded claims by DiIulio and others had already had an impact.

Perhaps the most critical evidence could not be assessed for years, which is whether juvenile violent crime would continue to increase as predicted. By the time that the superpredator theory became widely known, juvenile homicide and other violent crime was beginning to decline, and by the end of the 1990s it was clear that the dire forecasts were wrong.

The most forceful repudiation of the superpredator myth came from Franklin Zimring, a professor of law and director of the Earl Warren Legal Institute at the University of California at Berkeley. Referring to the predictions made by Wilson (1995) and DiIulio (1996), Zimring stated in his book, *American Youth Violence*, that "the current argument that a fixed percentage of a population of males will constitute a predatory menace in the year 2010 is a classic case study of compounded distortion" (Zimring, 1998, p. 60).

Zimring went on to explain that DiIulio's (1995) prediction that 6 percent of the males in the surging juvenile population will be superpredators was based on a famous study of delinquency (Wolfgang, Figlio, & Sellin, 1972) that examined court records for all 9,945 boys who were born in Philadelphia in 1945. The researchers found that about 6 percent of the boys in this age cohort accumulated five or more police contacts by age 18, and that these boys accounted for about 60 percent of all offenses, and about one-third of the violent crime, committed by all 9,945 boys in the group. Other studies found that a similarly small proportion of boys are chronic offenders who generally commit a high proportion of offenses.

According to Zimring, (1998), one of DiIulio's mistakes was to assume that the six percent found among boys who were born in 1945 and grew up in Philadelphia was a proportion that could be generalized to any community and any generation. It seems particularly dubious that the six percent figure found in the Philadelphia study could be applied to the nation's entire population of boys growing up fifty years later: No law of nature or quality of society fixes the proportion of juveniles who will become chronic delinquents at six percent.

Another mistake was to characterize the six percent of boys who were chronic delinquents as superpredators. There is no evidence that six percent of the Philadelphia boys who turned eighteen in 1963 were a group of heartless robbers, rapists, and murderers. Certainly the juvenile violent crime rate was much lower in Philadelphia in 1963 than in the 1990s. Furthermore, many of Philadelphia's chronic juvenile delinquents had not been arrested for *any* violent crimes, but simply got into trouble repeatedly for offenses such as truancy, underage drinking, and larceny.

Moreover, Zimring (1998) noted that DiIulio had ignored obvious contradictions between his conclusions and readily available facts. For instance, DiIulio pointed to the increasing level of violent juvenile crime already evident by the early 1990s to support his call for action, but this increase had nothing to do with an increasing juvenile population, as the teenage population actually *declined* during these years. Clearly, violent juvenile crime was being accelerated by factors other than the size of the population, and these factors were more powerful than demographic influences—which makes it unreasonable to speculate that violent juvenile crime would soar in the next ten years based on population size alone.

Finally, DiIulio's (1996, p. 1) prediction that "By the year 2010, there will be approximately 270,000 more juvenile superpredators on the streets than there were in 1990" was based on a flawed calculation. DiIulio based his estimate on the demographic prediction that the number of boys under 18 in the United States would grow from 32 million to 36.5 million by 2010. This would mean an increase of 4.5 million and six percent of this number would be 270,000. This way of estimating how many extra superpredators will be on the streets plaguing society, however, is not based on the number of *teenage* boys, but the total number of *all* boys under age 18, extending down to infants—a distortion that Zimring (1998, p. 49) wryly refers to as "the case of the terrifying toddlers." "His prediction wasn't just wrong," Zimring later said, "it was exactly the opposite. His theories on superpredators were utter madness" (Becker & Pedrick, 2001).

All of the debate about the numbers of superpredators begs a more basic question: What is a superpredator? Where did the term "superpredator" come from, and what does it mean? The term cannot be found in psychiatry's diagnostic manual of mental disorders (DSM-IV-TR, American Psychiatric Association 2000) and studies of superpredators cannot be found in the academic, medical, or criminological journals—because it has no basis in scholarly research. The term is generally credited to DiIulio, but he published no studies demonstrating that such youth exist or what diagnostic criteria might be used to distinguish them from other delinquents. Instead, he (DiIulio, 1995, 1996) variously attributed the origin of the term to a prison inmate he interviewed and to a reporter's use of the term in a story about juvenile gangs he read in the *Boston Globe*.

In 1999, DiIulio's collaborator Wilson conceded that the prediction of a virulent juvenile crime wave was wrong, "So far, it clearly hasn't happened. . . . That is a good indication of what little all of us know about criminology" (Steinberg, 1999). Ultimately, both the U.S. Surgeon General (U.S. Department of Health and Human Services, 2001) and the U.S. Department of Justice (2000) issued reports declaring the juvenile superpredator to be a myth.

In 2001, shortly after he was appointed director of the new White House Office of Faith-Based and Community Initiatives, DiIulio acknowledged that he wished he had never developed the superpredator theory and become a leading advocate of sending violent juveniles to prison. In the *New York Times* (Becker & Pedrick, 2001, February 9), he is quoted as saying, "If I knew then what I know now, I would have shouted for prevention of crimes."

Although the predicted juvenile crime wave never materialized, researchers are still tempted to draw upon the fear of youth violence to bolster their arguments. For example, in the 2004 *Handbook of School Violence*, a researcher (Lupton-Smith, 2004) attempted to justify the need for peer mediation programs in schools by citing a report from the University of Colorado's Center for Study and Prevention of Violence that stated, "The adolescent homicide rate has more than doubled in the past several years." The adolescent homicide rate had doubled over a period of about five years when, in 1994, the Colorado center published its report. Even though there is often a time lag of several years for most crime (and education) statistics, there is no justification for citing a report that is ten years out of date when more current data are readily available.

Juvenile arrests for homicide declined steadily from a high point of 3,284 in 1993 to just 783 by 2003 (Federal Bureau of Investigation, 1984–2004). The homicide *rate* (corrected for the changing size of the juvenile population) for 14- to 17-year-olds actually dropped from 31.3 arrests per 100,000 in 1993 to 9.0 arrests per 100,000 in 2002 (Bureau of Justice Statistics, 2004). In other words, rather than doubling, the juvenile homicide rate actually dropped by more than two-thirds.

THE SCHOOL SURVEY HOAX

The belief that America had produced a generation of young superpredators dovetailed nicely with the perception that schools had become dangerous places. Each report of another violent incident at a school seemed to confirm a radical change in the safety of all schools. In reaction to one incident in a New York school, the cover of *Newsweek* magazine (March 9, 1992) brazenly presented "A report from America's classroom killing grounds." The use of hyperbole such as "killing grounds" is an obvious attempt to reach a sensational conclusion.

The perception that schools were dangerous seemed to be confirmed by a widely publicized report on school problems (O'Neill, 1994) that compared a teacher survey of school problems conducted in 1940 with a more recent survey. The 1940 survey of "top problems of public schools" listed: (1) Talking, (2) Gum chewing, (3) Making noise, (4) Running in the halls, (5) Butting in line, (6) Wearing improper clothing, and (7) Not putting paper in wastebaskets. The harmless transgressions of 1940s students were in stark contrast to the modern list: (1) Drug abuse, (2) Alcohol abuse, (3) Pregnancy, (4) Suicide, (5) Rape, (6) Robbery, and (7) Assault.

The two surveys seemed to be compelling evidence of the sinister nature of the new generation of students and proof that today's schools are hopelessly crime-ridden. Social commentators pounced on the report; well-known political pundits such as William Bennett, Rush Limbaugh, Carl Rowan, and George Will used the lists to support their judgments about the state of American education and society. Authorities in other fields, from evangelist Billy Graham to former Dallas Cowboys football coach Tom Landry to financier Michael Milken, also used the lists to support their arguments. Ann Landers and Dear Abby quoted them, as did Barbara Bush and numerous politicians, ministers, and social commentators. The lists appeared in *Time, Newsweek, The New York Times,* and *The Wall Street Journal,* and all the major television networks aired them (O'Neill, 1994a, 1994b).

None of the authorities or news agencies that cited these surveys explained how they were conducted or accurately identified where they came from. In the fast-paced information age, when complex stories are routinely compressed into sound bites, there was no mention of the report's methodology—not even the size of the samples, where the surveys were administered, or who conducted the study. Once one news report cited the study without explaining its origin, others simply cited that report without determining its source.

A skeptical professor at Yale University, Barry O'Neill, thought that the existence of two surveys with such markedly contrasting results—and no description of their origin—was suspicious. He began tracking down references to the study, and in the process found over 400 examples of people quoting it. Curiously, there were over 250 different versions of the lists, some with different items or ranked in a different order.

Eventually, O'Neill traced the lists to their source, T. Cullen Davis of Fort Worth, Texas (O'Neill, 1994a, 1994b). Mr. Davis was a wealthy oil businessman who, in 1977, was arrested and charged with the murder of his ex-wife's boyfriend and her daughter. After he was acquitted, he became a born-again Christian who lobbied against sex education and the teaching of evolution in Fort Worth schools. Sometime around 1981, he constructed the lists as part of his campaign. The lists circulated among authors and speakers in the Christian conservative movement until 1985, when *Harper's Magazine* gave them national publicity. Soon others began to cite the surveys, and in the process, made changes here and there that made the lists shorter and more compelling. In 1987, Senators John Glenn and Christopher Dodd read them in a hearing and on the Senate floor, and they appeared in the *Congressional Quarterly.*

Asked how he arrived at the lists, Mr. Cullen told O'Neill, "They weren't done from a scientific survey. How did I know what the offenses in the schools were in 1940? I was there. How do I know what they are now? I read the newspapers" (p. 48, O'Neill, 1994a).

The story of the concocted school surveys was documented in 1994 by O'Neill (1994b) in a professional journal, *School Administrator*. The deception was revealed to the public in an article by *The New York Times Magazine* in March 1994 (O'Neill, 1994a) and other news reports followed. The National Education Association further exposed the report's mythical status in paid advertisements it published in *The Washington Post* and other newspapers. More than a decade later, details of the hoax can be found on Web sites that feature urban legends and on O'Neill's own Web site http://www.polisci.ucla.edu/faculty/boneill.

O'Neill felt that the lists reflected the conviction of every generation that the next generation represented a decline in traditional standards and values, and so would prove to be irresistible. For this reason, he predicted that the lists would continue to be cited, despite being publicly discredited.

O'Neill was right. More than a decade after being repeatedly exposed as false, the school survey report continues to be cited. In 2005, an amazingly diverse range of organizations posted web articles that touted the lists to support their views. Here are a few examples:

- Green at Work, an environmental organization that publishes a business magazine (Bonda, 2005)
- International Agency for Economic Development, a charitable organization working with the United Nations
- Leadership University, which describes itself as part of the "Telling the Truth Project"
- Modern Reformation Online, a theology publication (Hart, 1994)
- The Reason Foundation, a public policy think tank (Volokh with Snell, no date)
- Turn Off the Violence (2005), a nonprofit organization that wants to reduce children's exposure to media violence.

OUR SCHOOLS ARE SAFE

The question, "How safe are our schools?" can be addressed in multiple ways, but the answers should be based on facts rather than images of mass shootings. Although some schools are less safe than others, the facts consistently show that American schools are remarkably safe.

One way to answer the question, "How safe are our schools?" is to compare how many violent crimes occur in schools versus other locations. The Virginia

State Police (2005) report the locations of crimes for each person arrested in their state. Although Virginia is only one state (national data of this type are not available), the results in Figure 2–1 make it clear that violent crimes are far more likely to occur outside of school than at school. Overall, there were 21,982 arrests of persons for serious violent crimes (murder, aggravated assault, forcible sexual assault, and robbery) in 2004; the most common place for a violent crime to occur was at a home or residence (44%), followed by a highway or road (22%), and then some type of commercial establishment such as a store, restaurant, or office (15%). Only 621 of these crimes—2.8 percent—happened at schools or colleges. The Virginia data combine crimes taking place at all schools, including college campuses, so the percent of arrests in K–12 public schools is even lower.

One limitation of arrest statistics is that many crimes are not reported to the police, or even if reported, do not result in an arrest. Arrest statistics are good sources of information about crime trends, e.g., how much crime is increasing or decreasing, or whether crime occurs more in one place than another, but they are not the best indicator of the total amount of crime that occurs.

To determine how much crime occurs, it is necessary to survey people directly and ask whether they have been victims of some kind of crime. Since

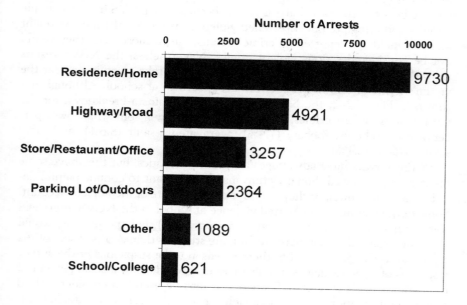

FIGURE 2–1.   Locations of serious violent crimes in Virginia.

1973 the U.S. Department of Justice has administered the National Crime Victimization Survey (NCVS) for this purpose (U.S. Department of Justice, 2004). Twice each year, U.S. Census Bureau personnel interview a nationally representative sample of 42,000 households comprising nearly 76,000 persons ages 12 or older. Each person is asked standard questions about the kinds of crimes, if any, they have experienced, regardless of whether these crimes were reported to the police.

In July 2005, the Bureau of Justice Statistics (2005) released results for 2003. According to the NCVS, there were 4.9 million crimes of violence in the United States in 2003, including 1.5 million acts of physical violence and 3.4 million threats or attempts to commit violence. There are some important differences between the NCVS and Virginia statistics. The NCVS includes a broader range of violent crimes, such as simple assaults and threats of violence that would not have been included in the Virginia arrest statistics, and the NCVS also uses different location categories than the Virginia State Police (both figures combine some categories used in the original reports in order to make the charts easier to compare). In addition, the NCVS only surveys persons age 12 and older, so that the crime victimization rates of younger children, which are generally lower than for adolescents, are not included.

The NCVS results in Figure 2–2 suggest a higher proportion of violence in schools (14%) than the Virginia arrest data (2.8%) in Figure 2–1. The difference between the two charts is largely because the NCVS includes simple assaults and attempted or threatened violence, which are the most frequent kinds of incidents reported by crime victims, but in most cases they would not be considered serious violent crimes. Nevertheless, the NCVS results show that violent crimes are much more likely to take place in or near the victim's home or another residence, as opposed to at school. Although not shown in Figure 2–2, the NCVS report also contains a breakdown for the most serious violent crimes, and these results show a somewhat lower percentage for schools: robbery (7.4%), aggravated assault (8.6%), and rape/sexual assault (2.1%).

Victim surveys have advantages over arrest statistics, but they have some disadvantages, as well: Some victims may be reluctant to confide painful details to an interviewer, or they may give an inaccurate or incomplete account. Some of the victims who reported violence at school in the NCVS interviews were adults (teachers, administrators, parents, etc.), but the majority would have been students since there are far more students than adults at school. As discussed in Chapters 4 and 5, there is reason to be suspicious of the survey responses of some teenagers; it only takes exaggerations by a small percent of respondents to skew results. Therefore, it may be useful to consider a third source of information about school violence, one that is not vulnerable to respondent bias: homicides.

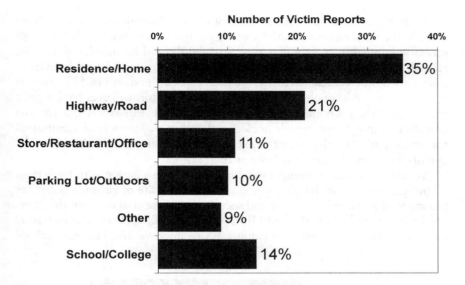

FIGURE 2–2.   Locations of violent crimes in the United States.

Although homicides represent only the most extreme cases, they are often used as a barometer of violent crime, because data on homicides, while not flawless, are more accurate and complete than other crime statistics. According to a study conducted by the Centers for Disease Control and Prevention (CDC; cited in DeVoe et al., 2004), there were 234 school-associated homicides of students from July 1992 through June 2000. The CDC defined school-associated homicide broadly to include all violent deaths of students that occurred at school or on school property, at a school-sponsored event, or traveling to or from school or a school-sponsored event. (In this book "at school" will be defined the same way unless stated otherwise.) Although 234 deaths seems like a lot, it is useful to compare this number to the 24,406 homicides of persons ages 5 to 19 during roughly the same time period. In other words, over the eight years from 1992 to 2000, there were 103 times more deaths outside of school than at school; fewer than one percent of homicides of school-age children took place at school.

The number of school homicides can be placed in perspective by considering other causes of death in the student-age population. In 1999—the year of the Columbine shooting—17 students were murdered at school (National School Safety Center, 2005). In that same year, however, there were 21,373 deaths of persons 5 to 19 years old (Anderson, 2001), so that school homicides constituted .0008 percent of the total deaths.

As shown in Figure 2–3, the number of school homicides is miniscule compared to the other causes of death for young persons (Anderson, 2001). Although school administrators may fear that a student could be murdered at their school, it is far more realistic to be concerned about accidental injuries—especially motor vehicle accidents—which caused the death of 575 times as many students. Although very few school administrators will ever have a child murdered at their school, most high school principals will experience the loss of a student in a motor vehicle accident. Another way for school administrators to look at this is that they can expect about 575 student deaths due to accidents for every student murdered at their school.

Although schools are comparatively safe places, in a nation with more than 50 million students in 100,000 schools, even a low rate of violence generates too many victims. School safety and security is an essential concern that cannot be minimized or overlooked (Trump, 1998, 2000). School administrators have a legitimate interest in seeking ways to improve and maintain school

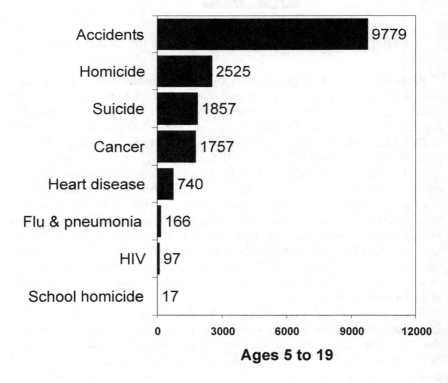

FIGURE 2–3.   Selected causes of death in 1999.

safety. From this perspective, it is reassuring to see that violent crimes in schools are in fact decreasing. According to the latest available information from the National Center on Education Statistics (DeVoe et al., 2004), NCVS interviews with 12 to 18 year old victims of crime show that serious violent crime (robbery, aggravated assault, rape and other sexual assaults) in public schools declined substantially from 1995 to 2003. In 1995, approximately 7 tenths of one percent of students reported criminal victimization at school in the past 6 months, in comparison to just 2 tenths of one percent in 2003.

When simple assaults are added to the NCVS crime figures to measure overall violent crime, there is a similar pattern: the 1995 rate was 3 percent of students and the 2003 rate was 1.3 percent. In other words, there appears to have been a two-thirds reduction in the number of students who report being victims of violent crime at school from 1995 to 2003. Chapter 7 will review some of the violence prevention efforts in schools that contributed to this reduction.

Despite the overall safety of American schools—and the improvements that were observed from 1995 to 2003—a high profile incident can radically change public perceptions. A Gallup poll taken after the Columbine shooting found that two-thirds of Americans believed that a similar incident was "very likely" or "somewhat likely" to happen in their own community (Saad, 1999). Almost one in five students reported being frightened enough to stay home from school, and 5 percent said their school actually closed for a day or more in response to a threat (Gallup, 1999). Would it have helped for parents and students to understand that heart disease kills 44 times more students, and that almost ten times as many students die of the influenza and pneumonia, than are murdered at school? Perhaps cold statistics would not lessen the understandable fears of those who watched the terrible scenes of violence at Columbine High School, but school authorities and public officials should be prepared to take a more objective and less emotional approach.

3

What Caused the School Shootings?

October 1, 1997
Pearl High School
Pearl, Mississippi

16-year-old Luke Woodham shot and killed his mother, then drove to school and opened fire in the school lobby, killing a former girlfriend and another girl, and wounding seven other students. Five other teenagers were charged with conspiracy and accessory to murder. Some students brought cameras to school because they were warned that something was going to happen in the lobby. Woodham fled the scene, but surrendered to authorities in the school parking lot.

December 1, 1997
Heath High School
West Paducah,
Kentucky

14-year-old Michael Carneal opened fire in the school lobby, shooting into a group of about 40 students who were participating in a morning prayer circle. Three girls were killed and five other students were wounded. After firing eight shots, Carneal put down his handgun and surrendered to the student leader of the prayer group and the school principal. Many students, including at least two of the victims, had been warned not to be in the school lobby that morning. In addition to the handgun, Carneal brought four rifles wrapped in a blanket into the lobby and offered them to a group of boys who had helped plan the shooting. The boys refused the guns, but stood nearby and watched.

March 24, 1998
Westside Middle
School
Jonesboro, Arkansas

11-year-old Andrew Golden pulled the school fire alarm and then joined 13-year-old Mitchell Johnson in an ambush attack on students and teachers as they exited the school building. Firing hunting rifles from a hill about 100 yards behind the school, the two boys shot fifteen persons, killing four girls and a teacher. After a few minutes, the boys fled the scene but were apprehended by police as they headed toward the Johnson family van, which Mitchell had taken. In the weeks prior to the shootings, both boys had made boastful statements to other students that something big was going to happen and that some people were going to be killed.

May 21, 1998
Thurstone High
School
Springfield, Oregon

15-year-old Kip Kinkle murdered his parents at home and then went to school, where he opened fire in the school cafeteria, killing two and wounding twenty-one others, before being wrestled down by students. In a police interrogation he reported a history of hearing voices telling him to kill. Two days prior to the shootings, Kinkle had been found to have a pistol in his locker. He had been arrested and charged with a felony, then released to his parents.

May 20, 1999
Columbine High
School
Littleton, Colorado

18-year-old Eric Harris and 17-year-old Dylan Klebold planned to set off two 20-pound propane bombs in the school cafeteria and then shoot survivors as they fled the building. When their bombs failed to explode, they went on a shooting rampage in the school, killing twelve students and a teacher before committing suicide. For approximately a year prior to the shooting, the boys had prepared for the attack, purchasing weapons and constructing at least 90 bombs. They made numerous threats to kill their classmates and posted angry statements on a Web site such as, "God, I can't wait til I can kill you people. Feel no remorse, no sense of shame. I don't care if I live or die in the shoot-out. All I want to do is kill and injure as many of you . . . as I can. . . ." (Columbine Review Commission, 2001).

Fears of school violence soared after a series of highly publicized school shootings that started in 1997 with the Pearl, Mississippi shooting and culminated in the 1999 Columbine tragedy. After each incident, the public was exposed to numerous images of bloody victims and interviews with traumatized survivors. Nationwide television coverage of Columbine began during the incident, while students were still hiding in the school and police were trying to locate Harris and Klebold.

Exhaustive media coverage fostered the perception that America's schools had become dangerous places. As mentioned in Chapter One, shortly after the Columbine shooting, a Gallup poll found that two-thirds of Americans believed that a similar incident was "very likely" or "somewhat likely" to happen in their community (Saad, 1999). More than one-third of teenagers aged 13–17 agreed that there were students at their school who were "potentially violent enough to cause a situation such as the one that occurred at Columbine High School" (Gallup, 1999).

One year later, a poll by the Pew Research Center (Nagy & Danitz, 2000) found that 71 percent of parents felt that the Columbine shooting had changed their view of how safe their child was at school. Fewer than half (40%) of parents regarded their child as "very safe" at school, and 50 percent described their child as only "somewhat safe." Because the perception of school safety is easily influenced by frightening but isolated incidents like school shootings, it is useful to consider how often such incidents actually occur. In a nation with 119,000 schools, it is easy to focus attention on a few schools where these shootings occurred and lose perspective on the thousands of schools where no such incidents have taken place.

HOW MANY HOMICIDES OCCUR AT SCHOOL?

The National School Safety Center maintains a record of school homicides in its "Report on School Associated Violent Deaths" (NSSC, 2005). This report consists of a list of incidents compiled from newspaper clipping services dating back to the 1992–93 school year. The NSSC report describes a surprisingly large number of cases: For the twelve complete school years from 1992–93 to 2003–04, there were 347 incidents that resulted in 400 deaths.

Although the NSSC report is a good source of information about school homicide trends, the cases listed in the report must be reviewed carefully because they span a wide variety of circumstances. These 347 incidents do not mean that 347 angry students charged into schools on a rampage like at Columbine. On the contrary, the overwhelming majority of cases involved situations quite unlike those in the high profile cases. Not only are homicides extremely rare events in schools, the most highly publicized homicides are the least representative.

Nearly three-fourths (289) of the deaths were shootings, fourteen percent (57) were stabbings, and five percent (20) were beatings, and the remainder a variety of other types. Beyond a simple breakdown by cause of death, it is difficult to classify the incidents into neat, nonoverlapping categories. Some incidents occurred at school, while others occurred off school grounds. Some deaths were homicides and others were suicides. And while the public image of a school homicide focuses on student perpetrators and student victims, this was not always the case. In some cases the victim was a student, in other cases the perpetrator was a student, in some cases both the victim and perpetrator were students, and in still other cases neither the victim nor the perpetrator was a student. An analysis of the diverse circumstances of these incidents can shed light on the different safety and security issues that schools must consider.

The NSSC report includes deaths that were *associated* with school, but did not necessarily occur *at* school. Incidents may have occurred near school property, at a school-related function, or while students were traveling to or from school. Altogether, only 233 (58%) of the deaths took place on school property, either during the school day or at a school function after regular school hours.

Deaths that take place off school property pose especially difficult safety and security issues. Twenty-four deaths took place on a school bus, and 143 others took place off school property. In one case, a 15-year-old middle school student was stabbed by another student at the school bus stop after he got off the bus. In another incident, a 15-year-old boy and his girlfriend rode to his home on the school bus, and after they went into the house, he shot himself in the head. In still another case, a 19-year-old was suspended from school and two hours later he was shot and killed by a gang member approximately one mile from school. Such cases raise questions about the boundaries of school responsibility for student violence. Perhaps they should not even be considered "school-associated deaths."

Even more difficult to prevent are cases in which a student was a victim of robbery or rape while traveling to or from school. In these cases students were victims of adult predators who had no relationship to the school. Although schools are often regarded as legally responsible for students as they travel to and from school, it is not clear how far this responsibility extends and what schools can do to prevent these sorts of violent events.

A further complication is that not all of the deaths included in the report were murders; there were at least 72 suicides, some by students and others by school staff members. Such cases call for preventive measures such as training staff to recognize signs of depression.

Some incidents did not involve students in any way. In one case a superintendent hung himself at a high school and was found by the custodian. There were multiple cases in which an estranged husband came to school and shot his wife, and several incidents in which a school employee (or former employee) killed a supervisor. Such cases fall into the general domain of workplace violence rather than school safety.

In some cases the deaths occurred on school property but had little association with the school. For example, a 24-year-old man was stabbed to death during the night on a school tennis court, a hotel security guard shot himself on a school's athletic field, and a gun battle erupted between rival gang members, ages 21 and 22, on a street leading to a school. Neighborhood crime obviously can intrude upon schools, but this does not reflect a lapse in school safety. Overall, there were 56 deaths in which neither victims nor perpetrators were students. Only 226 (57%) of the 400 deaths were homicides of students and only 170 (43%) were homicides committed by students. There were only 18 rampage-type incidents in which a student killed more than one person or killed at least one person and attempted to kill others. With this information as background, consider some of the common myths about school homicides.

MYTH 1: Student homicides are increasing.

FACTS: Incidents of student-perpetrated homicides at school peaked in the 1992–93 school year. There were actually more incidents in the years prior to the 1997 shooting at Pearl High School. Media attention to later shootings created the perception that school homicides were increasing.

MYTH 2: Student homicides are likely to occur at any school.

FACTS: The intense publicity given to several school shootings created the false impression that such crimes were so pervasive that they were likely to occur in one's own community. Judgments of the likelihood of a dangerous event are often subjective and can be influenced more by emotion than by an objective consideration of statistical probability. Humans instinctively pay more attention to events and images that provoke fear or outrage than to dispassionate numbers. We judge an event by its emotional salience rather than by its statistical prevalence. This is why so many parents and students believed that a Columbine-type shooting could occur at their school, even though such events are statistically rare.

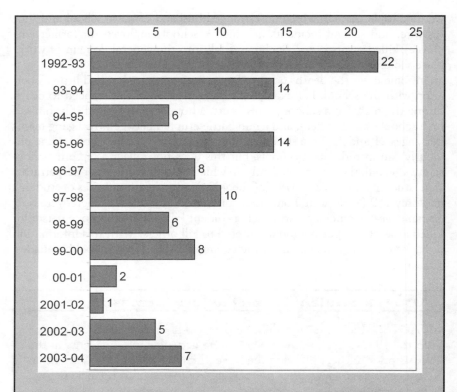

FIGURE 3–1.   Student-perpetrated homicide incidents at school.

Again using cases tabulated from the NSSC report (2005), there were 103 instances in which a student murdered someone at school during the 12 school years from 1992–93 to 2003–04. This means 8.58 incidents per year—which may seem like a lot, until one considers that there are 119,000 public and private schools in the United States (U.S. Department of Education, 2002). The likelihood that any one school will experience a student-perpetrated homicide is 8.58 divided by 119,000, or .0000721. Therefore, the average school can expect a student-perpetrated homicide about once every 13,870 years (1 divided by .0000721).

MYTH 3: Columbine was the worst incident of school violence in U.S. history.

FACT: Columbine High School is often described as the worst act of school violence in U.S. history, but an even bigger tragedy occurred almost 80 years ago in the small town of Bath, Michigan (May, 1999; Pawlak, n.d.). On May 18, 1927, Andrew Kehoe, treasurer of the Bath school board, set off a series of bombs that destroyed a school and killed 45 persons, including 37 schoolchildren. Mr. Kehoe, who was enraged because the tax levied to pay for the new school was going to cause him to lose his farm, volunteered to do maintenance work at the school and, over a period of months, secretly planted dynamite throughout the building. On the last day of school before summer recess, he parked nearby and watched the explosion from his pickup truck. Afterward, Mr. Kehoe called out to the school superintendent. When the man approached, Kehoe set off dynamite loaded in his truck, killing himself and the superintendent. Authorities later discovered that Kehoe had murdered his wife and rigged additional bombs at their home, which destroyed the house and barn at the same time the bombs went off at school. The Bath school massacre initially received national media coverage, but this attention was abruptly eclipsed three days later, on May 21, 1927, when Charles Lindbergh completed the first solo flight across the Atlantic.

MYTH 4: School homicides only take place in the United States.

FACT: School homicides have taken place in other countries, but do not receive much publicity in the United States. For example, on April 26, 2002 in Erfurt, Germany, 19-year-old Robert Steinhauser stormed into Johan Gutenberg Gymnasium armed with a 9 mm Glock pistol and a shotgun (CNN, April 27, 2002; Kim 2002). During the next 20 minutes he used the pistol to kill two girls, 13 teachers, a school secretary, and a police officer. One teacher succeeded in pushing Steinhauser into a room and locking the door, where he killed himself. He had failed an examination required for graduation, been caught forging a doctor's letter to excuse his absences, and expelled. Steinhauser, who hid the expulsion from his parents, had warned at least two students to stay away from school on the day of the shooting.

Three days after the shooting in Germany, in Vlasenica, Bosnia-Herzegovina, 17-year-old Dragoslav Petkovic went to his school and killed two teachers before committing suicide (Associated Press, April 30, 2002). The timing of this shooting strongly suggested a copycat effect, similar to what has been seen in the United States when one shooting inspired another student to do the same.

MYTH 5: School homicides are committed only by males.

FACT: Male students commit the vast majority of school homicides, but some have been committed by females. One of the earliest shooting rampages, for instance, was committed by 16-year-old Brenda Spencer, who in 1979 began firing into a San Diego elementary school from her house across the street (TheSanDiegoChannel.com, 2002). Using a .22 caliber rifle that her father had given her for Christmas, she killed the school principal and custodian and wounded eight students and a police officer. When asked why she committed the shooting, Spencer said, "I don't like Mondays." This reply inspired the Boomtown Rats to compose the controversial hit song "I don't like Mondays." Spencer was sentenced to 25 years to life in prison. Years later, she told her parole board that she had been physically and sexually abused by her father. She remains in prison.

Here are some other examples of school homicides committed by girls (NSSC, 2005): In 1993, 19-year-old Lawanda Jackson shot her former boyfriend in the back of the head with a pistol at Sumner High School in St. Louis, Missouri. In 1995, 17-year-old Marsha Mayfield of Holly Springs, Mississippi stabbed another girl to death in the hallway of Holly Springs Highs School. In 1996, two sisters stabbed another girl to death at Wichita Falls High School in Wichita Falls, Texas.

FBI (2004) statistics show that more than 90 percent of juveniles arrested for murder in the United States are male, as are more than three-quarters of juveniles arrested for aggravated assault. Males of all ages commit more violent crimes than females, but crimes by girls should not be overlooked.

THE SECRET SERVICE STUDY
OF SCHOOL SHOOTINGS

Shortly after the 1999 Columbine massacre, the U.S. Secret Service announced that it was going to conduct a study of school shootings (Vossekuil et al., 2002). It might seem curious that the Secret Service would be interested in school violence, but agency researchers thought that their special expertise in investigating potentially violent persons might be relevant to understanding students who attacked their classmates. The agency had just completed a landmark study of persons who threatened to attack public officials (Fein & Vossekuil, 1999), and had established a National Threat Assessment Center for the purpose of developing techniques and procedures for dealing with such persons. The Secret Service's approach—termed "threat assessment"—is discussed in Chapter 9.

The Secret Service study concentrated on what it termed "targeted school violence." Violence is "targeted" if the aggressor identifies a specific individual or group to be attacked. A spontaneous fight between two individuals, for example, would not be a targeted act of violence.

The Secret Service further limited its study (Vossekuil et al., 2002) to incidents in which a student or former student used a lethal weapon and chose a school as the site for the attack. This excluded student violence off school property, as well as violent incidents that were related to gang or drug trade activity that coincidentally occurred at school. Within these narrow parameters, the Secret Service identified only 37 incidents between 1974 and June 2000. In only 27 of these incidents did the attackers actually kill someone at school; in the remaining cases the attackers used a weapon to injure someone. This is a low number of incidents over a period of 25 years, especially when compared to the 347 incidents identified by the NSSC over a 12-year period using much broader criteria.

The Secret Service conducted a descriptive study of the 37 incidents using qualitative methodology that included a review of all available documents and interviews with ten of the student perpetrators. Two or more reviewers coded all of the documents to address several hundred questions that covered the attacker's motives and plans, mental state, life circumstances, and a wide range of other factors. The researchers then met to review and discuss their observations and reach general conclusions. A qualitative study like this is a valuable first step in conducting research in a new area and can be useful in generating hypotheses, but is not considered the most rigorous approach in social science research because so much depends on the subjective judgment of the researchers. The report states that "Researchers were cautious not to overreach in drawing conclusions from this information" (p. 10).

Characteristics of attackers. Despite the methodological limitations in this kind of study, the observations based on the Secret Service study are instructive. Most (81%) of the attackers acted alone, although in four cases the student had assistance in planning the attack; in three cases, two or more students acted together. Most of the attackers used a firearm—typically a handgun—and although half of the attackers carried more than one weapon, three-quarters of them used only one weapon during the attack. The attackers ranged in age from 11 to 21.

The researchers concluded that there was no profile or set of characteristics that described all or even most of the attackers. The cases receiving the most media attention generated the perception that all of the attackers were Caucasian, but only three-quarters were white; there were five African-American, two Hispanic, one Native Alaskan, one Native American, and one Asian student. Nearly two-thirds came from two-parent families.

The academic standing of the attackers varied considerably, although almost half of them were A and B students and only two were known to be failing school. The students were generally not regarded as discipline problems at school. Nearly two-thirds were regarded as never or rarely in trouble and only one-quarter had ever been suspended from school. Only four of the attackers had been expelled from school. In most cases, schools had not detected any marked change in the students' academic performance or behavior before the attack.

The attackers' social adjustment was harder to assess, but generally showed more signs of trouble. The largest group, about 40 percent, seemed to socialize with mainstream students, but the others were variously described as loners, lacking in friends, or part of a fringe group that was disliked by mainstream students. Almost three-quarters of the students felt persecuted, bullied, or mistreated by others prior to the incident. Several students were clearly identified by classmates as someone who was chronically teased or bullied. Not surprisingly, more than 80 percent of the attackers held some sort of grievance against someone, and at least 60 percent of the attacks were clearly motivated by revenge.

Most of the boys had demonstrated a preoccupation with fantasy violence through movies, books, or video games. Comparatively few adolescent boys are interested in writing, but more than a third of these boys wrote about violence in poems, essays, or journal entries. Nevertheless, the boys were not perceived as violent, and less than one-third had been known to act violently toward someone. Only five were known to have harmed an animal, and only one-quarter had been arrested for a juvenile offense.

What would trigger a change from violent fantasy to action? According to the Secret Service report, all but one of the attackers had experienced or perceived a major loss prior to their attack. These losses most often involved a perceived sense of failure or loss of status, and half of the cases, loss of a romantic relationship. In over 80 percent of the cases, observers commented that the boys had special difficulty coping with these losses.

Strikingly, most of the attackers had a history of suicidal attempts or thoughts prior to their attack. Most of them also had a documented history of serious depression, and about one-quarter had a known history of alcohol or substance abuse. Nevertheless, only one-third had received a mental health evaluation, and fewer than one-fifth had been diagnosed with a mental disorder. These observations suggest a group of boys that clearly were emotionally troubled but not receiving help.

Indications of the attack. One of the findings most strongly emphasized by the Secret Service was that the attacks were not impulsive acts but almost always carefully planned events. In some cases, the attacker had thought about the attack for as long as a year. The boy's preparation for the attack was often evident in behaviors such as asking friends for help obtaining a firearm or purchasing a coat that would conceal a rifle or shotgun. Some boys talked about different ways to injure or kill people. Others demonstrated a preoccupation with violence in their school writing assignments. These sorts of behaviors were sufficiently worrisome that in 88 percent of the cases, an adult was concerned about the boy.

Interestingly, the attackers did not directly threaten their intended victims, but they did let others know of their plans or intentions. In over 80 percent of the cases at least one person—typically a friend—knew that the student was thinking about or planning to attack others at school. In some cases, the student told one or more students explicitly when and where the attack would take place, and in a few cases, students purposely gathered to watch what would happen. Particularly disturbing was the finding that in at least 44 percent of the cases, the boys were encouraged or dared to carry out the attack. In various cases, friends assisted the boy in obtaining weapons or ammunition, helped plan the attack, or provided information on finding the intended victim at school.

Secret Service conclusions. The Secret Service concluded that "incidents of targeted violence at school" (Vossekuil et al., 2002, p. 31) were not impulsive acts, but events that had been planned days, weeks, or even months in advance. They emphasized that, although the attackers did not directly threaten their victims, they gave ample indication of their intentions in statements they made to others and through their preparations for the attack. These boys generally viewed themselves as victims of bullying or mistreatment by others, and their attacks followed a personal loss or failure. The clear implication of these findings is that the school shootings could have been prevented, if authorities had been alerted to what the boys were saying and doing before their attack.

CAUSAL QUESTIONS

The question "What caused the school shootings?" is deceptively simple. Philosophers and lawyers have long recognized that common-sense notions of one thing causing another break down under scrutiny (Hart & Honoré, 1985): An event is the product of a chain of prior events and occurs in the context of a complex set of conditions. Any change in the prior events or in the conditions surrounding the event could mean a different outcome. Some causal factors may be immediate and proximate to the event, and others may be distant and indirectly connected to the outcome. Some causal factors may be neither necessary nor sufficient to produce a certain outcome. Because causality is so complex, there is room for disagreement about the causes of any event, and emotionally charged events like school shootings are likely to generate considerable disagreement when different parties focus on different factors.

In the law, a causal question is often intended to mean "Who is to blame?" The simplest answer, favored from a law enforcement perspective, is that the person who commits a crime is responsible for his or her actions and therefore should be held accountable. It is a matter of finding the perpetrator and proving that he or she is the guilty party. This may be a satisfactory answer from a prosecutor's standpoint, but it fails to answer questions about why the person decided to commit the crime.

A prosecutor might go a step further and suggest a motive for the crime. An attacker, for instance, may have been angry and seeking revenge. He may have been seeking notoriety and bragged about what he would do. Such statements about motive do not really provide a sufficient explanation for the crime, however, since they only raise further questions about his or her decision-making process: Why would a young man (or woman) commit murder in order to achieve revenge? What would make him angry enough to kill? How could a person even consider such a course of action? These sorts of questions require one to examine the events that shaped the attacker's personality and character, as well as what conditions or circumstances affected his decision-making.

Questions about a person's decision-making process are unexpectedly complex. Even ordinary decisions, such as "What do I want to eat for lunch?" or "What will I do this weekend?" involve numerous factors that influence the decision-making process. A person deciding what to eat for lunch might consider how hungry he or she is, what restaurant options are available, and how much they cost. The person might consider whether he wants to eat alone or with friends, in which case he must consider their preferences, too. Similarly, a student who feels mistreated by others will be affected by how depressed and angry he feels, what options he perceives are available to him, and what the likely consequences of those options would be. He may also be influenced by peers who give him good or bad advice.

In addition to the obvious factors a person consciously considers, there may be subtle or indirect influences that are not consciously recognized. An over-weight person, for instance, may avoid high calorie foods. External influences such as advertising may depict certain foods as healthy or trendy. Even cultural heritage and upbringing plays a role in what kind of food is desirable. Similarly, a student with a frail self-image may be unusually sensitive to teasing and bullying. He may be influenced by social and cultural factors, for example, ranging from his religious background to the pervasiveness of violence in movies, music, and video games (see Chapter 6), that may shape his view of violence as a solution to his problems.

No one would assume that any one factor determines what a person chooses to eat for lunch, and even though the magnitude of the decision is much greater, one should not expect any one factor to explain why a boy would decide to commit an act of violence. Every act of school violence represents the culmination of a variety of factors that come together in a particular set of circumstances. Even so, it may be possible to identify factors that increase the risk of violence in the population as a whole, and some combination of these factors—a unique combination in every case—can produce the violence committed by an individual student. The Secret Service report both identifies a likely pool of factors and demonstrates that no single factor or set of factors can explain all cases. Recognizing that each case represents a unique combination of factors, it is possible to consider some of the factors commonly identified as responsible for school shootings.

WHAT DO THE POLLS SAY?

A year after the Columbine shooting, the Pew Research Center for the People and the Press (2000) conducted a national survey about the causes of school shootings. One question asked, "Now I have some questions about the recent school shootings like the one at Columbine High school in Colorado. . . . In general, what do you think is the MAIN reason why kids commit such violence?" Participants were given four options or the opportunity to offer their own explanation. The number one reason for the school shootings selected by participants was "poor upbringing by parents" (42%), followed by "violence in the media they are exposed to" (26%), "peer pressure from other kids" (14%), and "genetic or biologic tendencies toward violence" (4%). A small percentage offered some other explanation (7%) or gave no response (7%).

The survey question must have been frustrating to anyone who understands that complex events like school shootings cannot be reduced to a "main reason." Indeed, the idea that there is a "main reason" for the school shootings in itself represents a crude model of causality that is contrary to the more complex and varied picture described in the Secret Service report and other studies (Moore, Petrie, Braga, & McLaughlin, 2003). Moreover, the four choices offered by the survey represent factors that would influence an adolescent in vastly different ways and at different points along the chain of events that lead to a school shooting, from prenatal development to the moment of pulling the trigger.

How does one weigh the relative importance of genetics, a child's lifetime of experiences with parents, the vacillating fads and preferences of peers, and the hours spent being entertained by violent movies, music, and video games? Moreover, such factors surely interact with one another. For example, a boy with poor parental relationships might, as a result, be more susceptible to the influence of peers, and peer preferences affect what movies, music, and video games occupy the boy's free time.

Other important factors are not mentioned in the survey. For example, as noted in the Secret Service report, many of these boys felt themselves to be victims of teasing and bullying, and many of them were suicidally depressed. The absence of these important factors makes the four choices even more inadequate. Opinion surveys must use simple questions in order to gather information quickly over the telephone, but the result is that complex events are oversimplified. Public opinion is not so much measured by these questions as dissected into fragments that are pitted against one another.

The next set of questions in the poll illustrates a flagrant disconnection between perceived causes of school shootings and preventive actions. When asked, "In the end, who's mostly responsible for ensuring that children don't commit violent acts at school. . . . Is it mostly the schools' responsibility or mostly the parents' responsibility?" the general public overwhelmingly selected "parent responsibility" (85%) over "school responsibility" (9%). Yet, when asked to choose "the most effective way to prevent such things from happening," there were no options for strengthening families or helping parents to improve their child-rearing skills. The available options were:

- Increasing school security, such as installing metal detectors and hiring more guards (11%)
- Passing stricter gun control laws (6%)
- Paying more attention to kids' anti-social attitudes and behaviors (60%)
- Reducing violence in popular entertainment (13%)
- Other (6%)
- Don't know/Refused (4%)

If parents—by an overwhelming margin—are considered the responsible parties for ensuring that children do not commit acts of violence at school, why did the poll include no options directly aimed at parents? Why is "increasing school security" the first option? And "gun control" the second? None of the options specifically refer to parents or families (although presumably parents could be one of the parties to "pay more attention" to children's "anti-social" attitudes and behaviors). The framing of this question reflects how debate on school safety is steered toward politically controversial topics such as gun control and media violence, rather than moving toward a more complex and integrated understanding of the problem.

Survey questions are intended to reflect the agenda of public discourse, but they also shape that agenda by including certain options and omitting others. An option not included in the national surveys fades from public consciousness and soon ceases to exist as a policy option. The pollsters cannot claim that they did not anticipate what the survey results would look like, as they conduct numerous surveys and field-test questions before they use them. In the case of this survey, some of the same questions had been asked the year before in a *Newsweek* survey (Pew Research Center for the People and the Press, 2000).

Interestingly, the most notable change between the *Newsweek* survey after the 1999 Columbine shooting and the Pew survey one year later was that public support for "increasing school security, such as installing metal detectors and hiring more guards" dropped from 21 percent to 11 percent, while "paying more attention to kids' anti-social attitudes and behaviors" rose from 49 percent to 60 percent. This modest shift in public attitudes is especially meaningful in light of the subsequent Secret Service recommendation that schools pay serious attention to student threats of violence, which will be discussed in Chapter 9.

ARE THE PARENTS AT FAULT?

There is widespread sentiment that parents play a key role in keeping schools safe. This viewpoint extends to the courtroom, where victims of school shootings have filed lawsuits against parents of the attackers in Pearl, Paducah, Jonesboro, Littleton, and other communities. A cover story in the *New York Times Magazine* (Belkin, 1999) pictured the parents of Columbine victim Isaiah Shoels proclaiming, "They ask us if we blame the parents. Who else do we blame?" So far, however, no lawsuit has been successful in finding parents liable for the actions of their child in a school shooting; courts generally rule that parents are not responsible for their children's criminal behavior. The children alone are held responsible, and if they are old enough, they can be tried and punished as adults.

Are bad parents responsible for the school shootings? This is a moral question rather than a scientific one. Parents have legal and moral responsibility for their children, and it is their societal function to raise their children and prepare them for adulthood; thus it makes sense that society would want to hold them accountable when their children commit criminal acts of violence. From a scientific perspective, parents certainly play an important role in influencing their children, but studies have never found that parents account for the majority of variance in a child's behavior and parent influences are often over-estimated (Lytton, 2000).

School shootings are not like other forms of juvenile crime. The typical juvenile offender is raised in a family stressed by problems such as poverty, divorce, domestic violence, parental substance abuse, and child abuse and neglect (Lochman, 2004; Henggeler & Sheidow, 2003). In contrast the backgrounds of the attackers studied by the Secret Service are quite different. Although some of these students were raised in such adverse circumstances, a surprising number of families appeared to be relatively healthy and well-adjusted.

THE PADUCAH SCHOOL SHOOTING

One example of a seemingly healthy family is that of Michael Carneal, the 14-year-old who killed three students when he fired into a prayer circle at his high school. The 1997 school shooting at Heath High School in West Paducah, Kentucky has been the subject of considerable study. The police investigation released by the criminal court that sentenced Carneal to life in prison numbered over 2,000 pages in length and the National Research Council commissioned an investigation of school violence that included an extensive case study of the shooting (Harding, Mehta, & Newman, 2003).

The author conducted a forensic evaluation of Michael Carneal for his defense attorneys and testified at his sentencing, during which the court accepted his plea of guilty but mentally ill. The author's forensic evaluation included 20 hours of interviews with Michael, and dozens more with his parents and sister, four grandparents, other relatives, classmates, neighbors, and teachers. The author also had access to records from the police investigation, as well as evaluations conducted by experts for the prosecution and another defense expert. In addition, the author interviewed Michael again seven years later and was able to review the records of his psychiatric treatment in prison.

By all accounts, Mr. and Mrs. Carneal were concerned and dedicated parents. Prior to the school shooting, the Carneals were regarded by friends and relatives as a model family. Mr. Carneal was not only a successful lawyer, but one who was admired by his colleagues for the way he reserved time for his family. Ms. Carneal had a bachelor's degree, but elected to stay at home to raise their two children. The family had meals together, attended church together, and went on regular family trips and vacations. They lived in a well-kept, single-story home in a peaceful, wooded setting. There were no indications of marital conflict, substance abuse, child abuse, or any of the other family problems that one might suspect in a family where a teenager committed a terrible crime.

Michael was close to his mother and father, but somewhat distant with other relatives. He was respectful and obedient at home, and gave his parents little reason to be troubled by misbehavior. As he entered adolescence, they recognized that he was struggling with his self-image and peer relationships, and so tried to be supportive. He was shy and awkward and, at times, unusually fearful. Sometimes he was afraid to go out at night. Occasionally, he refused to sleep in his bedroom and slept on the couch instead. They noticed that whenever he took a shower, he stuffed towels in the bathroom floor vent and made the curious statement that he did not want anyone under the house to see him. Michael's parents did not know quite what to make of their son, but they did not suspect that he was showing signs of mental illness. They also did not know that in previous generations, several relatives had been institutionalized for severe mental illness—including one who had been violent toward others and eventually committed suicide.

If one judged Mr. and Mrs. Carneal by the example of their daughter, it would be impossible to find fault with their parenting. At the time of the shooting, Kelly Carneal was a senior at Heath High School. Well-regarded by her teachers, she was an honor student who later graduated as class valedictorian. She was musically talented, served as a section leader in the marching band, and made the all-state choir. She was also articulate, attractive, and popular with her peers.

His sister's exemplary qualities weighed heavily on Michael, who realized that he could not compete with her. He had to struggle to make good grades, and did not have her musical talent or poise, and was not popular. Michael's parents tried to avoid comparisons, but it was not necessary for them to point out what was obvious to him and everyone else. Even so, many boys grow up in the shadow of a more successful older sibling and find ways to cope. Michael occasionally bickered with his sister, but he did not hate her and the two of them got along well enough.

School bullying.   Michael suffered more from teasing and bullying by his peers than from rivalry with his sister. In middle school, Michael was a late bloomer: thin and awkward, with oversized glasses and no athletic talent. He became an easy mark for bigger boys who liked to push him around, spit on him, and make fun of him. He was especially troubled when a school gossip column said that he and a male friend "had feelings for one another." A few boys began to call him "gay," "faggot," and other sexually derisive terms.

Michael hoped that things would change when he started high school as a ninth grader, but instead the bullying only worsened. Larger boys continued to call him names and threaten him. They took food from his tray in the cafeteria and dared him to do anything about it. In science class, some of the boys would intentionally ruin his science experiments when the teacher left the room. In another class, several boys liked to put him in a headlock and grind their knuckles into his scalp. Other students experienced similar treatment, but they later reported that Michael seemed more troubled by it, and, as a result, may have been targeted more frequently.

Michael's parents knew about some of the teasing, but like many victims of bullying, he was embarrassed and reluctant to ask for help. Like many adolescents who long to establish independence, he did not want his parents to come to his aid. He did not believe that his parents could do anything to make the bullying stop and on the contrary, like many adolescents, he feared that their involvement would make matters even worse.

As discussed in Chapter 5, the bullying that Michael experienced is common in American schools, and his reluctance to seek help was typical of many victims, most of whom manage to endure the experience. What happens when the target of ordinary bullying is not a healthy child, but one who is predisposed to mental illness? Bullying that one student can tolerate may seem humiliating to another. Over time, Michael became increasingly depressed and began to think about killing himself. He found an old handgun in his father's closet, and considered using it to end his life. He took a sewing needle and gouged a large mark on his arm. In his depressed and paranoid state, he came to feel that all of his former friends had turned against him, and that students whispering and laughing in the hall were whispering and laughing about him. In the weeks before the shooting, he began to hear voices telling him to stand up for himself.

School authorities seemed to be either unaware of the bullying or unconcerned. They may have assumed that what they observed was good-natured horseplay. One school teacher, for instance, reportedly tolerated the hazing he witnessed because he regarded it as a harmless form of initiation and a school tradition. From Michael's perspective, however, his teachers did not care about him and were not interested in putting a stop to the bullying. This perception was further solidified when a gym teacher derided him for being a poor basketball player and humiliated him by making him play with the girls.

Peer influences. Michael noticed that many of the boys who teased him were popular with classmates and well regarded by teachers. They were referred to as "preps," a term used by students to refer to a favored or popular group of students. Although Michael and his sister might have been regarded as preps themselves, Michael began to feel alienated from the mainstream at Heath High School. Paranoia, alienation, and acute social anxiety are hallmarks of emerging mental illness.

In contrast to the preps, another group of boys who were not popular were called "freaks," and Michael found himself drawn to them. Why were the freaks appealing? The freaks were also harassed; they supported each another and seemed able to tolerate rejection by their classmates. In fact, they reveled in their marginal status and retaliated by rejecting the social conventions of their peers: they acted independent and defiant and would not participate in the morning prayer group in the school lobby or dress like the preppy students. Some claimed to be Wiccans rather than Christians, although it does not appear that any of them were sincere practitioners of this pagan religion, and used it for shock value.

Most important to Michael, the freaks did not make fun of him and seemed willing to accept him. If Michael could not be accepted by the mainstream group at school, he would turn to the marginal students in this group. It appeared that these older boys—juniors and seniors—took advantage of Michael's eagerness to please them and win their approval: They began to ask him to do small favors and soon he was bringing them gifts like CDs and cash from his father's wallet.

The freaks commiserated about their low status and the unfairness of school administrators who seemed to favor the preps, and they plotted ways to strike back or take revenge. They were most interested in the movie *Basketball Diaries*, in which a high school student—played by Leonardo DiCaprio—dreams of taking revenge against his school by going on a shooting rampage. In his dream, the student strides dramatically into a classroom, pulls out a shotgun hidden under his long, black trench coat, and opens fire on his teacher and the classmates who tormented him. In a grotesque distortion of reality, other students clap and cheer the student's actions. Although the movie emphasizes the unfortunate consequences that befell a youth who became involved in drugs and crime, these boys took a quite different message from the movie: They enjoyed talking about the shooting scene and speculated on what it would be like to commit a similar attack.

There are conflicting accounts as to whether the boys' conversations about shooting up the school were idle fantasies or specific plans. In at least one account to authorities, Michael reported that he and four other boys had planned to carry out the shootings together and that these older boys assigned him the job of obtaining guns for all of them. On other occasions, Michael disavowed this account and said that the others had nothing to do with the shooting. The boys themselves denied involvement in planning or carrying out the shooting, and, in the absence of convincing evidence, none was ever charged with a crime.

What is known is that, in the days and weeks before the shooting, Michael made a number of statements to students about "something big" that would happen and implied that he would be taking revenge on people. Some students heard what sounded like boastful statements that they did not take seriously. Other students, however, received more serious and specific warnings not to be in the school lobby the following Monday morning, which is when the shootings took place. None of the dozen or more students who heard Michael's threats and warnings went to an adult with this information. As will be discussed in Chapter 9, convincing students that they should report threats of violence is critically important to prevent similar acts of violence. In this case and other school shootings, the attack could have been prevented if school authorities had been informed of Michael's threats.

On Thanksgiving Day, Michael stole at least five firearms from a locked cabinet in a neighbor's house while they were away. He reported hiding the guns in his bedroom and practiced firing a pistol with one of his friends over Thanksgiving weekend before the shooting. Allegedly, Michael spoke with several "freaks" about the kind of guns he had stolen and each chose which one he would use.

The shooting.   On the day of the shooting, Michael carried two rifles and two shotguns into the school lobby wrapped in a blanket. He set the bundle down by the trophy case where the "freaks" were standing. Some of the boys realized that Michael had guns in the bundle, but none of them accepted his offer to take one. One commented that he "had balls" in bringing the guns to school. Michael also brought a bag of earplugs for the boys, which they also declined. Instead, the boys stood back and watched what happened next.

The prayer group of about 40 students formed a few feet away in the center of the lobby. They joined hands and were led in prayer by one of the students, Ben. Ben was a handsome, muscular senior who played on the football team. His father was pastor of a local church. Ben was also one of the students that Michael had warned specifically not to be in the lobby for the prayer group on Monday. Ben wondered whether Michael's warning was just foolish talk by a 9th grader who often said outlandish things to get attention, but he decided that he should be present in case there was some kind of trouble. Michael said that he warned Ben because Ben had been friendly to him.

The bell rang to signal students that it was time to head for their classes. The prayer ended and students dropped hands and bent over to pick up their books and bags. Michael left the bundle of rifles and shotguns alone. Instead, he reached into his book bag and pulled out a .22 caliber Ruger pistol. Fully loaded, the semiautomatic pistol could fire nine shots in rapid succession. Michael held the gun with both hands, arms extended straight in front of his face, and aimed into the crowd of students. It was the same pose he used in playing video games at home, where the object was to shoot as many figures as possible in rapid succession. In one of his favorite games, Nintendo's *Doom*, he often pretended that he was shooting the bullies at school.

Some authorities have claimed that Michael's practice at video games sharpened his aim and eroded the natural inhibition that one would have about shooting someone (Grossman & DeGaetano, 1999). The controversy over video games is discussed in Chapter 6. In any case, Michael was only a few feet from the first students he shot, so it is not surprising that his shots were on target: It would have been more difficult to miss everyone than to hit someone.

Michael fired eight shots, and each struck a different student. Three girls—ages 14, 15, and 17—were struck in the head and later died in the hospital. A 15-year-old girl was struck in the chest and paralyzed. Two other girls suffered less serious injuries to the shoulder and neck, and two boys suffered minor injuries to the neck and head. It all happened in about 10 seconds.

Still standing in the same spot where he opened fire, Michael put down his gun with one shot remaining. He said that when he saw the blood from the gunshot wounds, he came to his senses and stopped. Immediately after that, Ben came to him from one side, grabbed him by the shoulders and demanded, "What are you doing?" Michael looked at him and replied, "I can't believe I did that—please kill me now."

In a matter of seconds the school principal arrived and took control of Michael, leading him into an office. Once in the office, Michael told the principal that there were other guns in the blanket by the trophy case. The principal ran to retrieve them, leaving a teacher to supervise Michael. Soon the state police arrived and took him into custody.

The legal outcome. Michael's parents, along with everyone else, were horrified by what their son had done. They hired two of the best defense attorneys in Paducah, but instructed them to cooperate with the police investigation so that they could find out why this had happened. Just hours after the shooting, and with one of his attorneys present, Michael gave a videotaped statement to the police.

In his statement to the police, Michael seemed confused and uncertain, and said he did not know why he shot his classmates. When asked where he got the idea to commit the shooting, he referred to the movie *Basketball Diaries.* He talked about being teased and bullied at Heath High School, and he said that he acted alone and that the other boys were not involved. (In later interviews, Michael gave varied accounts of how much the other boys were involved and admitted that they had talked about shooting people at school, but in the end, he contended that he had acted alone.)

Michael was charged with multiple counts of murder and his case was promptly transferred from juvenile court to adult court. As a 14-year-old, under Kentucky law Michael was old enough to be tried as an adult and sentenced to life in prison. He could not be given the death penalty because the

U.S. Supreme Court had found that capital punishment of persons under the age of 16 was unconstitutional. (In 2005 the U.S. Supreme Court, in *Roper* v *Simmons*, extended this finding to include all persons under the age of 18.)

One of the first legal issues to consider was whether Michael's attorneys would raise an insanity defense. According to the Kentucky Penal Code, Chapter 504, "insanity" means "as a result of mental condition, lack of substantial capacity either to appreciate the criminality of one's conduct or to conform one's conduct to the requirements of the law" [504.060(5)].

A defendant who did not meet the criteria for insanity could be found "guilty but mentally ill at the time of the offense." The Kentucky Penal Code defines "mental illness" as "substantially impaired capacity to use self-control, judgment, or discretion in the conduct of one's affairs and social relations, associated with maladaptive behavior or recognized emotional symptoms where impaired capacity, maladaptive behavior, or emotional symptoms can be related to physiological, psychological, or social factors" [KRS 504.060(6)].

In separate evaluations with the author and psychiatrist Diane Schetky, M.D., Michael presented evidence of severe mental illness. In addition to symptoms of depression, he reported clearly paranoid delusions. He admitted covering the floor vent in the bathroom at home because he feared that a man was under the house and trying to get him. He became afraid to sleep in his bed at night because he feared that the man had a chainsaw and would cut off his legs from under the bed. After her son's arrest, Mrs. Carneal found that Michael had placed a variety of tools under his mattress; he explained that he thought the metal objects would protect him from the chainsaw. During his incarceration, Michael became fearful that a snake lived in the drain on the floor of his cell, and would come out to get him.

Michael reported hearing voices that criticized him, threatened him, and told him to do things. On the day of the offense, the voices told him that he needed to "Do this for yourself." The voices also told him not to tell anyone of their existence, and like many persons with an incipient mental illness, Michael was fearful of disclosing his symptoms. Like many persons in the early stages of schizophrenia, it was quite possible for people to interact with him and not know that his thought processes were disturbed.

Despite his psychotic symptoms, Michael retained a basic capacity to reason and communicate, and he could perform well on intelligence tests. He was polite and well-mannered in his interactions with authorities and he was well-behaved in the juvenile detention center.

The symptoms that Michael presented were consistent with an emerging mental illness such as schizophrenia, but this does not by itself demonstrate insanity. To be considered insane, it would be necessary to conclude that Michael lacked substantial capacity either to appreciate the criminality of his conduct or to conform his conduct to the requirements of the law. This legal language is usually interpreted to mean that an insane person did not adequately recognize that his behavior was wrong, or that if he did recognize his behavior was wrong, he was not able to control himself. Michael had some awareness that shooting his classmates was wrong, based on his statements after he stopped shooting and surrendered to authorities. The question of insanity for Michael would hinge on how *much* impairment he had in his understanding of the criminality or wrongfulness of his actions, and how much control he had over his behavior. Arguments for and against insanity could be made.

Ultimately, Michael—in consultation with his attorneys and parents—decided to forego an insanity defense and to plead "guilty but mentally ill at the time of the offense." Michael professed great remorse for his crimes and stated that he deserved to receive the maximum punishment. Under Kentucky law, as in most states with this plea, a verdict of guilty but mentally ill carries no special provision for mental health treatment or any difference in sentencing than for a person simply found guilty: Any person with a serious mental illness is entitled to treatment whether found guilty or guilty but mentally ill. Moreover, Michael's plea did not come with a reduction in sentence, as he received the maximum sentence under Kentucky law for a person his age. (In Kentucky, a person sentenced to life in prison can be considered for parole in 25 years.)

Michael was incarcerated in juvenile facilities until he turned 18. On his 18th birthday, he was transferred to an adult institution. Since entering prison, he has completed his high school education and has begun taking college correspondence courses. He has continued to suffer intermittently from paranoid delusions and auditory hallucinations, and has been hospitalized several times for psychotic and suicidal behavior. He has not been violent toward others, and is generally regarded as a polite and well-behaved inmate.

LESSONS FROM PADUCAH

Although every case has unique characteristics, the Paducah case provides some important lessons for the prevention of school shootings. First, no single factor can be considered the necessary or sufficient cause of Michael's decision to go on a shooting rampage. Even though parents are obviously the most important influence on a child—and the public generally blames parents of students who attack their schools—the Paducah case shows that poor parenting is not always a factor. By all accounts, the Carneals were good parents, and no one would have found fault with them prior to the shooting. One could contend that Michael's parents should have recognized his emerging mental illness, but the symptoms of mental illness are often subtle, and many parents have been stunned to discover that their son or daughter has been quietly delusional or experiencing undetected hallucinations for weeks or even months.

Certainly, Michael's developing mental illness was a critical factor that affected his reasoning and judgment, and made him more vulnerable to other influences. Perhaps Michael's mental illness was the factor that replaced the role often occupied by an abusive or disturbed family. Although most youth who commit serious acts of violence do not have the severity of mental illness that Michael experienced, such cases exist and cannot be ignored (Cornell, 1999).

Moreover, many of the attackers studied by the Secret Service exhibited serious depression accompanied by suicidal thinking. Even if these students were not delusional, suicidal depression distorts judgment and perception of reality, so that there seems to be no hope and no alternative to a violent course of action. Unfortunately, depression is a pervasive problem affecting as many as 8 percent of adolescents (U.S. Department of Health and Human Services, 1999), and schools typically do not have sufficient staff to identify and work with such students, a subject that will be reconsidered in Chapter 10.

The years of teasing and bullying that Michael withstood is another important factor, one that the Secret Service observed in many other school shootings (Vossekuil, Fein, Reddy, Borum, & Modzeleski, 2002). Victims of bullying experience chronic feelings of shame and helplessness that, over time, generate growing anger and resentment, and culminate in an overwhelming desire for revenge that can blind judgment and consideration of the consequences of one's actions. In Michael's case, bullying not only fueled his anger toward the school; it likely contributed to the onset of his mental illness as well.

Peer influences are yet another consideration in school shootings. Although most students acted alone, many of them were assisted by peers. It is a disturbing observation that in many cases, such as Luke Woodham's attack in Pearl, Mississippi, one or more youths deliberately encouraged a depressed and vulnerable boy to lash out rather than seek help. Although the boys that plotted with Michael Carneal were never charged with crimes for their actions, the influence they exerted over him is evident.

Peers can also be positive, protective influences. School shootings can be prevented when students are willing to seek help for a classmate who is depressed or who threatens an act of violence. As will be discussed in Chapter 9, the FBI study of school shootings (O'Toole, 2000) found that shootings have been prevented because students took such actions. Schools can teach students to distinguish between seeking help for a friend and snitching on a classmate.

Peers can also be a positive influence when it comes to school bullying. One of the standard goals of anti-bullying programs is to encourage a school climate in which students recognize the destructive impact of bullying and consciously agree not to condone or support it, even as passive bystanders. In schools like Heath High School, tragically, bullying had become an accepted part of the culture (Unnever & Cornell, 2003).

LEGAL DISPOSITION OF SCHOOL
SHOOTING CASES

The legal system has long had an ambivalent attitude toward the punishment of juvenile offenders (Bonnie, 1989). Although the juvenile justice system was designed to reform and rehabilitate juvenile offenders, the case of juvenile murder has never fit this paradigm, and in many cases, these juveniles are transferred to adult court. As a result, juveniles charged with murder can receive an astonishingly wide range of consequences, depending on their age and the jurisdiction of their crime. Those who remain in juvenile court can be incarcerated until they reach young adulthood, but those who are tried as adults can be incarcerated for life. Juveniles convicted of murder frequently receive lengthy prison sentences that match those received by adult offenders (Cornell, Staresina, & Benedek, 1989). In the case of school shootings, the legal consequences are equally diverse, and have ranged from incarceration until age 21 to life in prison.

October 1, 1997 *Pearl High School* *Pearl, Mississippi*	After the jury rejected Luke Woodham's insanity defense, the judge sentenced him to two consecutive life sentences for murder and seven 20-year sentences for aggravated assault.
December 1, 1997 *Heath High School* *West Paducah,* *Kentucky*	Michael Carneal pleaded "guilty but mentally ill" and received a life sentence with parole eligibility in 25 years. In prison, he has been treated for paranoid hallucinations and delusions associated with schizophrenia.
March 24, 1998 *Westside Middle* *School* *Jonesboro, Arkansas*	Eleven-year-old Andrew Golden and 13-year-old Mitchell Johnson were too young to be tried as adults. As convicted juvenile offenders, they can be incarcerated only until age 21.
May 21, 1998 *Thurstone High* *School* *Springfield, Oregon*	Kinkle's attorneys initially planned an insanity defense to the murder charges, but later accepted a plea bargain for a 25-year prison sentence. The judge then added 86 more years for attempted murder of 25 other students and the officer. Altogether, Kinkle was sentenced to 111.67 years without possibility of parole.
May 20, 1999 *Columbine High* *School* *Littleton, Colorado*	Eric Harris and Dylan Klebold committed suicide.

4

How Many Guns in Our Schools?

Fourteen-year old Bobby was a freshman at Patrick Henry High School. He had been teased and picked on by his classmates in middle school, but now, in the larger high school, he felt smaller and more vulnerable than ever. He eagerly joined the marching band, but soon found that new band members were hazed by senior members as part of "band initiation" during the annual summer band camp. The band director was vaguely aware of some teasing and horseplay among his students, but he regarded it as part of the band's tradition and nothing to be concerned about.

As the school year continued, Bobby expected the initiation to be over, but his hazing continued. Every day he dreaded going into the instrument storage room before and after band rehearsal. The older boys liked to catch him in the instrument room, shut the sound-proof door, and "have fun" with him. Some days they would just tease him, but sometimes they would push him around, choke him in a headlock, or humiliate him by pulling down his pants.

Bobby grew steadily angrier with the boys who hazed him, but he felt helpless to stop it: He was not big enough to fend the boys off and he was ashamed to ask for help. Besides, who would he tell? The band director seemed to know what was going on, yet did nothing about it. If he told anyone else at school, he would be teased as a tattletale. Finally, he couldn't tell his parents, because he feared they would complain to the school, which he felt would just make matters worse.

One day it occurred to Bobby that the best way to make the hazing stop was to go into the storage room with a gun in his backpack. He could pull out the gun and turn the tables on the boys. It was gratifying to imagine what he would say to the boys and what their frightened faces would look like. He knew where he could get a gun . . . .

HOW IS YOUTH VIOLENCE
RELATED TO GUNS?

Gun rights advocates often say, "Guns don't kill people; people kill people."
Gun control advocates retort, "Guns don't kill people; they just make it real
easy." These slogans play upon the distinction between two essential elements
of any crime: motive and method. A person must have a motive for committing a crime and then must have a method of carrying it out. In the debate on
gun control, one side points out that only people have motives to kill, while the
other side points out that guns provide a highly lethal method of doing so. Both
sides are right—but only because they address different aspects of the crime.

The debate between conservatives who favor unfettered gun access and
liberals who favor gun regulation reflects a fundamental difference in perspective on the causes of human behavior. The conservative view is that individuals are responsible for their own behavior and must be held accountable
for their choices. Social and environmental factors are given less weight as
causes of human behavior because people act according to their free will. The
liberal view places much more emphasis on social and environmental factors
as having a causal influence on human behavior. Just as in the controversy
over media violence, the debate hinges on differing notions of causality.

Social scientists, who—not surprisingly—are overwhelmingly liberal
(Redding, 2001), conduct research on the social and environmental factors
that affect human behavior. They pay much less attention to the concept of
free will, perhaps because it is an unobservable event that is difficult to con-
ceptualize and measure. Also, free will is so subjective that it does not fit easily into an objective scientific model. B. F. Skinner—one of the most influential psychologists of the 20th century—took an extreme position when he
provocatively argued in his famous book *Beyond Freedom and Dignity* that free
will was an illusion (Skinner, 1971). From his perspective as a "radical behav-
iorist," decisions and choices that seem to be an exercise of free will are actually the product of operant conditioning—learned responses to environmental reinforcement. More recently, psychologist Daniel Wegner (2002) of
Harvard University contended that free will is an illusion that helps us or-
ganize our experiences and develop an adaptive sense of responsibility.

Although most social scientists do not accept Skinner's most radical conclusions, most social science research attempts to show that certain social or
environmental conditions produce certain kinds of behavior, without attempting to measure the intervening stage of a person's willful decision to act
in a certain way. They try to stick to human behavior that can be observed
and objectively measured rather than mental processes that cannot be readily
observed or measured. When psychologists do study mental processes, they
tend to focus on learning experiences, attitudes, values, or perhaps reasoning
processes, that are associated with certain behavioral outcomes (but also see

Wegner, 2002). For instance, various psychological theorists (Berkowitz, 1993; Huesmann, 1994) assert that children learn to engage in aggressive behavior as a response to frustration or because they have observed aggression in others. Some aggression may be reactive to conflict or frustration, while other aggressive behavior may be proactive, in the sense that it is goal-directed and instrumental. (For a comprehensive review of the psychology of youth aggression and violence, see Moeller, 2001).

The epidemic of juvenile murder. From 1984 to 1993, juvenile murder soared in the United States. In 1984, law enforcement agencies reported 973 arrests of juveniles for murder; this number increased each year until 1993, by which time it had more than tripled to 3,284 (FBI, 1984–1994). The increase in juvenile murder arrests could not be attributed to an increase in the teenage population, because the teenage population had declined during this period. The increase could not be attributed to improved policing that resulted in the arrest of more perpetrators, because the percent of homicides resulting in an arrest dropped from 74 percent to 66 percent (FBI 1985–1994).

As discussed in Chapter 2, the increase in juvenile homicide stimulated scholarly theories that the younger generation was filled with "superpredators" who were vicious, cold-hearted killers (DiIulio, 1995; Zimring, 1998). Other scholars who suggested that the increase in violence was linked to juvenile access to firearms were branded as liberal apologists for juvenile offenders (Ludwig & Cook, 2003). Casting the issue in political terms as a conservative versus liberal debate makes it difficult to look objectively at the facts.

MYTH 6: Juvenile homicide has nothing to do with guns.

FACT: Examination of juvenile homicide arrests in the United States provides insight into the link between juvenile homicide and guns. Unlike assaults, murder data include the type of weapon used in the crime (Snyder, Finnegan, Wan, & Kang, 2002). If murders were being committed by a new, more heinous generation of youths, one would expect an increase in all forms of murder, such as stabbings, strangulations, and beatings, as well as guns. However, the data unequivocally implicate guns as a critical factor in the homicide increase: The number of murders committed with knives, blunt objects, and other weapons (including beatings without a weapon) remained essentially unchanged, while only shootings increased (see figure below). The increase in juvenile homicide can be accurately described as an "epidemic of gun violence" (Wilkinson & Fagan, 2001; Wintemute, 2000).

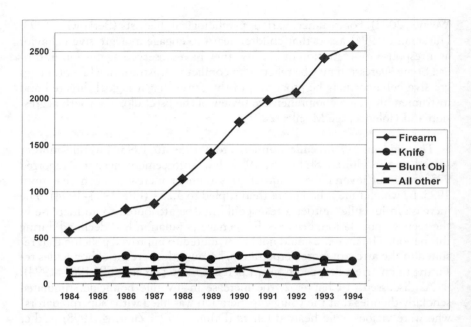

FIGURE 4–1.   Weapons used in juvenile homicides.

   The dramatic rise in gun homicides, which peaked in 1994, indicates that possession of a firearm played a significant role in juvenile murder (U.S. Department of Health and Human Services, 2001; Wintemute, 2000). In fact, a plausible hypothesis is that the murder rate increased *because* more juveniles were carrying guns and using them to settle disputes. In other words, teenagers were not more aggressive or predatory than in past generations: they were simply better armed, and as a result, more likely to inflict a fatal injury on their antagonists.

   What kinds of firearms were used during this epidemic? Although handguns represent only about one-third of the firearms possessed by civilians in the United States, at least 80 percent of the firearms used in juvenile homicides were handguns (Cook & Ludwig, 1996). Handguns are clearly the weapon of choice in juvenile homicides. Moreover, the type of handgun is important. During the 1980's there was a rapid transition in the type of handguns that were available to youth: from revolvers to semiautomatic pistols (Wintemute, 2000). Studies in Chicago, Los Angeles, Philadelphia, and Milwaukee found large increases in the use of pistols in homicides (Wintemute, 2000). In 1992 more homicides were committed with 9 mm pistols than in the entire decade of the 1980's (Diaz, 1999).

The transition from revolvers to pistols helps explain why homicides increased. Revolvers fire slowly because the ammunition is contained in a cylinder that revolves after each shot in order to place a new cartridge into position for firing. Semiautomatic pistols, in contrast, hold ammunition in a magazine that fits into the handle of the gun. After the pistol is fired, a new cartridge quickly snaps into place. Because of this, revolvers are typically heavier, contain less ammunition, and most importantly, fire at a slower rate. This makes them less deadly than pistols, which are lighter, hold more ammunition, and can fire rapidly. In addition, revolvers typically carry only six rounds, but many pistols can carry twenty or more rounds. The rapid fire of multiple rounds has a dramatic effect on the shooter's likelihood of hitting a target, because it is possible to spray an area with bullets, assuring that at least some of the shots are accurate.

The newer pistols not only carried more rounds, they carried larger caliber bullets. Larger bullets inflict considerably more damage. Studies of emergency medical care during the 1980s showed that the caliber of bullets extracted from shooting victims increased, and that a larger percentage of these victims died at the scene (Wintemute, 2000). The percentage of victims killed at the scene due to pistols increased, while the percentage killed by revolvers decreased. Speed of fire, number of rounds, and caliber of bullets make pistols more effective killing tools than revolvers.

There were at least two other advantages of pistols that contribute to their lethality. A pistol can be loaded in seconds simply by changing the magazine, whereas a revolver must be reloaded one cartridge at a time. Second, the new semiautomatic pistols were small enough to be easily concealed in a pocket or tucked into a waistband. This meant that youths could carry them easily and have them available in the event that a dispute or conflict arose.

Why was there an increase in the availability and use of semiautomatic pistols? The answer is largely economic and can be understood by examining changes in the gun industry during the 1980s. In a bid to recover from economic hard times, American gun manufacturers began to produce large quantities of semiautomatic pistols (Wintemute, 2000). The pistols were relatively inexpensive, but generated profits through volume sales to distributors. American manufacturers enjoyed a competitive advantage over manufacturers from other countries because the Gun Control Act of 1968 imposed standards for imported handguns that did not apply to domestic firearms. American-made firearms were (and are) largely exempt from regulation regarding design or performance, and the Consumer Product Safety Commission was (and still is) prohibited by law from regulating firearms or ammunition (Wintemute, 2000).

Pistols were widely available to youth because of the loose nature of the firearms market. Guns could be purchased from a multitude of dealers under largely unregulated conditions. Prior to 1993, the cost of a dealer's license was just $10 per year, so that almost anyone could become a licensed dealer and sell firearms out of his or her home or car (Wintemute, 2000). Remarkably, by 1992 the United States had more gun dealers than gas stations (Sugarmann & Rand, 1992). The Bureau of Alcohol, Tobacco, and Firearms (1993) estimated that it would take ten years to inspect all the licensed dealers, which meant that gun dealers had little reason to be concerned about government regulation or oversight. Not surprisingly, studies have found a high rate of legal violations among gun dealers, such as failure to keep a record of sale or obtain a required state license (Wintemute, 2000).

Gun dealers are not the only source of handguns for youth; guns can be bought and sold without a license by anyone not engaged in the gun dealing business, and hobbyists and sportsmen are not required to maintain records. At thousands of gun shows every year, individuals can purchase firearms in relative anonymity (Wintemute, 2000). The result is a large pool of weapons that can easily circulate into the hands juveniles. By 1994 there were an estimated 65 million handguns and 127 million other firearms in American households (Cook & Ludwig, 1996).

THE FEAR OF 135,000 KIDS WITH GUNS

The news media so dramatized the increase in youth gun violence that it seemed that our nation was plagued by an entire generation of murderous, armed youth. In 1992 *Newsweek* (March 9, 1992) published a frightening cover depicting emergency workers wheeling a body to an ambulance with the chilling headline: "Kids and guns: A report from America's classroom killing grounds." A 1993 cover of *Time* magazine (August 2, 1993) contained a shadowy image of a boy in a t-shirt pointing a shotgun and the headline, "Big shots: An inside look at the deadly love affair between America's kids and their guns." The same week, *Newsweek* ran a similar cover of a boy in a t-shirt running with a rifle and the headline: "Teen violence: Wild in the streets."

The fear of armed youths in the streets soon became a fear of armed students in American schools. The American public was bombarded with claims that schools were full of students carrying guns. Perhaps the most widely reported assertion was that "Nearly 135,000 guns are brought into schools every day" (National School Boards Association, 1993, p. 3). This figure is equivalent to about one gun in every school, every day.

The "135,000 guns in schools every day" statistic has been cited to buttress a wide variety of policies and reforms. For example, it has appeared in reports by such organizations as the National School Boards Association (1993), the Family Research Council (Maginnis, 1995), the American Sociological Association (Levine & Rosich, 1996), and the National Crime Prevention

> ## Myth 7. Students bring 135,000 guns to school every day.
>
> **FACT:** The claim that students bring 135,000 guns to school every day is one of the most widely cited statistics in the field of school safety, yet the organizations and authorities making this claim consistently fail to explain how it was determined and many provide an inaccurate citation for its source. As described below, the scientific basis of this claim is highly questionable.

Council (1995). The statistic appeared in *The New York Times* (Leary, 1990) as early as 1990, yet fifteen years later it continues to be widely cited as current knowledge. A Google search for "135,000 guns" on February 1, 2005, produced 112 hits. Law enforcement, education, health, and religious organizations routinely proclaim that 135,000 guns are brought into American schools every day.

Where did the "135,000 guns" statistic come from and how was it determined? None of the organizations quoting the "135,000 guns" statistic explained how it had been determined. None of them offered any reservations about its accuracy. It was simply presented as a fact attributed to a reputable source. But what source? This statistic has been attributed to a variety of different sources.

- At the outset of its 1993 report on violence in schools, the National School Boards Association (p. 3) wrote "About 135,000 guns are brought into schools every day." There is no explanation for this statistic.
- In 1994, Senator Diane Feinstein of California quoted the 135,000 guns statistic in a speech praising the President's zero tolerance initiative, and attributed it to the National School Safety Center (see http://www.ibiblio.org/pub/archives/whitehouse-papers/1994/Oct/1994–10–22-Feinstein-on-Zero-Tolerance-for-Guns-in-Schools-Memo).
- In 1995, Robert Maginnis of the conservative Family Research Council attributed the "135,000 guns are brought into schools every day" statistic to the 1993 National School Boards Association report.
- In 1996, the respected American Sociological Association released a report entitled "The Social Causes of Violence" (Levine & Rosich, 1996). This scholarly analysis accepted at face value the claim that "some 135,000 guns are brought into school each day" and attributed it to "a 1993 survey conducted by the Harris Poll for the Harvard School of Public Health" (p. 28).

- Shortly after the 1999 Columbine shootings, Senator Carl Levin of Michigan introduced juvenile justice legislation with a press release that repeated it twice, "135,000 guns are brought into U.S. schools every day according to an estimate by the National School Boards Association. 135,000 guns every day brought into our schools" (http://levin.senate .gov/newsroom/release.cfm?id;eq209429).

- A 2001 article on gun violence in schools published in the journal, *Law & Policy* attributed the claim that "each day 135,000 students carry guns to school" (Redding & Shalf, 2001, p 298) to Robert Maginnis's 1995 report for the Family Research Council (see above). The article makes the point that if there are 135,000 guns in school every day but only about 6,000 students expelled each year for bringing a firearm to school, then school security must be seriously deficient.

- The website of the National Crime Prevention Council in 2005 says that the 135,000 guns figure came from the Centers for Disease Control and Prevention, but gives no further information (National Crime Prevention Council, 1995).

Where did the ominous "135,000 guns" figure come from? The American Sociological Association gave the most specific source for the statistic, attributing it to "a 1993 survey conducted by the Harris Poll for the Harvard School of Public Health" (Levine & Kosich, 1996, p. 28). Multiple inquiries to staff and faculty at the Harvard School of Public Health could not identify anyone who knew of such a report.

Fortunately, an article in *Education Week* (Lawton, 1993) mentioned that the Harris poll was funded by the Joyce Foundation. The Joyce Foundation was able to find a copy of the 25-page report, the 12-page survey it employed, and 267 pages of statistical tables presenting the survey results (Sydney Sidwell, personal communication, January 26, 2005).

The Harris survey was conducted on a representative sample of 2,508 students (grades 6–12) from 96 schools around the country. The survey was conducted in April and May of 1993. The report from this survey (LH Research, Inc., 1993), however, does not say anything about 135,000 guns being brought to school every day. The closest the survey comes to such a figure is, "15 percent say they have carried a handgun on their person in the past 30 days, and 4 percent— 1 in 25—say they have taken a handgun to school this past year" (p. vi).

Did someone infer that if one student in 25 brought a gun to school at least once, sometime during the school year, then there must be 135,000 handguns brought to school on a daily basis? There are about 180 days in the average school year, and in 1993 there were about 25 million students in grades 6–12 (NCES, 1995). If 4 percent of these students—1 million students—brought a handgun to school on one occasion, the average number of handguns per day would be just 5,556. The only way that 4 percent of students could generate 135,000 guns per day is if they brought a gun to school an average of 24 times per year.

Multiple organizations claimed the source to be the 1993 report by the National School Board Association (NSBA), but the NSBA report does not explain the basis for this number. Staff members at the NSBA (Linda Embry, personal communication, February 10, 2005) suggested that the source might be found in a footnote indicating that several statistics on school violence were "compiled by the Center for Demographic Policy" (NSBA, 1993, p. 12).

The Center for Demographic Policy is part of the Institute for Educational Leadership, which is a not-for-profit, nonpartisan organization whose mission is to "improve education" (http://ielorg.fatcow.com/about.html). The former co-director of the Center for Demographic Policy, Dr. Harold Hodgkinson, emphatically denied that the Center could have provided any statistic on the number of guns brought to school (personal communication, February 14, 2005).

A librarian at the National School Boards Association (Dottie Gray, personal communication, February 16, 2005) subsequently turned up a 1991 article in *U.S. News & World Report* (Witkin, 1991) that stated,

> A 20-state survey of 11,000 adolescents found that 41 percent of the boys could obtain a handgun if they wanted to. An extrapolation of surveys by the National School Safety Center suggested that 135,000 students carried guns to school daily in 1987. Officials at the center think that figure is higher today (p. 26).

The survey mentioned in the *U.S. News & World Report* article was the National Adolescent Student Health Survey (American School Health Association, 1989), which surveyed 11,419 8th and 10th grade students in 1987. One survey question asked students to "Think back over the last 12 MONTHS. While at school, how often did you carry a handgun?" Students could mark their reply as "Never," "Less than once a month," "A few times a month," "A few times a week," and "Nearly every day." Approximately 2.6 percent of the boys admitted bringing a handgun to school, including almost one percent (.8) who claimed to have brought a handgun to school "nearly every day."

The Director of the National School Safety Center, Dr. Ronald Stephens, was familiar with the 135,000 guns statistic. He stated, "First, the 135,000 figure did not come from any research or any public announcement from NSSC. The 135,000, to my understanding and recollection, was based upon an extrapolated estimate benchmarked against other studies such as the National Adolescent Student Health Survey" (personal communication, February 18, 2005). The National School Safety Center multiplied the percent of students claiming to bring a gun to school every day by the number of students in the United States and the result was 135,000. Dr. Stephens concluded, "The bottom line is that there is no definitive study to affirm this statistic. Whenever NSSC was contacted about this we would consistently report the same answer to the media. For some reason, that quote would never appear in the articles. It is almost as though someone wanted to keep the information alive."

The mystery of the origin of the 135,000 guns statistic appears to be solved, but the greater mystery is how such a statistic could circulate for over fifteen years.

HOW DO WE DETERMINE HOW MANY YOUTH ARE CARRYING GUNS?

According to the Centers for Disease Control and Prevention (CDC), in 1990 five percent boys in grades 9–12 had carried a gun in the past 30 days (Centers for Disease Control, 1991). A news report that one in twenty high school boys carried a gun in the past month sounds alarming, because in the context of a story about juvenile crime it conjures an image of a young armed criminal. However, the CDC survey question simply asked, "During the past 30 days, on how many days did you carry a gun?" The survey made no distinction between use of a gun for criminal purposes and legitimate gun-carrying for hunting or sporting purposes.

Questions about carrying a gun to school.   Some surveys did ask students about carrying a gun to school. The well-known Monitoring The Future survey is administered annually by the University of Michigan to a nationally representative sample of students, and includes a question about carrying a gun to school. A recent survey asked 5,426 students, "During the LAST FOUR WEEKS, on how many days (if any) did you carry a gun to school?" A total of 167 students claimed to have carried a gun to school, including 81 who claimed to have brought a gun on ten or more days. This means that about 3 percent of students, or one in 32, claimed to have brought a gun to school.

How do we really know how many students took a gun to school? Researchers must rely on what the students report, and since the surveys are anonymous, students are free to claim whatever they want. Some students may be telling the truth, but others may be amusing themselves by giving a provocative response. Still others may be bored with the survey and mark it at random. And, of course, there may be students who are bringing a gun to school but do not want to report it, because they fear that the survey might not be anonymous after all. There is no conclusive way to tell whether students are telling the truth, so researchers must trust students to be honest. And while the majority of students may be honest, it only takes a small percentage—just one class clown per classroom—to produce alarming results.

From this perspective, it is interesting to consider some other responses to the Monitoring The Future survey. The tenth-graders were asked how many times they drank an alcoholic beverage during the last 30 days. There were 132 students who claimed to have drank on 10–19 occasions, 42 who claimed to have drank on 20–39 occasions, and 27 students who claimed to have drank an alcoholic beverage 40 or more occasions—literally more than once a day. The tenth-graders were also asked if they had "used marijuana (weed, pot) or hashish (hash, hash oil)" during the last 30 days. There were 122 students who claimed to have used these drugs on 40 or more occasions—again, more than once per day. Even allowing for a high incidence of alcohol and drug abuse among high school students, it seems likely that some of these students were amusing themselves by giving an exaggerated answer.

The researchers who conducted the National Adolescent Student Health Survey (NASHS) survey—the survey used to extrapolate the "135,000 guns" estimate—expressed reservations about the accuracy of student responses. They acknowledged that "Undoubtedly, some students misrepresented their actual behaviors and attitudes when responding to the survey. Distortions in both over- and under-representing certain behaviors are likely to occur with an adolescent population. However, based on the procedures and observations described, it is likely that distortions in the data represent exceptions rather than rule" (American School Health Association, 1989, p. 15–16).

The NASHS researchers believed that they minimized dishonest reporting by assuring students that their answers were anonymous and that no teacher or school staff member would ever see their responses (American School Health Association, 1989). Although the researchers intended these assurances to encourage honesty, an experienced educator might think otherwise. As any substitute teacher knows, when the regular teacher is not in charge, some students will take advantage of the situation and behave inappropriately. The promise of anonymity probably encourages most students to give honest answers, but other students will see an opportunity to entertain themselves by marking the survey with extreme answers.

Consider, for instance, some of the extreme answers regarding sexual assault obtained with the NASHS (American School Health Association, 1989). Students were asked if anyone had raped them or attempted to rape them in the past year at school. Approximately six percent of girls claimed that someone had raped or attempted to rape them, including two percent who claimed to have been victims three or more times in the past year at school. Could it really be true that two percent of girls in the 8th and 10th grades were rape victims three or more times in one year? An extrapolation from this survey result would mean that millions of rapes or attempted rapes take place in U.S. schools every year. Moreover, four percent of boys claimed to have been rape victims, too, and half of these boys claimed to have been sexually assaulted three or more times. Crime statistics consistently show that females are victims of rape far more often than males, but the NASHS results—if considered accurate—indicate that almost as many boys as girls are raped in American schools.

Investigations of self-report exaggerations.   One group of researchers at the University of California, Santa Barbara challenged the accuracy of student self-report surveys. They obtained access to the CDC's highly influential Youth Risk Behavior Survey (YRBS) data and found some unusual response patterns that had not been reported in the official studies by the CDC (Furlong, Bates, & Smith, 2001). The California group found that there was a group of students who claimed to have carried a weapon to school 6 or more times in the past month (the most extreme response). While this might be a credible response in some cases, a large proportion of these students gave other extreme responses, such as exercising vigorously seven days per week and participating on three or more sports teams. The researchers concluded that a group of students simply gave extreme responses to survey questions regardless of item content.

Another approach to examining the honesty of student self-report is to *ask* students whether they are being honest. Some surveys simply ask students whether they are telling the truth with an item such as, "I am telling the truth on this survey." Of course, students who are inclined to lie on the survey may also lie in response to this item, so it will not detect all dishonest students, but what about those students who admit that they are lying? Certainly the responses of these students are suspicious and should be red-flagged. The author's study with colleague Ann Loper at the University of Virginia (Cornell & Loper, 1998) examined surveys from 10,909 students in grades 7, 9, and 11 and found that 5.8 percent of students admitted they were not telling the truth on the survey. About one-third of these admittedly dishonest students also claimed to have brought a gun to school.

The use of validity screening procedures can substantially reduce estimates of the prevalence of student involvement in high risk behavior such as fights, drug use, and gangs. In the University of Virginia study (Cornell & Loper, 1998), approximately one-fourth of the surveys failed to meet validity screening criteria that included detection of students who omitted demographic information, indiscriminately marked items all in the same way, or gave inappropriate answers to validity questions (e.g., answering "No" to "I am telling the truth on this survey"). The deletion of invalid self-report surveys reduced the estimated 30-day prevalence of fighting at school from 28.7 percent to 19.2 percent. Similarly, the estimated prevalence of self-reported drug use at school dropped from 25.1 percent to 14.8 percent, gang membership dropped from 8.4 percent to 5.2 percent, and carrying a knife at school dropped from

18.4 percent to 7.7 percent. Nevertheless, even the best screening procedures are unlikely to identify all false reports. The question of weapon carrying at school cannot be definitively answered using student self-report alone, and will require more extensive research than has been undertaken to date.

THE MISUSE OF GUN SURVEY STATISTICS

Both conservative and liberal organizations seize upon student survey statistics to inflame public fears that schools are full of armed students. Ironically, both liberal and conservative organizations used the same exaggerated reports to reach opposite conclusions. The typical article begins by citing frightening statistics about the numbers of students carrying guns or shooting at one another, followed by an anecdotal account of a horrific crime intended to represent what these statistics mean in human terms. After setting the stage so dramatically, the author points the finger of blame. For conservative organizations, the cause of school violence might be a perceived breakdown in traditional values or the lack of two-parent families. Liberal organizations might blame social conditions such as poverty and racism, or the lack of gun control. Both conservative and liberal organizations could be partially correct in their concerns, but because they are based on inaccurate characterizations of the conditions in American schools, their arguments rest on quicksand.

Misuse of the Youth Risk Behavior Survey. A good example of the misuse of the YRBS findings can be found in an article entitled, "Guns in School, What Can You Do?" (Klammer, 2000), which was published by American Catholic.org and, in 2005, was still available on the internet (http://www .americancatholic.org/Newsletters/YU/ay0700.asp). The facts and fears mingled in this article might well persuade parents to remove their children from public schools and send them to a Catholic school. The opening paragraph, for instance, makes two frightening claims:

> According to a report by the Department of Education, over 6,000 students were expelled in 1996–1997 for bringing guns into their public schools. A 1990 survey by the Centers for Disease Control reported that one in 20 high school students had carried a gun in the past month.
> Why did those kids feel the need to carry a gun to school? (Klammer, 2000)

Readers might assume that the Centers for Disease Control had found that one in 20 high school students were carrying a gun *to school* in the past month, since the statement follows a sentence about bringing guns into public schools. The opening sentence of the next paragraph makes the implication even stronger by asking, "Why did those kids feel the need to carry a gun to school?" Any reader would conclude that one in 20 high school students had brought a gun to school in the past month.

However, the survey used by the Centers for Disease Control did not ask students whether they had taken a gun to school, but simply whether they had *carried* a gun, period. Any student who had used a gun while hunting would have answered "yes" to this question, as would any student who went target-shooting or had some other legitimate reason to carry a gun. Klammer's article distorts the survey finding in a way that makes public schools seem dangerous.

Klammer's claim that "over 6,000 students were expelled in 1996–1997 for bringing guns into their public schools" is also not quite correct. In fact, 6,093 students were expelled for bringing a *firearm* to school (Sinclair, Hamilton, Gutman, Daft, & Bolcki, 1998). The definition of a firearm in this report includes explosive devices such as fireworks and bombs. Moreover, as the report clearly warns readers, some of the states—such as Ohio, Colorado, and Missouri— erred in making their reports and included expulsions for all weapons in their data. In other words, some of the "firearms" were actually items such as knives and brass knuckles. So how many of these 6,000 expulsions were for guns, as distinguished from firecrackers, knives, brass knuckles, or some other weapon? It is impossible to say, but clearly it is not accurate to say there were 6,000 ex-pulsions for guns. All firearms are not guns and, in this case, some of the weapons were not even firearms.

Most states provided a breakdown of what type of weapon was associated with each expulsion, but a few states only reported the total number of ex-pulsions. As a result, the researchers could determine the type of firearm in only 3,497 cases. Of these cases, only 65 percent involved guns. Therefore, a rough estimate might be that the total number of times a student was caught bringing a gun to school was closer to 4,000 than 6,000. Certainly, even one student bringing a gun to school is too many, but to put these numbers in per-spective, with a school population of 51 million, 4,000 represents approxi-mately one out of every 12,750 students.

Misuse of Louis Harris Poll statistics.   The conservative Family Research Council issued a report, "Violence in the Schoolhouse," that was laden with alarming statistics used to buttress its argument that the deterioration of the American family was the cause of pervasive school violence (Maginnis, 1995). Ten years later, the Schoolhouse report is still widely cited and can be found on the internet (http://www.townhall.com/spotlights/archive/9–11–95/is94e5cr .html). Perhaps the most disturbing claim in the Schoolhouse report was that "11 percent of schoolchildren had been shot at by a gun in the past year." Could it really be the case that, in just twelve months, one of every nine schoolchildren had been shot at by a gun?

MYTH 8: 11 percent of schoolchildren have been shot at by a gun in the past year.

FACT: The basis for this alarming claim is a single anonymous survey of 2,508 students with no verification of the truth or accuracy of their responses. As described below, the results of the survey were extrapolated to represent national norms.

The Family Research Council based its claim that "11 percent of school-children had been shot at by a gun in the past year" on a reputable source, a Harris Poll conducted for the Harvard School of Public Health and funded with a grant from The Joyce Foundation (LH Research, 1993). This is the same poll that the American Sociological Association erroneously claimed as the source for its "135,000 guns" in schools statistic.

The Harris Poll was conducted on a representative sample of 2,508 students (grades 6–12) from 96 schools. The survey asked students to complete an anonymous questionnaire that would be mailed to researchers without their teachers reading their answers. One survey question asked, "Over the past year, has anyone shot at you with a gun, or not?" Students could answer by checking boxes labeled "been shot at," "not been shot at," or "not sure." Of 2,505 respondents to this question, 285 students—11 percent—checked "been shot at." Interestingly, the same percent was found for public, private non-Catholic, and Catholic schools, and students in middle schools were slightly more likely to be shot at (12%) than high schools (11%). More males (17%) than females (5%) reported being shot at.

How plausible are students' answers to questions about being shot at? In 1993 there were approximately 25 million students enrolled in grades 6 through 12 (National Center for Education Statistics, 1995), and 11 percent of this total would mean that roughly 2.75 million students had been shot at in the past year. Pollsters should have realized that it is beyond credibility that 2.75 million children actually were shot at in one year.

Moreover, the Harris survey asked those who students claimed they had been shot at whether they had been "seriously injured when you were shot at." Nine percent of students who had been shot at said that they had been seriously injured. If these statistics are accurate, then it would mean that almost one percent of all students (grades 6–12) in the United States (.09 × .11 is .0099) were seriously injured by a gunshot. In other words, there would have been about 247,500 students injured by gunshots in a single year.

The Harris researchers could have assessed the plausibility of their figures by considering how many young people nationwide are injured by gunshots each year. The U.S. Consumer Product Safety Commission calculates injury rates by surveying hospitals across the country. Although their figures are only estimates, they indicate that approximately 13,281 children ages 11 to 18 were injured by guns from May 1, 1992 to May 1, 1993. The estimate of 13,281 may seem like an extraordinary number of injuries, but it is far smaller than the 247,500 indicated by the Harris survey. The number of gunshot injuries as determined by the Harris survey is 18 times the number estimated by the U.S. Consumer Product Safety Commission. Clearly, the Harris survey results are not credible.

Another source of corroborating information is the National Center for Injury Prevention and Control (NCIPC). Their online system (http://www .cdc.gov/ncipc/) provides statistics dating back only to 2000, so a direct comparison with 1993 is not possible. However, it is noteworthy that in 2000 the NCIPC recorded just 8,491 gunshot injuries in a population of 36.6 million children ages 10 to 18.

The Harris survey next asked students whether the person who shot at them was "caught and punished." Approximately 16 percent of the students who were allegedly shot at said that their assailant was caught and punished, and another 9 percent said their assailant was "caught but not punished." It is not clear what "caught" means, but if being caught means being arrested, this would be a staggering number of arrests. If there were truly shooting incidents involving 11 percent of all students in the United States, and 25 percent of these incidents resulted in an arrest, this would mean that in one year, 2.75 million students were shot at and 687,500 persons were arrested (assuming that all those who were punished were arrested) for these shootings. This is plainly implausible when considered in comparison to national crime statistics. In 1993 there were only 442,075 persons arrested for aggravated assault in the United States (FBI, 1994). In other words, the estimate of persons punished for shooting a student exceeds the total number of persons arrested for any form of aggravated assault in the United States.

The Family Research Council was not the only organization to cite the Harris poll statement that 11 percent of children had been shot at by a gun. This dubious statistic was quoted in the opening of an article in *Education Week* (Sommerfeld, 1993), a well-regarded publication that touts itself as "American Education's Newspaper of Record." The article reported that the Harris poll findings were publicized at a national conference sponsored by the federal departments of Education, Justice, Health and Human Services, and Housing and Urban Development (Sommerfeld, 1993). To its credit, the *Education Week* article expresses some reservations about the validity of the Harris Poll, stating, "Some experts and educators, however, dismissed the grim findings as being unrealistic, attributing the high numbers to youthful bravado" (p. 21).

What did the Harris researchers say about the accuracy of their survey? The survey report gives no indication that researchers used any of the standard methods to screen surveys for random or exaggerated responses. For instance, there were no validity check questions. On the contrary, the researchers simply assert that the students were honest:

"Perhaps more than any other group, we are deep in debt to the 2,508 young people themselves who with characteristic bluntness and honesty answered some of the most personal questions about their own personal security that might be asked" (LH Research, 1993, p. v).

How do the researchers know that the young people taking the survey were honest? They do not say.

Misuse of statistics to support liberal causes. Liberal organizations also seized upon the youth gun issue to support their causes. On its Web site, the Brady Center to Prevent Gun Violence (http://www.bradycenter.org/stop2/facts/fs5 .php, accessed January 6, 2005), lists a series of ominous statistics under the heading "Guns in our nation's schools." Consider two:

- "In a 1997 survey, 9 percent of high school students had carried a weapon to school during the 30 days preceding the survey; 6 percent had carried a gun."
- "In the 1993–94 school year, Virginia school officials discovered 373 guns."

The source for the first claim, that 6 percent of high school students had carried a gun to school in the 30 days preceding the survey, is given as "Youth Risk Behavior Study, Centers for Disease Control and Prevention, 1997." However, inspection of the 88 items in the 1997 Youth Risk Behavior Survey (Centers for Disease Control and Prevention, 1997a) reveals that students were never asked whether they carried a gun *to school.* One question (Q13) asked "During the past 30 days, on how many days did you carry a gun?" Of the 16,262 responses to this question, 1,110 or 6.8 percent claimed to have carried a gun on one or more days. Perhaps this is the figure cited by the Brady Center.

There is an additional question on the 1997 YRBSS (Q14) that *includes* carrying a gun to school; "During the past 30 days, on how many days did you carry a weapon such as a gun, knife, or club on school property?" There were 1,309 positive responses to this question, indicating that 8 percent of students reported carrying a weapon of some type, but not necessarily a gun. The claim made on the Brady Center website appears to be based on a faulty reading of the YRBS survey results. (The Brady Center did not reply to an inquiry about these statistics.)

The second claim by the Brady Center, that 373 guns were found in Virginia schools during the 1993–94 school year, is also suspect. According to Virginia's annual report of school crimes and disciplinary violations, there were 373 *firearms* violations for the year (Virginia Department of Education, 1995). At that time, the Virginia reporting system defined "firearms" in a manner that could include guns, BB guns, pellet guns, starter pistols, and even bombs, fireworks, rockets, and other explosive devices. In addition, according to Marsha Owens, school safety specialist and author of the Department of Education report (personal communication, 2003), some school divisions may have reported water guns, cap guns, and other toy guns under this category.

How many of the 373 firearms violations were actually gun violations? It is not possible to say, but in subsequent years Virginia revised its definition of a firearm and began reporting a more differentiated breakdown of violations. The newer statistics give some indication of how many "firearms" were actually guns. During the 2002–2003 school year there were just 45 violations involving handguns and 7 involving rifles or shotguns (Virginia Department of Education, 2004). Tellingly, there were 362 violations for "look-alike guns," 115 violations for "fireworks," 71 for "weapon designed or converted to expel a projectile," 37 for "explosive devices," and 37 for "other firearms." If all these categories are combined, guns represent less than ten percent of the 674 total violations. Obviously, school statistics on how many "firearms" were brought to school cannot be trusted to mean guns.

HOW MANY GUNS ARE ACTUALLY FOUND IN SCHOOLS?

Although there is no foolproof way to determine how many students bring guns to school, it is possible to count how many students are *caught* with guns at school. The federal government requires all states receiving federal funds to expel for at least one year any public school student who brings a firearm to school (although schools can modify the expulsion on a case-by-case basis in extenuating circumstances; U.S. Department of Education, 2004). Schools must report an annual tally of the number of students disciplined for firearms violations, which the federal government summarizes in an annual report. National data for the 2001–2002 school year were released in 2004 (U.S. Department of Education, 2004), and indicate that 2,554 students were found to have a firearm at school. Over half (57%) of these students were in high school, 30 percent in junior high or middle school, and 13 percent in elementary school.

As noted above, a firearm does not necessarily mean a gun. The federal definition of a firearm includes not only guns, but explosive devices such as bombs, grenades, rockets, or starter pistols (U.S. Department of Education, 2004). The most common firearm was a handgun (50%). Only 12 percent of the firearms were rifles or shotguns and 38 percent were for some other explosive device. The federal definition explicitly excludes toy guns, cap guns,

BB guns, or pellet guns, making it clear that there was no intention to require schools to expel students for possession of such objects. Unfortunately, school administrators in Virginia and other states may have expelled students from school under the mistaken belief that federal law required them to do so.

With a total public school enrollment of 48,264,624, the percentage of students found to have a firearm was .0000529 percent and the percent found with a gun was .0000328 percent. This means there was approximately 1 firearm-related expulsion for every 19,000 students and 1 expulsion for possession of a gun for every 30,000 students.

The number of guns actually found in schools is obviously far fewer than the number that students claim they brought to school in self-report surveys. The contrast between the number of students found with a gun and the number estimated by researchers is extreme. Even if one chooses a relatively low estimate of the number of students who claim to have brought a gun to school, there is a huge discrepancy. Consider the relatively low estimate obtained from researchers at the University of Illinois at Urbana-Champaigne (Williams, Mulhall, Reis, & DeVille, 2002). In this survey of 22,000 Illinois students in grades 6, 8, and 10, only about 1.2 percent of students claimed to have brought a gun to school in 1998.

Even a small percent like 1.2 percent translates into a large number of guns statewide. In 1998 Illinois had a public school enrollment of 1,008,610 students in grades 6 through 12 (NCES, 2000), so approximately 12,103 students would have carried a gun to school statewide.

In 1998, Illinois expelled 83 students for bringing a handgun, rifle, or shotgun to school (U.S. Department of Education, 1999). That means that if projections from the Illinois survey are correct—and the students told the truth on their survey—school authorities caught only 83 out of 12,103 students who brought a gun to school. It is likely that school authorities did not catch every student who brought a gun to school, but is it plausible that there were 12,020 missed cases and that the detection rate was only one out of every 146 guns? More likely is that student self-reports of gun carrying at school were grossly exaggerated.

WHAT CAN WE DO TO REDUCE GUN VIOLENCE?

The problem of gun violence is serious, even if the statistics are inaccurate. Exaggerations are counter-productive because they distort our understanding of the problem, create a climate of fear in our schools, and lead to misguided policies. If the gun problem is so pervasive and the danger so great, it seems necessary to impose draconian policies such as zero tolerance—expelling every child who brings a gun—or even a toy gun—to school. A more accurate assessment of the problem, however, could lead to more effective prevention, as discussed in Chapter 8.

Many groups have developed strategies to reduce youth gun violence. There are two main approaches: educational programs and intensified law enforcement. Educational programs are designed to educate students or parents about firearm safety and dissuade them from carrying, storing, or using guns inappropriately. This is a primary prevention approach that starts with elementary or middle school children and might not show effects on crime rates for years to come. In contrast, field-based law enforcement programs target gun violence in high-crime communities. These programs tend to combine strong warning messages with intensive policing and aggressive prosecution of offenders, with the goal of producing immediate reductions in gun crime.

Educational programs.   There are dozens of educational programs developed by well-meaning organizations who want to teach gun safety to children. The National Rifle Association (NRA; no date), for example, developed the "Eddie Eagle Gun Safety Program" for children up to grade 6. The program emphasizes a "just say no" approach to dangerous behavior such as playing with a firearm. No study has demonstrated the effectiveness of the Eddie Eagle program, although the NRA claimed credit for the 13 percent nationwide reduction in gun-related injuries to children from 1991 to 1992 (Hardy, 2002). National trends are influenced by a multitude of factors, of course, and no program can claim to be effective without a controlled study.

One study examined a "just say no" program similar to the Eddie Eagle program (Hardy, Armstrong, Martin, & Strawn, 1996). This program randomly divided 48 preschool children and their parents into two groups: Half of the children and their parents listened to a police officer lecture on the dangers of guns, while the others served as a control group. The children in the "just say no" program solemnly promised never to touch a gun if they found one. Afterwards, these children and the control children were allowed to play in a room where they found a gun. Children in both groups were equally likely to play with the guns.

Despite the absence of evidence for its effectiveness, the National Rifle Association (no date) asserts that the program has helped reduce gun accidents. On its website, the NRA posted the question: "Have there been any evaluations of the program's impact in published/unpublished literature? If not, how do you measure its impact?" The second question, "If not, how do you measure its impact?" indirectly acknowledges that no evaluation has demonstrated the program's impact, but the answer provided by the NRA implies otherwise:

One study published in the *Journal of Emergency Nursing Online* (October 2001) named The Eddie Eagle GunSafe® Program the best of 80 gun accident prevention programs evaluated. Beyond that, the effectiveness of the program is evident in several ways. First, according to the National Center for Health Statistics and the National Safety Council, fatal firearms accidents among children have dropped 91 percent since 1975. NRA believes that gun accident prevention programs such as Eddie Eagle are a major reason for the dramatic decline. Second, we often receive letters from parents whose children have encountered guns in unsupervised situations and avoided an accident by doing exactly what Eddie Eagle had taught them: "STOP! Don't Touch. Leave the Area. Tell an Adult." Third, the program has been honored or endorsed by groups such as the National Safety Council, the National Sheriffs' Association, the Department of Justice, and bipartisan support from 24 state governors. Finally, the mere fact that 22,000 schoolteachers and law enforcement officers have taught the program to 17 million children verifies the popularity of the program with those who deal with child safety issues every day (accessed February 5, 2005 at http://www.nrahq.org/safety/eddie/fact.asp).

The NRA cites a "study published in the *Journal of Emergency Nursing Online*," but this study was not a scientific evaluation of whether the programs worked. Rather, it was a descriptive article that reviewed different programs and complimented the Eddie Eagle program for its educational materials and printing format. The NRA's statement that the Eddie Eagle program has won the praise of many organizations and has been widely implemented falls short of proof that it is effective. And although fatal firearms accidents among children may have dropped 91 percent since 1975, there is no scientific basis for the NRA to claim that the Eddie Eagle program is a "major reason" for the decline.

Marjorie Hardy (2002), a professor of psychology at Eckerd College, argues that "just say no" programs are unlikely to be effective because merely telling children what they should do is too weak an intervention. She contends that effective programs must teach children to understand the *reasons* for gun safety practices and to develop skills to resist temptation and peer pressure.

At the other end of the political spectrum from the NRA, the Brady Center to Prevent Gun Violence developed a skills-based program called Straight Talk about Risks (STAR). This program is aimed at educating students from kindergarten through 12th grade about the risks of firearm injury and includes age-appropriate lessons to encourage students to resist peer pressure, identify risks, and seek help when necessary. While there is some evidence that this type of approach increases children's knowledge of gun safety, there is no definitive evidence that such programs change children's behavior (Hardy, 2002).

Still another educational approach attempts to convince parents to store guns more safely or even to remove them from their homes. The American Academy of Pediatrics, in conjunction with the Brady Center to Prevent Gun Violence, developed a gun safety program that encourages physicians and nurses to educate parents about gun safety. Called Steps to Prevent Firearm

Injury (STOP), this program emphasizes the dangers of having a gun in the home and stresses the need for safe gun storage.

Researchers at the St. Vincent Mercy Medical Center in Toledo, Ohio evaluated the STOP program by providing educational messages to 1,617 families that brought children in for annual school physicals (Oatis, Fenn Buderer, Cummings, & Fleitz, 1999). A year later they queried roughly one-quarter (23.6 percent) of the families who returned for another visit to see if there had been any reductions in gun ownership or changes in gun storage precautions. There were slight decreases in gun ownership and storage of loaded guns, but the differences were not statistically significant. Although these were disappointing results, it remains unclear whether the intervention might have been effective if the educational message had been repeated or reinforced over time, and if the researchers had gathered follow-up data from a larger proportion of the families who came to the medical center.

Unlike in the field of entertainment violence, where a large body of research supports unequivocal conclusions, the field of gun violence suffers from serious deficiencies in both quantity and quality of research. Educational programs to prevent gun violence have not been adequately studied. According to a 2005 landmark report of the National Research Council's "Committee to Improve Research Information and Data on Firearms,"

> ... there is almost no empirical evidence that the more than 80 prevention programs focused on gun-related violence have had any effect on children's behavior, knowledge, attitudes, or beliefs about firearms. The committee found that the data available on these questions are too weak to support unambiguous conclusions or strong policy statements. (National Research Council, 2005, p. 2)

The National Research Council report does not conclude that gun-violence prevention programs do not work; the problem is that in almost all cases prevention programs have been implemented without rigorous evaluations of their effectiveness. The limited research that has been conducted suffers from deficiencies that make it inconclusive. Quality research is an expensive and burdensome activity that is not sufficiently valued by the organizations that design and implement violence prevention programs.

Law enforcement programs.   There is more reason for optimism with law enforcement approaches to gun violence. Some studies have found immediate benefits to a concerted effort by law enforcement authorities to reduce youth gun violence.

The most highly regarded attempt to reduce youth gun violence is Boston's Operation Ceasefire, also called the Boston Gun Project (Braga, Kennedy, & Tita, 2002; Kennedy, Braga, & Piehl, 2001; National Research Council, 2005).

This program won the Ford Foundation Innovations in Government award and the International Association of Chiefs of Police Webber Seavey Award. The program began in 1995, at a time when Boston had about 60 different neighborhood groups—loosely organized gangs—that were engaged in a series of vendettas that resulted in numerous shootings and killings. Between 1991 and 1995, Boston averaged 44 homicides of persons under age 24 per year, as well as many more non-lethal shooting incidents.

In response to years of almost weekly murders, a group of police officers, youth workers, and researchers devised a plan to stop the gun violence among the rival neighborhood gangs. The plan involved a coordinated effort to interrupt the cycle of violence by communicating to gang members that there would be a massive crackdown on gun violence and on gun trafficking to juveniles. The message delivered by police, probation, and parole officers was that there would be relentless pursuit, arrest, and punishment of anyone involved in juvenile gun violence. This was repeated citywide by youth workers, church leaders, and other community authorities, and further augmented by increased enforcement of curfews and other restrictions for juveniles on probation. Gang members were told that authorities would "pull every lever" legally available to prosecute gun offenders. This approach has come to be known in criminal justice circles as the "pulling levers" strategy (Braga, Kennedy, & Tita, 2002).

Like most violence prevention efforts, resources were devoted to implementing the program rather than evaluating its effectiveness. There was no comparison group, which would be required for a rigorous evaluation. Instead, researchers could only examine crime rates before and after the program was undertaken. Nevertheless, the drop in gun-related crimes was remarkable: Boston youth homicides declined 63 percent. There were substantial declines in firearm-related assaults (25%) and shot-fired calls (32%). Boston's drop in youth homicide was larger than declines seen in most other cities, and could not be explained by changes in employment, youth population, or citywide violence trends (Braga, Kennedy, & Tita, 2002).

The apparent success of Boston's Operation Ceasefire inspired similar programs in many other cities, including Minneapolis; Baltimore; Indianapolis; the Boyle Heights section of Los Angeles; High Point, North Carolina; and Stockton, California. All of these "lever pulling" programs involved an intensive effort to stop gun violence associated with drug-dealing or conflicts between neighborhood groups or gangs. These programs have not been rigorously evaluated—which is a major shortcoming of many law enforcement programs—but local crime statistics show substantial declines in the targeted neighborhoods (Braga, Kennedy, & Tita, 2002).

The program in Baltimore is particularly noteworthy because during the early 1990s homicides were averaging more than 300 per year—nearly one a day, a rate that was among the highest in the United States. Researchers estimated that there were 325 drug groups in Baltimore that ranged from highly structured criminal organizations to loosely organized neighborhood groups that sold drugs. The most violent drug market areas were targeted for intensive enforcement and aggressive prosecution. This message was communicated to gang members, suspected or known drug dealers, and community residents through individual contacts, public forums, and fliers posted in the area. Although a citywide evaluation has not been completed, analyses of the program's effect in the high crime community of Park Heights showed a 74 percent reduction in shootings and a 22 percent reduction in homicides (Braga, Kennedy, & Tita, 2002).

Law enforcement efforts appear to have been successful in reducing the most frequent and notorious forms of gun violence committed by drug dealers and gang members. The increased availability of highly lethal guns made this problem particularly acute in the early 1990's, and there has been substantial progress in reducing these kinds of crimes (Blumstein & Wallman, 2000). But what about other forms of gun violence committed for different motives? Not all young gun users are gang members or drug dealers. How does the availability of guns influence a young person's decision-making under stressful circumstances?

DOES THE TRIGGER PULL THE FINGER?

It is easy to see how possession of a gun makes one more dangerous, since guns easily inflict more serious injury than fists or knives, but could the presence of a gun have an additional, stimulating effect that makes someone more aggressive? Noted psychologist Leonard Berkowitz contended, "Guns not only permit violence, they can stimulate it as well. The finger pulls the trigger, but the trigger may also be pulling the finger" (Berkowitz, 1968, p. 22). A well-established body of psychological research started by Berkowitz shows that the mere presence of a gun stimulates more aggressive behavior, particularly if someone is already frustrated or angry. Such findings would have provocative implications for gun regulation policies.

One of the most remarkable studies of the psychological effects of guns was conducted by Berkowitz and LePage (1967) at the University of Wisconsin. This study demonstrated how the presence of a gun could stimulate more aggressive behavior in a person who was already in an angry state of mind. This study was so provocative that it requires a detailed explanation. Two male students were brought into a laboratory where the experimenter told them that they would be participating in an investigation of physiological reactions to stress. In reality, one student was a confederate of the researcher and only pretended to be participating in the study. The experimenter told the students that each would take turns working on a series of problems and that his partner would evaluate the quality of his work by giving him a series of mildly painful electric shocks—up to ten shocks for poor performance. In fact, the student was randomly assigned to receive either one shock or seven shocks, regardless of the quality of his work. Students who received seven shocks understandably became angry.

When it was the student's turn to evaluate the quality of his partner's ideas, the student was taken to a room where he could press a telegraph key that he was told would shock his partner. One group of students saw a revolver and a shotgun lying on the table next to the shock key, and another group saw two badminton racquets. In both instances, the experimenter shoved the objects aside and said that they had been left there by someone who was doing a different experiment. A third group of students found nothing on the table other than the telegraph key. The experimenter then left the room so that the student could evaluate his partner's work and administer electric shocks accordingly.

As expected, the students who were made angry by receiving seven shocks gave more shocks—typically 4 or 5—than the students who only received one shock, who tended to give 2 or 3 shocks. The most startling finding, however, was that the men who were exposed to guns gave an average of 5.8 shocks in comparison to the men who saw nothing (average of 4.6 shocks) or saw only a pair of badminton racquets (average of 4.7 shocks). This result shows that the mere presence of guns had an effect on an angry person and stimulated him to engage in a more aggressive action against an antagonist.

Researchers around the world became intrigued by the results of this study, which came to be called the "weapon effect." No single study can produce conclusive results, and so other studies were necessary. These studies used different strategies and research designs, and produced varying results, but overall indicated support for the basic finding that exposure to a gun increased aggressive behavior, particularly if the person was angered or disinhibited in some way (Berkowitz, 1993, 1994). A weapon effect has been found for pictures of guns, toy guns, weapons other than guns, and even just weapon names (Anderson, Benjamin, & Bartholow, 1998; Berkowitz & Frodi, 1977; Leyens, & Parke, 1975; Page & O'Neal, 1977; Turner, Simons, Berkowitz, & Frodi, 1977). The presence of a weapon appears to increase mental processing of aggressive thoughts and make aggressive ideas more accessible to consciousness (Anderson, Benjamin, & Bartholow, 1998).

Some researchers challenged the validity of the weapon effect by contending that the subjects probably suspected what the study was about and simply complied with the experimenter's expectation that they give more electric shocks. However, a series of studies found the opposite: persons who did suspect what the study was about actually tended to inhibit their aggression; the weapon effect was strongest in persons who were unaware of the purpose of the study (Simons & Turner, 1974, 1976; Turner & Simons, 1974).

A study at the University of Zagreb in Croatia (Zuzul, 1989, cited in Berkowitz, 1993) found an effect of both toy guns and real guns on the sub-sequent play behavior of 6-year-old children. Children who had been frus-trated and then shown either toy or real guns were more likely to push and hit their classmates on the playground than children who were frustrated but not shown any guns. Most interesting was that some children were told a story implying that the adult had a permissive attitude toward aggressive behavior and others heard a story implying a strict attitude; the children who heard from the adult with the disapproving attitude toward aggression did not dis-play as strong a reaction to the guns as did the other children. In other words, adults could lessen the effects of gun exposure if they conveyed disapproval for aggressive behavior.

The Croatian study provides support to both sides of the gun control de-bate: Advocates of gun control can cite the adverse effect of gun exposure on children, while advocates of gun freedom can point out that evidently the children's behavior is not automatic, but can be influenced by the example set by adults.

In conclusion, guns played a critical role in the epidemic of juvenile homi-cide our nation experienced in the 1980s and early 1990s, but the role of guns is easily misconstrued if motive and method are not clearly distinguished. Guns provide youth with a highly lethal method of settling disputes, but they are not the cause of those disputes. Guns provide youth with a means of com-mitting robberies, but they are not the cause of the robbery. The motives for killing someone precede the influence of the weapon, even if the presence of weapons has an aggravating effect on the aggressor's decision-making process.

Because motive and method are essential ingredients of any violent act, there will always be legitimate multiple perspectives on the problem of gun vi-olence, and compelling arguments can be made for limiting juvenile access to guns as well as for addressing the underlying social problems and psychologi-cal factors that lead young people to choose a violent course of action. Fourteen-year-old Bobby would be much better off if he had no access to guns, but he would be better still if he attended a school where bullying and hazing were not a rampant part of the school's culture. The problem of bullying is an-alyzed in the next chapter.

5

What Can We Do about Bullying?

Fifteen-year-old Mickey dreaded Mondays so much that every Sunday evening his stomach started to churn at bedtime. He tossed and turned much of the night. Sometimes he had nightmares. The next morning he could honestly claim to feel sick, and several times he managed to convince his parents to let him stay home from school. But after a few weeks his parents became suspicious of his complaints and made him go to school anyway. "Why don't you want to go to school?" they would ask.

"I just don't feel good—I feel sick," was his consistent reply.

Mickey lived with his family in a nice home in a middle-class suburban neighborhood. He attended a high school with a good reputation: Few students dropped out of school, and the majority went to college. There were no gangs, few students rarely got into serious trouble; they were mostly interested in sports, music, and school dances.

Mickey had never been a great student, but this year his grades had fallen from Bs and Cs to Cs and Ds. He hated going to school, and once he got there, he kept a low profile. He sat in the back of the classroom and skipped lunch in order to stay out of the cafeteria. But nothing he could do stopped the teasing. The other boys liked to tease him and make fun of him, and sometimes the girls would laugh as well, even the one he really liked. His face turned red when he was embarrassed, and sometimes he stammered when he was upset. Mickey never told his parents about the teasing at school. He never told them how much he hated being "gay" and "queer." His parents knew none of this until they read the suicide note.

On his 16th birthday Mickey went to school late on a Sunday night. He stood
in front of the security camera at the main entrance to the school, doused himself with gasoline, and set himself on fire.

Why did Mickey kill himself? The simplest answer is that he was driven to
kill himself by the relentless teasing of his peers. His suicide letter said that he
could not take it anymore. Certainly the boys who teased him were shocked
at his death. They protested that they never intended such an outcome—they
were just "having fun." Nevertheless, the boys felt guilty and remorseful for
their actions.

Millions of students are teased without committing suicide, of course, so an
explanation of why Mickey killed himself must consider other factors. Perhaps
Mickey was more sensitive than other boys, and less able to shrug off ridicule.
Perhaps he lacked the coping skills of other boys, who fend off teasing with a
clever retort. If he had been stronger or more confident, he might not have
made such a good target. Shy and introverted, he did not make friends easily,
and had no close friends to stand up for him or console him. He wasn't smart
or athletic or talented in some way that would provide him with a reservoir of
self-respect. Instead, he withdrew and brooded on the insults.

Mental health practitioners would say that Mickey had a major depression
(American Psychiatric Association, 2000) with symptoms of depressed mood,
feelings of worthlessness, suicidal ideation, sleep problems, and loss of energy.
A psychiatrist would say that his brain suffered from biochemical malfunction,
with deficiencies in serotonin or dopamine neurotransmitters which regulate
mood, energy, and the experience of pleasure. Whatever biological changes
might be observed in his brain, once Mickey entered a state of depression with
suicidal thinking, his view of the world became darker and more pessimistic.
He began to feel hopeless. As he wrote in his letter, the world was full of stu-
pid people and he didn't want to be part of it any longer.

NEW INTEREST IN BULLYING

Bullying has become one of the hot topics in education. Public interest in bul-
lying was stimulated by the school shootings of the 1990s. Fourteen-year-old
Michael Carneal shot eight students at Heath High School in Paducah,
Kentucky after being bullied and taunted by larger boys (Harding, Mehta, &
Newman, 2003). Thirteen-year-old Mitchell Johnson and his accomplice,
eleven-year-old Andrew Golden, allegedly had been teased and picked on by
other students before they killed five and wounded ten at Westside Middle
School in Jonesboro, Arkansas (Fox, Roth, & Newman, 2003). Both the FBI
and Secret Service studies of school shootings (O'Toole, 2000; Vossekuil,

Fein, Reddy, Borum, & Modzeleski, 2002) concluded that 2/3 of the students who opened fire on their classmates were motivated by a desire to take revenge for bullying.

In recent years, at least 17 states have enacted laws that direct schools to tackle the problem of bullying (Jamisa Murray, personal communication, December 3, 2004). Thousands of schools have implemented bully prevention programs, and many new state laws mandate that all schools in a given state address the problem (Limber & Small, 2003). Bullying prevention is rapidly becoming part of the standard school health curriculum, alongside programs to prevent drug use, cigarette smoking, and teen pregnancy (Olweus, Limber, & Mihalic, 1999; Whitaker, Rosenbluth, Valle, & Sanchez, 2004).

Accordingly, educational publishing companies have been quick to provide schools with numerous prepared programs to reduce bullying, with titles such as "The Bully Free Classroom" (Beane, 1999), "Bullyproofing Your School" (Garrity, Jens, Porter, Sager, & Short-Camilli, 1994), "Bully Busters" (Horne, Bartolomucci, Newman-Carlson, 2003), and "Taking the Bully by the Horns" (Noll & Carter, 1998). School counselors are barraged with advertisements for curriculum packages, books, videos, posters, and other materials intended to reduce bullying.

Research on bullying has escalated dramatically; a PsycINFO search using keywords "bully" or "bullying" located 300 published articles in the past 30 years (1975–2004); 90 percent (271) of these studies were published in the past 10 years, and more than three-fourths (229) in the past five years.

Of course, most bullying does not lead to homicide or suicide. Bullying can encompass a wide range of interactions between students so it can be difficult to judge when harmless teasing becomes vicious verbal abuse or when playful pushing and shoving crosses the line into physical assault. Student responses to bullying are highly subjective, and teasing that one student would dismiss might be devastating to the self-esteem of another. Even in the aftermath of school shootings, teachers and classmates found it difficult to gauge the severity of bullying that had taken place (Moore, Petrie, Braga, & McLaughlin, 2003).

The difficulty of distinguishing bullying from less serious forms of peer conflict, or even playful teasing and horseplay, cannot be overemphasized. On the one hand, teachers often fail to recognize bullying when it is taking place, leaving students with the impression that they do not care about bullying and will do little to stop it (Unnever & Cornell, 2003). On the other hand, a multitude of studies proclaim that school bullying is a pervasive problem that affects millions of students at all grade levels in virtually every school (Espelage & Swearer, 2004). The ambiguity of bullying has ramifications that affect every aspect of the problem, from estimates of its magnitude to the ability to determine whether bullying prevention efforts are successful.

WHAT IS BULLYING?

Bullying can be defined most simply as repeatedly humiliating another person who is perceived as weaker or less capable than the bully. Humiliation can be accomplished by physical intimidation or assault, or by verbal abuse that ridicules or demeans someone. Bullying is a repetitive action that instills anxiety and dread in the victim.

In order for bullying to take place, the aggressor must be in a position of dominance or superiority over the victim. Among boys, dominance is often achieved because one boy is larger or stronger than the other, or because several boys outnumber their victim. Among girls, physical size may not matter as much as social status and popularity. In all cases, the bully exudes confidence and arrogance that intimidates the victim. Bullying does not occur between two equals, which distinguishes it from ordinary conflict between peers.

Because bullying is such a broad concept, it is difficult to distinguish from other forms of peer aggression and play. Physical bullying seems easiest to identify because it involves discrete acts of violence and can be readily observed. Even so, physical bullying can include the *threat* of violence, which can be conveyed in words or even implied with a gesture or a glance.

Moreover, bullying must be judged in its social context, with knowledge of the intentions and feelings of the participants. This means that bullying can be difficult to distinguish from playful behavior; common horseplay and teasing among friends can seem like bullying to an observer. Even the participants may have differing perceptions of their behavior: Teasing remarks can be misunderstood or taken more seriously than they were intended, and sometimes playful wrestling can escalate into physical bullying. Accused bullies may rely on the defense that they were "just playing around" or "didn't mean" what they said.

In recent years, bullying researchers have paid more attention to social forms of bullying, which are typically engaged in by girls. Variously termed "relational" or "social" aggression" (Bjorkqvist, Lagerspetz, & Kaukinian, 1992; Crick & Grotpeter, 1995; Underwood, 2003), social bullying occurs when a girl (or boy) is shunned and excluded by others. Social bullies may conspire to humiliate their victim by discouraging others from associating with her and spreading rumors that mock or demean her. Several popular books, such as *Reviving Ophelia* by Mary Pipher (1994), *Odd Girl Out* by Rachel Simmons (2002), and *Queen Bees and Wannabes* by Rosalind Wiseman (2002) have drawn attention to this phenomenon, as have movies such as *Mean Girls* and *Welcome to the Dollhouse,* which portray the experience of girls who suffer at the hands of popular, socially dominant girls.

With these complications in the definition and demarcation of bullying, it is no wonder that it is difficult to measure bullying and determine how much of it occurs at school. Are victims of verbal bullying affected in the same way as victims of physical bullying? Is so-called social bullying really just another form of bullying, or should it be identified as a separate problem? Do bully prevention programs really work? None of these questions can be answered without research that clearly measures bullying and distinguishes it from other forms of student interaction.

HOW MUCH BULLYING OCCURS AT SCHOOL?

The standard way to measure how much bullying occurs at school is to administer an anonymous survey to students and ask them if they have been bullied. This simple, direct approach has great appeal to researchers because it is quick and inexpensive. However, bullying is such a broad and ambiguous concept that a questionnaire is unlikely to yield precise and reliable data. Questions about bullying tend to be general and over-inclusive, so that students may report even mild teasing and horseplay between friends as bullying. The result is that estimates of bullying are likely to be inflated.

In 2001 the *Journal of the American Medical Association* published a study that has been widely cited as a benchmark for how much bullying occurs in the United States (Nansel et al., 2001). The study was conducted by the National Institute of Child Health and Human Development (NICHD) using a survey developed by the World Health Organization. The survey was administered in school classrooms to a nationally representative sample of 15,686 students in grades 6 through 10.

The NICHD survey concluded that 29.9 percent of students in the United States—three of every ten students—are either victims or perpetrators of bullying. Approximately one of every five students—19.3 percent—were identified as bullies, and nearly one of every six—16.9 percent—were classified as victims of bullying. These figures include 6.3 percent of students who fell into both bully and victim categories.

Does this survey mean that one out of every five students in the United States is a bully? And that one of every six students is a victim of bullying? This is an alarmingly high rate of bullying, especially in the context of the high-profile cases of bully victims who committed suicide or homicide. Bullying has the connotation of repetitively cruel or mean-spirited behavior that has painful consequences for the victim and reflects serious adjustment problems in the bully—but is this what bullying means in this study?

The NICHD researchers did nothing unconventional or extraordinary; they used survey techniques and procedures found in most student studies. Students were given paper-and-pencil questionnaires to complete at their desks, and they were assured that their answers would be anonymous. Students answered questions about bullying after reading the following definition:

> We say a student is BEING BULLIED when another student, or a group of students, say or do nasty and unpleasant things to him or her. It is also bullying when a student is teased repeatedly in a way he or she doesn't like. But it is NOT BULLYING when two students of about the same strength quarrel or fight.

There are three essential criteria to consider in defining bullies: harmfulness, peer status, and frequency (Olweus, 1999). First, the action between students must be harmful—which the survey defined as "nasty and unpleasant." This definition is problematic because students often say unpleasant things to one another. A conscientious student taking the questions literally might admit to teasing a classmate even if the teasing was relatively innocuous. Teasing is a commonplace activity among children and adolescents, and although it may be nasty or unpleasant, it does not necessarily rise to the level of bullying.

Second, bullying is distinguished from ordinary conflict between peers because the bully has a position of superiority over the victim. Any definition that does not emphasize this criterion runs the risk of overestimating bullying: students will report on peer aggression that occurs between friends and classmates of comparable size. The survey definition instructs students to consider any "nasty and unpleasant things" that they say or do, but to not include quarrels and fights between students of "about the same strength." How can researchers be certain that students will carefully read this definition and understand that it excludes all "nasty and unpleasant things" that occur between students of comparable strength? The definition of bullying is complex, and there is no assurance that students will grasp the subtle distinctions that it requires.

Third, bullying is a repetitive, chronic activity, not a one-time event (Olweus, 1993). Surveys usually handle this criterion by asking students how frequently the bullying has occurred. In the NICHD survey, students were asked to mark how frequently the bullying had occurred during the current school term. Students could answer "none," "about once or twice," "sometimes," "about once a week," or "several times a week."

The researchers defined involvement in bullying as answering at least "sometimes." In other words, a student who says something nasty or unpleasant to another student *less than about once per week* is considered a bully. Similarly, a student who has had someone say something nasty or unpleasant to him or her, even if it is less than about once per week, is considered a victim of bullying. Can a behavior that takes place so infrequently be considered bullying?

In addition, the frequency scale does not address whether the student is bullied by the same student or different students. Bullying involves a repetitive interaction between two parties (Olweus, 1993), but when a student marks that he or she has been bullied "sometimes" or "about once a week" it is not clear that the same perpetrator is involved. Similarly, when a student admits bullying others by saying nasty or unpleasant things to others sometimes or about once a week, there is no assurance that the behavior was directed at the same victim.

Another weakness in the NICHD survey could lead to overestimates of the prevalence of bullying at school. The NICHD asked students separate questions about bullying at school and outside of school. There were four questions: two questions concerning being bullied at school or outside of school and two questions concerning bullying others at school or outside of school for an overall estimate of bullying *anywhere*. However, in the article published in the *Journal of the American Medical Association*, the NICHD researchers combined the answers for bullying at school and outside of school. The article only presents the total figures for bullying, and does not present how much bullying students reported occurring at school.

When the study was published, NICHD issued a press release with a title that implied the results referred to bullying in school: "Bullying widespread in U.S. schools, survey finds." The press release began, "Bullying is widespread in American schools, with more than 16 percent of U.S. school children saying they had been bullied by other students during the current term. . . ." (Bock, 2001). Nowhere in the published study can readers find the actual percentage of students who reported being bullied at school.

It is defensible for researchers interested in the psychological consequences of bullying to measure how much bullying students experience, whether at school or outside of school—but if researchers are particularly interested in bullying at school, then figures that report school-based bullying should be presented. Otherwise, educators and researchers who are interested in knowing how much bullying takes place at school might mistakenly use figures that include bullying that takes place outside of school.

When subsequent researchers cite figures for "student bullying" from the NICHD study, readers might assume that they refer to bullying at school. A Web of Science citation search identified at least 88 scientific publications citing the NICHD study by 2005. A review of the ten most recent publications and ten more selected at random found that none of them mentioned that the NICHD figures combined bullying in school and out of school.

The figures for bullying at school are about 15–20 percent lower than the overall figures reported in the article (Tonja Nansel, personal communication,

March 7, 2005). If one adopts a conservative definition of bullying and only counts behavior that occurs more than once a week, the rates are markedly smaller. Only four percent of students reported being bullied, and 4.6 percent reported bullying others.

These criticisms are not intended to indict the NICHD survey, but rather to illustrate limitations of methods commonly used to study bullying. All three criteria for defining bullying—harmfulness, peer status, and frequency—affect estimates of the prevalence of bullying. Definitions like the NICHD definition cast a broad net that inadvertently includes innocuous teasing, conflict between peers of comparable strength, and relatively infrequent acts. The result is that estimates of bullying are likely to include peer aggression and conflict that is not bullying.

THE OLWEUS SURVEY OF BULLYING

The most widely used bullying survey was developed by Dan Olweus, a Norwegian psychologist who conducted seminal work on bullying in his country. The Olweus Bully/Victim Questionnaire (Olweus, 1996; Solberg & Olweus, 2003) presents students with a standard definition of bullying:

We say a student is being bullied when another student or several other students

- say mean and hurtful things or make fun of him or her or call him or her mean and hurtful names
- completely ignore or exclude him or her from their group of friends or leave him or her out of things on purpose
- hit, kick, push, shove around, or threaten him or her
- tell lies or spread false rumors about him or her or send mean notes and try to make other students dislike him or her
- and do other hurtful things like that

These things may take place frequently, and it is difficult for the student being bullied to defend himself or herself. It is also bullying when a student is teased repeatedly in a mean and hurtful way. But we don't call it bullying when the teasing is done in a friendly and playful way. Also, it is not bullying when two students of about the same strength or power argue or fight.

This is a long and complex definition to expect students to comprehend and apply with precision. Most educators would balk at using such a difficult definition for instructional purposes. Yet after reading this definition, students are asked two key questions: "How often have you been bullied at school in the past couple of months?" and "How often have you taken part in bullying another student(s) at school in the past couple of months?" Students can choose among five possible responses: "I haven't been bullied/ bullied other students at school in the past couple of months," "only once or twice," "2 or 3 times a month," "about once a week," and "several times a week."

Solberg and Olweus (2003) recommended that a frequency of "2 or 3 times a month" should be sufficient to identify a student as a victim of bullying or as someone who bullies others. In other words, a student who is teased as infrequently as every other week can claim to be a victim of bullying. And a student who teases a classmate at least once every other week should, in good conscience, identify himself or herself as a bully. This appears to be a low threshold for bullying that, like the NICHD study, would generate a high estimate of bullying.

Consider the consequences of a low threshold definition of bullying. Not only are estimates of bullying inflated, but students identified as victims and bullies are quite heterogeneous. The resulting group of victims would include not only students who have been victims of serious and chronic bullying, but students who have not experienced much bullying as well. This means that research on the characteristics of bully victims would be obscured by the inclusion of students who have experienced only mild bullying. Of even greater concern is that responses from students identified as bullies—if such students are even willing to admit to bullying on the survey—would not be distinguishable from students who conscientiously identify themselves as bullies even though their actions may be relatively minor.

Subsequent bullying researchers frequently relied on the Olweus survey, which provides some degree of consistency across studies. But even when studies use the Olweus questionnaire, it must be translated into the student's language, and there may be meaningful differences in wording as well as cultural differences in the conceptualization of bullying (Smith, Cowie, Olafsson, & Liefooghe, 2002). Not surprisingly, studies have produced wide differences in the prevalence of bullying across samples.

Smith, Madsen, and Moody (1999) reviewed data from studies in Norway, Sweden, England, Australia, and Ireland, and found considerable variation in the percentage of children who reported being bullied both within and across countries. For example, the percentage of 11-year-old children who reported being bullied ranged from 3.1 percent in one Irish sample to 22 percent in one of the English samples. At age 13, the percentages ranged from 3.3 percent in a Norwegian sample to 21.3 percent in an Australian sample. It is not possible to determine whether these differences reflect true national differences or are artifacts of measurement.

Eslea et al. (2003) compared rates of bullying and victimization in seven countries, all using some form of the Olweus questionnaire. The percentage of students classified as bullies ranged from 2.0 percent in China to 16.9 percent in Spain. The percentage of students classified as victims ranged from 5.2 percent in Ireland to 25.6 percent in Italy. Similarly, the percentage of students who claimed no involvement in bullying ranged from 91 percent in Ireland to 50.8 percent in Spain. The researchers pointed out that these differences are so large that it is unlikely they indicate true national differences in behavior.

ARE BULLYING SURVEYS ACCURATE?

Most bullying surveys are administered on an anonymous basis; that is, students do not put their names on the survey. As a result, there is no way to verify whether the students who claim to be victims of bullying are actually victims, and no way to confirm whether the students who claim to be bullies are actually bullies. Similarly, there is no way to determine whether all of the victims and all of the bullies in a school are identified by the survey; some may have declined to admit their involvement and others might not realize that the behavior they are engaged in is a form of bullying. There is no way to tell if the anonymous bullying survey is accurate.

It seems remarkable that there is no body of research demonstrating the validity of bullying surveys. Even evidence in support of the Olweus survey has been slow to emerge. The instructions accompanying the Olweus Bully/Victim Questionnaire state, "We have made lots of analyses on the internal consistency (reliability), the test-retest reliability and the validity of the Olweus Bully/Victim Questionnaire on large representative samples (more than 5000 students). The results are generally quite good. . . . Unfortunately, most of this psychometric information has not yet been published, due to lack of time" (Olweus, 2002, p. 1). In a 2003 study of their self-report instrument, Solberg and Olweus acknowledged that self-report surveys are vulnerable to both under- and over-reporting of bullying, but described it as "a big and complex issue that cannot be treated satisfactorily within the scope of the present article" (p. 264).

The most direct way to validate bullying surveys is to corroborate self-report with an independent source of information. Even though the surveys would have to be administered without the protection of anonymity, students could be assured that their answers were confidential and protected from disclosure. Then the names of students (or code numbers that protect student identity) who reported themselves to be perpetrators or victims of bullying could be compared to other sources of information, such as school records, interviews conducted with school staff, or peer reports. While arguably there is

no true "gold standard" for bullying that can be compared to self-report, vali-
dational studies would provide a much needed source of support for a method
that used literally around the world and forms the bedrock for conducting and
evaluating bullying prevention programs. Such studies have been done with
self-report measures of juvenile crime and delinquency (Huizinga & Elliott,
1986; Piquero, Macintosh, & Hickman, 2002).

In summary, bullying has become a hot topic in American education, as
well as in other countries, but the measurement of bullying is problematic.
The definition of bullying is complex and excludes commonplace teasing and
horseplay that might occur among peers rather than between a bully and victim. Unfortunately, self-report surveys of bullying are likely to produce inflated
estimates of bullying unless students make a number of careful distinctions
about the quality and frequency of the behavior, as well as the relative size and
power of the two parties involved in the behavior. Studies have not demonstrated that the students who claim to be victims of bullying are actually victims, or that all of the actual victims in a school are identified by the survey.
Similarly, the use of self-report surveys to identify bullies has not been validated. The reliance on self-report surveys has important implications for the
kinds of prevention programs used in schools as well as for the evidence of
their effectiveness, as will be discussed in the remainder of this chapter.

CAN SCHOOLS PREVENT BULLYING?

Many authorities claim that bully prevention programs are highly effective.
Two federal agencies, the Substance Abuse and Mental Health Services
Administration (SAMHSA) of the U.S. Department of Health and Human
Services, and the Office of Juvenile Justice and Delinquency Prevention
(OJJDP) of the U.S. Department of Justice have designated the Olweus
Bullying Prevention Program as a "Model Program" (SAMHSA, n.d.). SAMHSA
declares that the Olweus program has "proven results" that include:

- A 30 percent to 70 percent reduction in student reports of being bullied
  and bullying others; results that are largely parallel with peer ratings and
  teacher ratings
- Significant reductions in student reports of general antisocial behavior
  (e.g., vandalism, fighting, theft, and truancy)
- Significant improvements in classroom order and discipline
- More positive attitude toward schoolwork and school

Closer inspection of the "proven results" for the Olweus program adds
some important qualifications to this characterization of the program's effec-

tiveness. According to the SAMHSA report (SAMHSA, n.d.), the results were based on a study of ten schools in Oslo, Norway conducted in 1999 and 2000. Can it be assumed that a program in Norwegian schools will work equally well in other countries, including the United States? Research on bullying prevention, starting with the first national program in Norway, gives cause for doubt.

In 1983, Norway began a nationwide effort to reduce bullying in response to public outcry over three separate incidents in which 10- to 14-year-old boys who were victims of bullying committed suicide (Olweus, 1993). The Norwegian government distributed educational information on bullying to teachers and parents, and all primary and junior high schools were invited to administer the Olweus Bully-Victim survey to measure bullying before and after implementing the new program (Roland, 2000). Separate evaluations of the bullying prevention effort were conducted in 42 schools in Bergen and 37 schools in Rogaland County (Roland, 2000).

The evaluation of bully prevention in Bergen received international attention because Olweus found large reductions in bullying in several waves of follow-up surveys (Olweus, 1991, 1993). For example, after 20 months, student reports of being victimized by bullying had dropped 52 percent for boys and 62 percent for girls. Olweus (1993) summarized the studies as demonstrating a reduction of bully/victim problems "by 50 percent or more" (p. 113).

The evaluation of bullying prevention in Rogaland was conducted by Norwegian researchers Erling Roland and Elaine Munthe (Roland & Munthe, 1997). Their evaluation found far less positive results and received far less attention. For example, the overall rate of bullying in Rogaland schools actually increased 24 percent for boys and 14 percent for girls. Reports of victimization decreased 12.5 percent for girls, but increased 44 percent for boys (Munthe, 1989; Roland & Munthe, 1997).

Both Olweus (1999) and Roland (2000) pointed out important differences between the bullying prevention efforts in Bergen and Rogaland that might explain why there were such striking differences in outcome. Although all schools received the same materials and instructions from the government, researchers had closer contact with the Bergen schools, and it seemed that these schools mounted a more concerted effort to reduce bullying. In contrast, the Rogaland schools received less support and did not seem to make as serious an effort to implement the program. A small number of Rogaland schools that seemed to embrace the program did experience modest reductions in bullying.

What about studies outside Norway? In England, the Sheffield Anti-Bullying project was conducted in 23 schools from 1991 to 1993. This project differed from the Olweus bullying prevention program because the programs were individualized by each school. Overall, the Sheffield project had only modest effects: In primary schools, there was a 7 percent reduction in students who reported bullying others and a 17 percent increase in the number of pupils who reported not being bullied; and in secondary schools, there were reductions of only 3–5 percent in both categories (Smith, 1997).

A Canadian anti-bullying program modeled after the Olweus approach had mixed results in four Toronto elementary schools (Pepler, Craig, Ziegler, & Charach, 1994). After fifteen months, the percent of children who reported being bullied in the previous five days declined from 28 to 23 percent, although the percentage who reported bullying others rose from 16 to 21 percent. The proportion who reported being bullied more than once or twice in the past term also increased—from 12 to 15 percent—but the change was not statistically significant.

The Canadian researchers also examined how completely the schools implemented the bully prevention program, and documented substantial changes, such as increased supervision of playgrounds and lunchrooms, classroom meetings on racism and bullying, parent newsletters and parent meetings. The schools also instituted conflict mediation on the playground and mentoring groups for students in older grades. In two schools, social workers led discussion groups on bullying, and in one school students developed an educational video on bullying. Eighty-nine percent of teachers reported talking to bullies about their behavior, and 94 percent had talked to victims. Overall, it appeared that the schools made a concerted effort to reduce bullying, but obtained relatively modest results.

In the United States, a two-year controlled study of South Carolina schools that implemented a modified Olweus program produced largely disappointing results (Melton et al., 1998). Conducted in 39 schools from 1995 to 1997, the study found that student reports of being victimized by bullying did not change in Year 1 or Year 2. There was a 20 percent decline in student reports of bullying others after one year, and no further change after two years. There were no changes in overall measures of antisocial behavior. Clearly, educators should not assume that the results obtained by Olweus in Oslo can be readily obtained in American schools.

The South Carolina study is particularly important because the researchers collaborated with Olweus in authoring a "blueprint" model for how bullying prevention programs should be conducted in the United States (Olweus, Limber, & Mihalic, 1999). The Olweus Bullying Prevention Program endorsed by the federal government is based on this work. In fact, the SAMHSA (n.d.) endorsement of this program states that "Professor Olweus worked closely with a number of colleagues in the United States, notably Dr. Sue Limber and Dr. Gary Melton at Clemson University in South Carolina, to implement and evaluate the program in the United States" (p. 3). This carefully worded statement says nothing about the results of Limber and Melton's effort to implement and evaluate the program in the United States—and the

SAMHSA description of the "proven results" of the Olweus Bullying Prevention Program makes no mention of the South Carolina findings.

A team of Canadian and English researchers (Smith, Schneider, Smith, & Ananiadou, 2004) published an important review of school-wide bullying prevention programs in *School Psychology Review*, the leading journal of the U.S. National Association of School Psychologists. The researchers reviewed all of the studies they could find—fourteen—that either used the Olweus Bullying Prevention Program or were modeled on it and shared its core features. Eight of the studies used control groups, including four studies that randomly assigned either classes or schools to intervention and control conditions. All but one study relied on student self-reports of bullying and victimization as their outcome measures.

What did the researchers find? Each study conducted a series of statistical tests to see what effect the program had on bullying, victimization, or other desired outcomes for one or more time periods. Overall, bullying prevention programs had little or no effect on bullying. The largest effect observed was a single condition in one study that produced an effect size that was classified as "medium." For self-reported bullying, all of the studies produced effects that were negligible or negative (meaning that bullying increased).

The researchers' conclusion is noteworthy because it contradicts the federal endorsement of the Olweus Bullying Prevention Program and bucks the prevailing trend toward implementing bully prevention programs:

> The widespread enthusiasm for the whole-school approach, and its enactment into law in some jurisdictions, can be based only on the perceived urgent need to intervene and on the few studies indicating success. The dramatic success of the Olweus program in Norway has not been replicated elsewhere. There are a few instances of significant improvement following program implementation, though not nearly as striking, and there are many nonsignificant findings and some results opposite to the expected direction. (Smith, Schneider, Smith, & Ananiadou, 2004, p. 557)

The researchers do not call for the abandonment of bullying prevention efforts, but they point out the need to recognize the limitations of current knowledge, and to conduct more careful research on how programs are implemented and monitored. It is possible that many schools did not fully implement the program or pursue its goals with the level of commitment necessary to make a substantial impact.

One recommendation that merits serious consideration is that "Researchers should collect data on outcomes from other sources in addition to students' self reports, such as observations from teachers, classmates, administrators, and even parents" (Smith, Schneider, Smith, & Ananiadou, 2004, p. 558).

Because bully prevention programs rely almost exclusively on student self-report surveys, the determination of their success or failure rests on shaky ground.

THE HAZARDS OF BULLY SURVEYS

As discussed earlier, student self-report surveys can be unreliable measures of bullying for a variety of reasons. Some students might exaggerate, while others might deny, their involvement in bullying. Even if they attempt to answer the survey honestly, students must make subjective judgments about the distinction between playful teasing and verbal abuse, and between harmless horseplay and physical bullying. In the case of social bullying, they must decide whether choosing not to associate with a classmate or leaving someone out of a social invitation constitutes shunning that person. And in all cases, they must remember to exclude from consideration conflict between peers of equal strength and only count instances where the aggressor is stronger than the victim. All of these complications make the determination of bullying a challenging task for students that would be formidable even for their teachers.

Because student surveys are so vulnerable to measurement error, relying on them to determine the success of a bully prevention program is hazardous. If students cooperate and answer the survey honestly and accurately, they will provide useful information, but this information will be obscured by the degree to which other students provide false or mistaken information.

The balance between accurate and inaccurate information is commonly referred to as the signal-to-noise ratio, an analogy to radio reception. If a survey includes too much noise, the signal may be faint or even go undetected. For example, consider a hypothetical school—Jefferson Middle School—where the administrators decide to institute a bullying prevention program. The school follows the usual procedure of administering a baseline survey at the beginning of the year, implementing the program, then conducting a follow-up survey at the end of the year. Suppose that one percent of Jefferson students are victims of bullying and report it accurately on the survey, but an additional ten percent of students inaccurately report being victims of bullying. Of this ten percent, perhaps half of these students dislike taking surveys or for some reason intentionally answer the survey incorrectly. The other half of the students mark the survey inaccurately because they did not understand that the definition of bullying excluded teasing and fighting between students of equal strength. The result is that the student survey indicates that eleven percent of students are victims of bullying, even though the true incidence is one percent, and the signal-to-noise ratio is ten to one.

Because the estimate of bullying obtained by the student survey is inflated tenfold, there is no chance that the follow-up survey at the end of the school year will show that the bullying prevention program was effective. Even if the program eradicated bullying from Jefferson Middle School, the decline in student reports of bullying would be small relative to the inflated estimate. If student reports of bullying dropped from eleven percent to ten percent, depending on the sample size, a statistical analysis would show the results to be negligibly small or statistically insignificant, just like the results reported by most studies (Smith, Schneider, Smith, & Ananiadou, 2004).

Even worse, reports of bullying could *increase* at Jefferson Middle School. Researchers have observed that bullying prevention programs might sensitize students to the issue of bullying and increase their reporting (Pepler, Craig, Ziegler, & Charach, 1994; Smith, Ananiadou, & Cowie, 2003). Students who initially did not realize that what was happening to them constituted bullying—as well as students who did not want to admit they were being bullied at the time they completed the baseline survey—might come forward and report bullying on the follow-up survey. In addition, some students invariably start using the term bullying to describe peer conflicts and disputes that are not bullying.

WHAT CAN BE DONE TO IMPROVE THE ACCURACY OF BULLY SURVEYS?

Surveys should be carefully screened for signs of inaccurate or exaggerated reporting. For example, surveys can include questions that permit researchers to examine the consistency of student answers. Jennifer Cross and Rebecca Newman-Gonchar of Colorado State University (Cross & Newman-Gonchar, 2004) screened school surveys for the presence of inconsistent responses to items with the same content (e.g., answering "never" when asked what age they belonged to a gang but "yes" to the question, "Have you ever belonged to a gang?") and extreme responses (e.g., claiming to have used LSD 20 or more times in the past 30 days). Surveys with three or more inconsistent and/or extreme responses were identified as "suspect."

Although only a small percentage of surveys were identified as suspect— 2.7 percent in one sample and 4.4 percent in a sample that used a different survey—the presence of these suspect surveys inflated estimates of victimization and high-risk behaviors. For example, estimates of the percentage of students carrying a handgun at school in the past 30 days jumped by a magnitude of 30—from .1 percent to 3.2 percent—in one survey; in another survey, reports of physically attacking or harming someone went from 9.9 percent to 15.8 percent. In one high school, the proportion of students who reported having been bullied was 45.7 percent, but after suspect surveys were removed from the sample, the proportion dropped to 25.0 percent, which is a reduction of more than 45 percent (Cross & Newman-Gonchar, 2004). There is relatively little research on the factors that influence how a classroom of students will respond to a survey—whether they will take it seriously and complete it honestly. Cross and Newman-Gonchar (2004) pointed out that teachers must be well-prepared and motivated to administer the survey, they must have clear instructions and adequate time, and they must be willing and able to persuade the students to take the survey seriously. Otherwise, students may not respond honestly or take care to complete it accurately.

Cross and Newman-Gonchar (2004) observed striking differences in survey results between schools that used trained versus untrained survey administrators. In some cases the teachers were not given adequate instructions or advance notice that they would be administering a lengthy survey. Although this was not a controlled study, their post hoc observations were provocative; 28 percent of surveys obtained by untrained administrators failed to meet validity standards, whereas only 3 percent of those obtained by trained administrators were considered invalid.

USE OF PEER REPORT TO IDENTIFY VICTIMS OF BULLYING

Another strategy for improving student surveys is to broaden their focus on self-report to include peer report. A peer report survey asks students to identify classmates who are victims (or perpetrators) of bullying, either by writing their names or circling their names on a class list (Cornell & Brockenbrough, 2004). The number of times a student is nominated by peers is used as an index of the student's victim status, and a cut-off may be used to classify a student as a victim or non-victim.

The simple advantage of peer report over self-report is that scores are based on information from multiple students. Statistically, this approach should decrease measurement error and produce a more reliable result. In other words, although one student might make an erroneous judgment about a classmate's involvement in bullying—such as circle a friend's name as a joke—the combined judgment of the class should be more accurate.

Peer nominations are still susceptible to many of the problems that plague self-report surveys, such as the difficulty of ensuring that students use a standard definition of bullying. Many students are identified as bullies or victims by one or two classmates, so an accurate cut-off must be determined (Cornell & Brockenbrough, 2004). The most common reservation about peer nomination is that teachers are reluctant to ask students to make judgments about one another, fearing that the exercise will stimulate teasing or cause anxiety. Of course, any bully survey raises similar issues. With appropriate classroom supervision, a peer nomination survey can be administered without such problems. Ideally, surveys should be accompanied by class discussion of bullying and the importance of seeking help to stop it.

Although peer nominations are not used very often in bullying research—Olweus discourages their use in favor of his self-report survey (Solberg & Olweus, 2003)—the peer nomination method is widely used and well-accepted in other fields, including research on peer aggression (Hawker & Boulton, 2000; Ladd & Kochenderfer-Ladd, 2002; Leff, Kupersmidt, Patterson, & Power, 1999; Pellegrini, Bartini, & Brooks, 1999; Perry, Kusel, & Perry, 1988). Several studies have supported the reliability and validity of peer-report measures of child victimization in middle and high school age children (Achenbach, McConaughy, & Howell, 1987; Ladd & Kochenderfer-Ladd, 2002; Nabuzoka, 2003; Perry, Kusel, & Perry, 1988). Peer nomination inventories have been used for diagnostic screening purposes to identify children with a wide variety of emotional and behavioral problems, including aggression, delinquency, hyperactivity, anxiety, and depression (Eron, Walder, & Lefkowitz, 1971; Weiss, Harris, & Catron, 2004).

Researchers have found only moderate correspondence between self and peer reports, generally in the range of .14 to .42 (Achenbach et al., 1987; Cornell, Sheras, & Cole, in press; Juvonen, Nishina, & Graham, 2001; Ladd & Kochenderfer-Ladd, 2002; Perry et al., 1988). In a study correlating self-report and peer report in 416 middle school students, Cornell and Brockenbrough (2004) found correlations of just .17 for bully victimization and .10 for bullying others. Furthermore, peer reports of bullying were more predictive of future school discipline problems than were self-reports. Students identified as bullies by their peers were more likely to receive office referrals for misbehavior, and more likely to serve detention and be suspended from school, than students identified by self-report.

The choice of instrument to assess bullying can have a powerful effect on the nature and course of the school's bully prevention effort. If school authorities rely on an anonymous self-report survey, they may learn how much bullying is occurring, but they will not know who is being bullied and by whom. With such limited knowledge, interventions naturally focus on school-wide rules and curriculum units on bullying. Meanwhile, counselors must wait for bullying to be reported before they can intervene with specific students.

Unfortunately, many students do not seek help for bullying and teachers often do not detect it (Unnever & Cornell, 2003, 2004). Notably, the Cornell and Brockenbrough (2004) study found that there were twelve middle school students identified as victims by at least ten classmates, yet only two of these students turned up as victims on the self-report survey. Why were these students unwilling to admit that they were victims of bullying? Perhaps they were in a state of denial or were ashamed of being victims. The same study found that only four of the twelve students were recognized by their teachers as victims. These findings suggest that peer nominations are a potentially valuable way to identify victims of bullying that are not identified by self-report and are not known to teachers.

In contrast to anonymous self-report, a peer nomination survey will give school counselors the names of possible victims. Counselors can use the names to assist them in observing and interviewing students to identify bullying. In this way, bullying prevention efforts can focus immediately on specific cases of bullying. To determine whether a program is effective, schools would not need to rely on self-report, but could use a combination of measures, including a follow-up peer nomination survey and interviews with students previously identified as victims of bullying.

HOW COULD THE SCHOOL HAVE PREVENTED MICKEY FROM KILLING HIMSELF?

Schools cannot eliminate all the teasing and taunting that occur everyday in schools, but they can act decisively when it becomes chronic and severe. Mickey's suicide could have been prevented if school authorities had known about the bullying and taken decisive action to stop it. Students should face stiff disciplinary consequences for bullying: In the most serious cases, bullying can constitute a criminal act punishable by the juvenile justice system. At the same time, victims of severe bullying need psychological assessment and mental health treatment, particularly if they have developed a clinical depression with suicidal features.

Most bully prevention programs emphasize a "whole-school" approach that attempts to change the school climate and basic pattern of student interactions through school-wide interventions. This approach is derived largely from the Olweus model (Smith, Schneider, Smith, & Ananiadou, 2004; Olweus, Limber, & Mihalic, 1999), and typically includes training on bullying prevention for all school staff, educational assemblies for the student body, revisions to the school discipline code, a classroom curriculum designed to instill anti-bullying attitudes, and an anonymous self-report survey.

The standard bully prevention model has little to say about work with individual bullies and victims. Because this model emphasizes group interventions and assesses bullying with an anonymous survey, the orientation is not aimed at resolving individual cases of bullying. Therefore, it is not clear how a whole-school approach would have helped Mickey, particularly in light of the equivocal evidence of its effectiveness.

What should school authorities do when they learn that a student is being bullied? The Olweus (1993) model says that school authorities should have a "serious talk" with bullies, but more guidance on how to deal with bullies is needed. What counseling approaches are effective with bullies? There is little research on the most effective ways to discipline bullies and to discourage them from continuing to bully (Cole & Cornell, in press), although some schools have experimented with school tribunals and restorative justice approaches (Smith, Ananiadou, & Cowie, 2003). Clearly, more work is needed.

There is also a need for work on encouraging victims to seek help. Several studies have found that students are not inclined to seek help for bullying, in part because they believe that teachers and other school personnel will not be willing or able to help them (Unnever & Cornell, 2003, 2004; Williams & Cornell, 2005). In light of the unwillingness of students to identify themselves as victims, peer reports may be a more effective alternative. If Mickey's school had administered a peer nomination survey, he could have been identified as a victim and school staff could have investigated and taken action.

To be effective, bullying programs must focus more on how to identify individual cases of bullying and what techniques are most effective in putting a stop to it. This would be a bottom-up approach, in contrast to the top-down approach that is currently in favor.

6

Are We Teaching Our Kids to Kill?

After his parents divorced, 15-year-old Daniel lived with his father and grand-mother in a small New England town. By all accounts, Daniel had a good rela-tionship with his grandmother, despite some occasional arguments and disagree-ments. Daniel was a marginal student who would rather spend his time watching horror movies and playing *Dungeons and Dragons* with a small group of friends. He was proud of the fantasy character he created for himself because his char-acter was nearly invincible and could kill almost any opponent.

Daniel also liked to play *Mortal Kombat*, a popular video game in which one can tear off the head or rip out the heart of an opponent. He had a collection of violent video games, and spent many hours playing them in his room. While playing video games, Daniel also liked to listen to heavy metal rock music. With his headphones turned up high, he could spend hours listening to songs with vio-lent lyrics such as "The Assassin" and "Bring Your Daughter to the Slaughter" by Iron Maiden, "No Remorse" by Metallica, and "After All the Dead" by Black Sabbath.

Another of Daniel's favorite activities was watching horror movies with his father; the two would laugh and marvel at the most gruesome scenes involving vampires, monsters, and deranged killers. Daniel particularly enjoyed watching *Faces of Death*, a quasi-documentary that presented scenes of real-life death that even his father found difficult to watch. Daniel watched it over and over again.

Daniel enjoyed reading horror novels, and had more than a dozen books by Stephen King (*The Dark Tower, The Tommyknockers*) as well as similar authors such as Dean Koontz (*Lightning, Midnight*) and Clive Barker (*The Damnation Game, The Inhuman Condition*).

Daniel and his grandmother had multiple quarrels over his neglect of his school work and the inordinate time he spent playing games, watching movies, and listening to music. One day after a particularly heated argument, Daniel locked himself in his room and spent the afternoon playing a violent video game and listening to heavy metal music. Then he turned to reading a favorite novel by Stephen King, *The Shining*, in which a deranged man attacks his family with an ax. Daniel had enjoyed the movie version, which starred Jack Nicholson as the madman. That evening Daniel crept quietly out of his room, found his grandmother alone in her bedroom, and without saying a word, chopped her to death with an ax.

What role did Daniel's preoccupation with violent entertainment play in his crime? Unlike many youth who commit violent crimes, Daniel was not a drug user, did not belong to a gang, and had no history of violent behavior except in fantasy. He was not exposed to crime and violence in his community and he was not a victim of abuse at home. He attended church regularly, albeit reluctantly. His shocked and grief-stricken father maintained that Daniel had an affectionate relationship with his grandmother before he murdered her. Extensive psychological evaluations found that he did not suffer from schizophrenia or other forms of mental illness. Although Daniel had experienced family conflict and his parents' divorce, these circumstances do not seem adequate to explain his actions. After the murder, he packed some of his favorite belongings and drove off in the family car. He checked into a motel under his own name and was quietly arrested the next morning. Daniel could offer no reason for his behavior beyond the explanation that he was angry at her. He insisted that he loved his grandmother and was sorry for what he had done.

Consider some ways that violent entertainment could have affected Daniel. First and most obviously, the fact that Daniel decided to use an ax to murder his grandmother suggests that he was influenced by *The Shining*. One could hardly argue that his choice of weapon was mere coincidence. One research team (Heller & Polsky, 1976) found that about one-third of their sample of juvenile offenders acknowledged committing crimes by using techniques they had observed on television.

Daniel also had a lot of experience killing people—in fantasy—and this experience may have predisposed him to resort to violence in a frustrating situation. Through video games he had practiced acts of violence over and over, to the point that they were almost automatic. He had been rewarded for his skill in killing others, which was a source of pride and won him the esteem of his peers. His repeated exposure to violence through gruesome movies may have desensitized him to the point that he no longer had the same inhibiting feelings of revulsion and horror that most people would experience in contemplating an act as cruel as chopping someone to pieces with an ax. Studies reviewed in this chapter support this hypothesis.

Daniel's music was passionate and stimulating, and frequently included morbid lyrics about suicide, homicide, and violent death. For thousands of years, music has been used to arouse aggressive passions, whether to inspire soldiers on the battlefield or excite athletes on the playing field. Perhaps music contributed to the emotional state that drove Daniel to kill.

But did Daniel's exposure to violent entertainment *cause* his murderous behavior? One might argue that Daniel's preoccupation with violent entertainment was itself a symptom of psychological problems and not a cause of his violence. One cannot clearly distinguish cause and effect in a single case. Case examples can aid in generating hypotheses, but only scientific studies can provide the evidence that is needed to answer such questions.

The scientific hypothesis that exposure to violent music or video could lead someone to commit an act of violence is one of the most controversial topics in social science. For decades, researchers have debated the complex issues involved in proving or refuting the seemingly simple hypothesis that exposure to entertainment violence could cause aggressive behavior. Even though now there is a broad, but not unanimous, scientific consensus that entertainment violence increases aggressive behavior, the topic remains hotly contested because of the social, legal, and economic ramifications of such a conclusion. If violent movies can produce real-life violence, should the movie industry be held accountable? Should the government restrict entertainment violence in the same way it protects consumers from other dangerous products?

One reason the answers to such questions are not clear is the difficulty in distinguishing between scientific *explanation* and moral *responsibility*. Daniel's use of an ax to murder his grandmother appeared to be connected to *The Shining*, yet this does not mean that Stephen King was responsible for Daniel's behavior. Daniel decided to use the ax, not Stephen King. In social science research, a *scientific* link cannot be presumed to have direct moral or legal ramifications. A scientific approach seeks to *explain* rather than *excuse* a person's behavior. Science and morality are different frameworks for viewing a person's behavior, and the existence of a scientific explanation for someone's behavior does not automatically excuse the behavior or eliminate a person's responsibility for his or her actions. Even the most depraved and morally reprehensible behavior has some kind of scientific explanation. Explanation does not rule out responsibility.

In principle, there is an explanation for every criminal act or, more generally, for all human behavior. The standards for legal and moral responsibility, however, are not concerned with whether an explanation exists, but what kind of explanation it is. If a person kills someone by accident, or in self-defense, this explanation may be considered sufficient to absolve the person of moral responsibility. And in some cases, a person might be so deranged by mental illness that he or she does not adequately comprehend what he or she is doing, in which case the person might be found not guilty by reason of insanity. Few, if any, social scientists believe that the scientific evidence showing the influence of entertainment violence on human behavior rises to the level of producing insanity.

It is also important to recognize that social scientists do not claim that entertainment violence is the *only* cause of violence, the *most important* cause of violence, or even *sufficient* to cause violence. Most social scientists who study this issue take the position that entertainment violence is simply a *contributing factor* that increases the risk of violence (U.S. Department of Health and Human Services, 2001). Violence is usually the product of multiple factors (Moeller, 2001). Entertainment violence is just one of many factors, but it is important because it is so pervasive and affects so many people. Critics often challenge the link between entertainment violence and aggressive behavior by arguing that there are other, more important causes of violence and that many consumers of entertainment violence do not engage in violent behavior; these are straw-man arguments that do not really contradict or refute the claims made by social scientists.

MYTH 9: Media violence does not increase aggression in children.

FACT: The evidence from hundreds of scientific studies clearly demonstrates that "viewing entertainment violence can lead to increases in aggressive attitudes, values, and behaviors, particularly in children. Its effects are measurable and long-lasting" (Joint statement on the impact of entertainment violence on children, 2000). The voluminous evidence on this topic will be summarized in this chapter.

WHAT IS THE SCIENTIFIC EVIDENCE THAT MEDIA VIOLENCE CAUSES VIOLENT BEHAVIOR?

Scientific studies of the link between television violence and aggressive behavior began in the 1950s. Because no single study can prove conclusively that entertainment violence causes violent behavior, researchers must accumulate evidence across a wide range of studies. These studies can be divided into three main types: experimental studies, cross-sectional studies, and longitudinal studies.

Experimental studies. True experiments are considered the scientifically most rigorous kind of study because participants are randomly assigned to different conditions which are controlled by the researcher. For example, a group of children is randomly chosen to watch a violent or a nonviolent video, then observed for signs of aggressive behavior. Since the researcher controls what conditions the children experience, any differences between children who watch the violent versus the nonviolent video must be due to the nature of the video. The researcher assigns children randomly to each condition to minimize the possibility of sampling bias. For example, if children could choose which video they wanted to watch, children who were predisposed to be aggressive might choose the violent video and less aggressive children the nonviolent video. The results of such a study would not be clear, since children who watched the violent video might engage in aggressive behavior because they were already predisposed to be aggressive and not because of the video's influence.

Nearly every college student who has taken an introductory psychology class has seen the old black & white films of Albert Bandura's famous Bobo doll studies at Stanford University (Bandura, Ross, & Ross, 1961, 1963). These studies demonstrated dramatically that young children who watched a video of an adult hitting and kicking a large, inflated Bobo doll would spontaneously imitate that behavior when placed in a room with the same kind of doll. Variations on this study showed conditions that predictably affected children's behavior; for example, children were less likely to imitate aggression that resulted in punishment and more likely to imitate aggression that was rewarded. The ability to produce and control children's aggression by altering what children observed provided strong evidence that television violence could have a similar effect.

Many laypersons assume that only realistic aggression affects children, and that unrealistic or humorous portrayals of aggression, such as cartoon aggression, is inconsequential (Gentile, 2003). This is an example of an intuitively plausible assumption that in fact is wrong. A comparison of different types of television programs found that cartoon and fantasy programs produced more aggressive behavior in children than any other type (Paik & Comstock, 1994). The effect of violent cartoons was demonstrated in a study by Kenneth Gadow and Joyce Sprafkin of the State University of New York at Stony Brook (Gadow & Sprafkin, 1987) in which elementary school students were randomly divided into two groups: One watched humorous cartoons with highly aggressive content—"Tom and Jerry" and "Bugs Bunny"—and the other watched cartoons with little aggression—"Fat Albert and the Cosby Kids" and "Lassie's Rescue Rangers." Raters who did not know which cartoons the children watched observed the children during lunch and recess. The children who had watched the violent cartoons were more aggressive than their classmates who had watched the non-aggressive cartoons.

Some plausible assumptions turn out to be true. Experimental studies have repeatedly found that TV violence has a greater effect on children who are already prone to aggression. For example, Wendy Josephson of the University of Winnipeg compared the effects of TV violence on boys who had been identified as highly aggressive or not highly aggressive by their teachers. Both groups of boys were divided into those who watched a television show with police violence or an exciting nonviolent show about bike racing, and then allowed to play a game of floor hockey (Josephson, 1987). Observers (who did not know which show the boys watched) rated the boys for aggressive behavior such as hitting, elbowing, and yelling aggressive remarks. The highly aggressive boys were most strongly affected by the violent television show and exhibited the most aggressive behavior playing floor hockey. However, even the less aggressive boys were affected by the violent television show, although to a lesser degree.

Still another study examined the impact of violent movies on boys living in a home for delinquent youth (Leyens, Camino, Parke, & Berkowitz, 1975). Boys in two cottages saw violent movies every night for five nights while boys in two other cottages saw nonviolent movies. The boys who watched the violent films engaged in more physical assaults on their peers.

Studies using experimental designs provide compelling evidence that television viewing has an effect on children's behavior, but have important limitations. First, these studies only look at short-term effects and so do not demonstrate a lasting impact on children. And second, of course, none of the children committed serious violent crimes in these studies. The fact that children become more aggressive in their play does not mean they will commit more serious acts of violence. Finally, critics also point out that studies conducted in a laboratory setting or as part of an experiment under strictly controlled conditions might not generalize to real-life television viewing in uncontrolled conditions. For these reasons, researchers must look at evidence from other kinds of studies.

Cross-sectional studies. A cross-sectional study involves the comparison of a diverse group of persons at roughly the same point in time. A cross-sectional study of entertainment violence, for instance, might survey a large group of children about their television viewing habits and see if there is a correlation between aggressive behavior and how much violence they watch. Studies have found that viewing television violence is correlated with self-reported aggression and delinquency (McLeod, Atkin, & Chaffee, 1972; Robinson & Bachman, 1972), peer ratings of aggression (Sheehan, 1983), and antisocial and criminal behavior (Belson, 1978; Heath et al., 1989).

Other researchers have attempted to explain how television violence might affect the judgment and reasoning of children so as to produce aggressive behavior. Their studies have found that children who watch more television violence are more likely to see violence as acceptable or morally justified and as an effective solution to conflict (Atkin, Greenberg, Korzenny, & McDermott, 1979; Dominick & Greenberg, 1972). Studies have also found that heavy television exposure has a desensitizing effect that lessens the viewer's emotional and physiological reaction to violent scenes (Cline, Croft, & Courrier, 1973) and even decreases response to real-life aggression (Thomas, & Drabman, 1975). Heavy viewers are also more likely to see the world as a dangerous and violent place (Gerbner, Gross, Signorielli, Morgan, & Jackson-Beeck, 1979; Pingree & Hawkins, 1981). All of these factors conceivably increase the likelihood that a person would engage in aggressive or violent behavior.

A cross-sectional study has the advantage that it can assess a large, diverse sample of children and that it can show a link between television violence and naturally occurring aggression in the real world; however, the trade-off is that researchers cannot control the effects of other variables that might be responsible for the aggressive behavior. For example, children from lower-income homes tend to watch more television than other children, and any number of factors associated with lower income (increased family stress, less parent supervision, poorer school achievement, higher crime neighborhood, etc.) could account for the increased aggression observed in this population. Also in cross-sectional studies, it is impossible to determine whether the link between television violence and aggressive behavior is a direct causal link or an artifact of other influences associated with television viewing habits.

There are statistical procedures to take into consideration the effect of other factors; for example, researchers can calculate the correlation between amount of television violence and aggressive behavior after controlling for the relationship with family income. Such procedures are never wholly satisfactory, however, and are based on simplistic assumptions about which variables matter and how they influence one another. In the real world, causal relationships are not simple and direct, but complex and bidirectional. For example, does television violence cause aggressive behavior, or do children who are predisposed to aggressive behavior for other reasons simply enjoy watching violence on television? Do children from low-income families spend more time watching television because it is relatively inexpensive, or because their parents are busy working and not available to spend time with them, or for other reasons? In the real world there may be hundreds of factors to consider, but most researchers limit themselves to a handful and construct a simple model based just on those variables.

Keeping in mind that measures of almost all important variables are imprecise, it is difficult to accurately determine how variables influence one another. How do you measure how much television violence a child has watched? It is impractical to monitor a child's television viewing day after day, so researchers rely on estimates based on what the child or the parent recalls, or records in a notebook for a limited period. And even if you knew what programs the child watched, how would you gauge how much violence was in the program? And how much the child paid attention to the program? The measurement of many other factors, such as family stress or neighborhood crime, is equally problematic. The use of imprecise measures will decrease the size of correlations and obscure what otherwise might be meaningful relationships. In other words, real-world studies are plagued by measurement problems and the impossibility of ever taking into consideration the myriad influences that exist in natural settings. The result is that cross-sectional studies, at best, can produce only small correlations suggesting a weak relationship between television violence and aggressive behavior. Such studies are biased toward *underestimating* the size of the relationship.

Longitudinal studies. Longitudinal studies examine changes in children over long periods. Such studies share many of the disadvantages of cross-sectional studies and are usually correlational rather than experimental, but nevertheless, they can provide convincing evidence of real-life effects.

Researchers studied a group of 63 four-year-olds for five years, periodically assessing their television viewing habits and aggressiveness. Preschoolers who watched the most television were most aggressive at age 9, even after controlling for the children's initial aggressiveness (Singer, Singer, & Rapaczynksi, 1984). These children were also the most restless and likely to view the world as a "mean and scary" place.

Psychologists Leonard Eron, L. Rowell Huesmann, and colleagues (Eron, Huesmann, Lefkowitz, & Walder, 1972) conducted one of the most influential longitudinal studies of the effects of television violence on aggression. When they began their ten-year longitudinal study of 875 eight-year-old children, they did not intend to study exposure to television violence, but were interested primarily in familial influences on child development. They asked about children's television viewing only because they needed a few questions as fillers between questions that were deemed more important (Huesmann & Eron, 1986). To the researchers' surprise, they found that exposure to television violence at age eight was predictive of aggressive behavior in boys, but not girls, at age 18. The correlation remained statistically significant even after controlling for the children's initial aggressiveness and intelligence, their parents' child-rearing practices, and family socioeconomic status. Even more impressive, a 22-year follow-up study of these boys found that television viewing at age 8 remained predictive of violent criminal behavior even at age 30 (Huesmann, 1986).

Huesmann and Eron (1986) conducted a second longitudinal study, this time sampling 1,683 1st grade children from five countries—Australia, Finland,

Israel, Poland, and the United States. The level of television viewing varied substantially across countries, but the overall pattern of findings demonstrated that television viewing was associated with aggressive behavior as the children reached 3rd and 5th grades. The relationship between television violence and aggressive behavior was strongest in countries with the highest levels of television viewing, United States and Finland. Interestingly, among Israeli city boys, who watched substantial television violence, the relationship with aggression was stronger than in any other nation, but the relationship was weakest in the sample of Israeli kibbutz-raised children. One possible explanation is that the kibbutz-raised children watched very little television violence, and violent programs were often followed by discussions of the social implications of violence.

Fifteen years later, researchers conducted a follow-up study on a Chicago subsample of these boys and girls, now in their early twenties (Huesmann, Moise-Titus, Podolski, & Eron, 2003). To measure aggressive behavior, the researchers interviewed spouses and friends and reviewed court records. Men who watched the most television violence as children—e.g., "Starsky and Hutch," "The Six Millon Dollar Man," and "Roadrunner" cartoons—were most likely to have assaulted their spouses, shoved someone in response to an insult, or been convicted of a crime. Women who watched the most television violence showed similar effects and were more likely to have thrown something at their spouses, assaulted someone who made them mad, or committed a crime. These findings held up even after controlling for the child's initial aggressiveness and intelligence, their parents' aggressiveness and parenting style, and their family's socioeconomic status.

Social impact studies.   Social impact studies investigate the impact of television violence on communities using a variety of cross-sectional and longitudinal designs. One study examined the rate of children's aggression in a remote Canadian community shortly after it had acquired television (Williams, 1986). First and second-grade children in this town, dubbed "Notel," were compared to two similar communities. One community, "Unitel," had a single television station and the other, "Multitel," had four stations. After two years, physical aggression by the children in Notel—who were newly exposed to television—had increased 160 percent, but was unchanged among children in Unitel and Multitel. The study found that both boys and girls, as well as children who were either high or low in initial aggression, were affected.

Epidemiologist Brandon Centerwall (1992) investigated the doubling of the U.S. homicide rate in the decades following World War II. In studies conducted for the Centers for Disease Control and Prevention, Centerwall compared homicide rates in South Africa, where television was banned until 1975, with the U.S. and Canada. The researcher examined only homicide rates among whites, because of the extreme living conditions of blacks in South Africa. From the introduction of television in 1945 until 1974, U.S. homicide rates increased 93 percent and Canadian homicide rates increased 92 percent. During the same period in South Africa, homicide rates declined 7 percent. But after television was permitted in South Africa, homicide rates began to increase; by 1987, the homicide rate had increased 130 percent.

In reports published in the *American Journal of Epidemiology* (Centerwall, 1989) and the *Journal of the American Medical Association* (Centerwall, 1992), Centerwall concluded that the introduction of television caused homicide rates to double in 10 to 15 years—the time that it takes for the first cohort of television-watching children to reach early adulthood, which is the peak time for the commission of homicide. This is a provocative and controversial claim, because it is difficult to conclude that the differences between South African homicide rates and the homicide rates in United States and Canada were due solely or even largely to television. Yet Centerwall contended that other societal and economic differences between these nations cannot explain his pattern of findings.

Another controversial series of studies examined the immediate impact of televised events on suicide and homicide rates. Sociologist David Phillips of the University of California, San Diego (1979) examined the day-to-day number of suicides in the United States and correlated changes in the suicide rate with television events. Confirming what mental health professionals have long suspected, he found that the suicide rate in the United States increases briefly following news reports of a suicide by a famous person. Another proxy indicator of suicide, single-car fatalities, also increases. Surprisingly, the suicide and single-car fatality rate even increases following the *fictional* suicide by characters in soap operas (Phillips, 1982).

Next, Phillips (1983) conducted a homicide study that would earn him an award from the American Association for the Advancement of Science. He examined the homicide rate before and after 18 major televised prizefights between 1973 and 1978. These prizefights all received national and international attention, at a period when prizefighters such as Muhammad Ali and Joe Frazier were at their peak of celebrity. Incredibly, there was a slight increase in homicides during the ten days following each boxing match, peaking on the 3rd day. Phillips concluded that the 18 fights stimulated a total of 125 homicides beyond what would be expected after controlling for normal changes (e.g., the day of the week and season). If homicides increased it is likely that other forms of assault also increased, but such assaults are difficult to measure with sufficient precision.

Social impact studies like those by Centerwall and Phillips attempt to demonstrate a causal connection between television violence and violent behavior on a large scale. Such studies are inconclusive because there are so many uncontrolled factors that might explain the results. Even so, they help compensate for the limitations of studies that have been criticized for studying mildly aggressive behavior, such as playground pushing and shoving.

Meta-analyses. With so many different studies yielding results of different magnitude, how does one summarize them and decide whether the relationship between television violence and aggression is large, small, or nonexistent? Social scientists use a complex statistical procedure known as *meta-analysis* to combine the results of different studies into an overall average. A meta-analysis can take into account that some studies used larger samples, and for instance, can determine how different study designs such as experiments versus cross-sectional studies affected the results. The most influential meta-analysis was conducted by Haejung Paik of the University of Oklahoma and George Comstock of Syracuse University (Paik & Comstock, 1994). Their analysis, which combined the results of 217 studies, concluded that, "All types of aggressive behavior, including criminal violence and other illegal activities, have highly significant, albeit, in some cases, small magnitudes of effect size associated with exposure to television" (p. 538).

When a research finding is described as "highly significant" it means that the statistical results were highly unlikely to have occurred by chance. A statistically significant result is usually defined as a result that could not have occurred by chance more than 5 times out of 100, which is referred to as the .05 level of statistical significance. The significance levels obtained by Paik and Comstock (1994) were smaller than .0001, which means that the likelihood that the results were due to chance was smaller than 1 in 10,000. No social scientist would question the statistical validity of a finding at this level.

Researchers are not only concerned with the statistical significance of a result, i.e., the likelihood that it could have occurred by chance, but with the size or magnitude of the effect, called the *effect size*. The distinction between statistical significance and effect size is important. Suppose, for example, that researchers compared one group of boys who were exposed to a violent television show with a group who watched a nonviolent show, and found that the boys exposed to violence scored higher on some measure of playground aggression. First, researchers would compare the average aggression score of the boys in the violent television group with the average score of the boys in the nonviolent television group, then conduct a statistical significance test to determine the likelihood that the difference between the two groups could have occurred by chance.

However, a result that is statistically significant might not be of practical significance; the difference between the two groups could be so small that in practical terms there was little difference between the boys in each group. This is why researchers follow a test of statistical significance with a measure of effect size. There is much less consensus among researchers about the proper way to calculate and evaluate an effect size. Traditionally, researchers described the effect size as the percent of variance accounted for by the result. For example, researchers might find that 10 percent of all the differences (variance) among boys in the study could be attributed to being in the violent versus nonviolent television group. Presumably the remaining 90 percent of variance among the boys is attributable to a combination of preexisting differences in aggressiveness, errors in measurement, and other factors.

The most common criticism of research on television violence is that the effect sizes are so small that they are trivial. In some studies the effect size was less than 5 percent of the variance; the average effect size found by Paik and Comstock (1994) was 10 percent. How important is an effect size that accounts for 10 percent of the variance in aggressive behavior? From a layperson's perspective, and from the perspective of scholars critical of television violence research (Freedman, 1984), 10 percent seems small compared to the remaining 90 percent.

However, conventional measures of effect size used in the social sciences give a false impression. In a surprisingly contrarian article, noted research methodologist Robert Rosenthal of Harvard University (1990) pointed out that even small effect sizes can have substantial consequences. For example, the discovery that aspirin can reduce the risk of fatal heart attacks was based on an effect size that accounted for approximately one tenth of one percent of the variance, according to the way that social scientists measure effect size. Judged from social science standards, this important medical breakthrough would have been dismissed as trivial, but cardiologists had the opposite reaction, and promptly began recommending aspirin for their patients. Rosenthal chided social scientists for being slow to revise their understanding of the importance of small effects.

Rosenthal (1990) recommended a different approach to measuring effect size, called the Binomial Effect Size Display, which estimates the percent of persons who would have a positive or negative reaction to some treatment or effect, such as exposure to high levels of television violence. Bushman and Huesmann (2001) applied this approach to the correlation of .31 obtained between television violence and aggressive behavior in one of the analyses conducted by Paik and Comstock (1994). By conventional methods, a correlation of .31 produces an effect size of .096, or approximately 10 percent of the variance. But using the Binomial Effect Size Display, a correlation of .31 is equivalent to finding that 65.5 percent of persons who are exposed to television violence exhibit aggressive behavior versus 34.5 percent of those who were not exposed.

Bushman and Anderson (2001) go even further, pointing out that the correlation between television violence and aggressive behavior is comparable to the correlation between smoking and lung cancer. In fact, the correlation between television violence and aggressive behavior is much larger than other well-established medical correlations such as the correlation between exposure to asbestos and laryngeal cancer or the correlation between calcium intake and bone mass. The problem is that social scientists have taken a dim view of low correlations, failing to appreciate their real-world significance.

Correlations in social science research are often small because real-world relationships are complex and influenced by many factors. No researcher contends that television violence is the only cause of violence or that every person exposed to television violence will be aggressive. Consider the effects of television advertising: No agency expects their commercials to convince everyone to buy their product, but if an ad influences just one in a thousand viewers, it would be highly successful (Medved, 1995). The effect size for such an ad would be miniscule—yet because ads are seen by millions, the results can be substantial. Similarly, even a small effect of television violence can have serious consequences when broadcast nationwide.

Even if the effect of a single viewing is trivial, the cumulative effect may not be. A decade-old study concluded that by the time the average American child completes elementary school, he or she will have seen over 8,000 murders and more than 100,000 other violent acts on television (Huston et al., 1992). The current generation of children, many of whom spend hours playing video games where they shoot, stab, or beat their opponent to death, can probably claim much higher levels of entertainment violence.

How much youth violence can we attribute to television? One of the most respected researchers in the field, psychologist Leonard Eron (1999) of the University of Michigan, addressed this question before the Senate Committee on Commerce, Science, and Transportation in hearings held in May 1999. He estimated that 10 percent of youth violence could be attributed to the effects of television alone. To put this estimate in perspective, consider that in 2003 there were almost 65,000 arrests of juveniles in the United States for serious violent crime (murder, aggravated assault, robbery, and rape) and another 170,000 arrests for other assaults (FBI, 2004). Since many crimes do not result in an arrest (and of course, some innocent juveniles are arrested), the actual number of juvenile violent crimes is unknown, but likely of a similar magnitude.

WHAT ABOUT VIOLENT MUSIC AND VIDEO GAMES?

That music affects mood would not seem to require scientific proof; nevertheless, researchers have started to investigate the effects of music on aggressive mood and behavior. Several studies have examined music videos, primarily using college students. These studies found that exposure to violent rap music videos increases aggressive attitudes, in particular a willingness to use violence in dealing with interpersonal problems (Johnson, Jackson, & Gatto, 1995; Peterson & Pfost, 1989).

Other studies have focused on the effects of violent lyrics in rap and heavy metal music, with mixed results (Wester, Crown, Quatman, & Heesacker, 1997). One study found little effect, perhaps because the lyrics are often not comprehensible to listeners (Ballard & Coates, 1995). Craig Anderson of Iowa State University and colleagues (Anderson, Carnagey, & Eubanks, 2003) conducted five experiments with college students on the effects of violent lyrics on aggressive thoughts and feelings. They found that violent songs produced hostile feelings, aggressive thoughts, and more aggressive interpretation of ambiguously aggressive words. Such studies are a good foundation for further research, but do not demonstrate that violent lyrics can cause violent behavior. The only study venturing into this domain was a report that removal of Music Television (MTV) from a forensic inpatient ward was followed by a decrease in aggressive behavior (Waite, Hillbrand, & Foster, 1992).

Video games.   Video games are the newest and potentially most dangerous form of entertainment violence. Video games not only present children with the same kinds of violent images seen in television and movies, but give them the opportunity to direct and control the violence as well; they are also directly rewarded for violent thoughts and actions. The intensity and realism of video games, combined with the player's control of the action, make them likely to have a more potent effect on children than any other form of violent entertainment (Dill & Dill, 1998).

Public concern skyrocketed when it was reported that several of the students who committed rampage school shootings were ardent video game players (Vossekuil et al., 2002). These observations gave rise to some extreme claims that video games somehow brainwashed young players so that they were devoid of compassion for their victims or became machines that killed by reflex. Overstatements such as these weaken the credibility of criticism that is based on empirical research. While research has shown that entertainment violence, including video games, desensitizes youth to violence and increases their aggressiveness, this does not mean they were brainwashed or rendered incapable of self-control.

Another claim is that video games improved the marksmanship of the youth who committed the school shootings. This claim is plausible, as Lt. Colonel Dave Grossman, a military expert on combat training, has pointed out, both the U.S. military and many law enforcement agencies use similar technology. Video simulators are used to train recruits in marksmanship and to prepare them to make quick decisions about when to fire their weapons.

TABLE 6–1.
Is there a scientific consensus on the impact of entertainment violence?

1972	U.S. Surgeon General, *Television and Growing Up*	"Thus, there is a convergence of the fairly substantial experimental evidence for short-turn causation of aggression among some children by viewing violence on the screen and the much less certain evidence from field studies that extensive violence viewing precedes some long-run manifestations of aggressive behavior." (p. 185)
1982	National Institute of Mental Health, *Television and Behavior*	"The research question has moved from asking whether or not there is an effect to seeking explanations for that effect." (p. 6)
1999	U.S. Senate Committee on the Judiciary, *Children, Violence, and the Media: A Report for Parents and Policymakers*	"The effect of media violence on our children is no longer open to debate. Countless studies have shown that a steady diet of television, movie, music, video game, and Internet violence plays a significant role in the disheartening number of violent acts committed by America's youth."
2000	Federal Trade Commission, *Marketing violent entertainment to children: A review of self-regulation and industry practices in the motion picture, music recording, and electronic game industries*	"Do industries promote products they themselves acknowledge warrant parental caution in venues where children make up a substantial percentage of the audience? And are these advertisements intended to attract children and teenagers? For all three segments of the entertainment industry, the answers are plainly, 'yes.' " (p. 2)
2000	American Academy of Child and Adolescent Psychiatry, American Academy of Family Physicians, American Academy of Pediatrics, American Medical Association, American Psychiatric	"The conclusion of the public health community, based on over 30 years of research, is that viewing entertainment violence can lead to increases in aggressive attitudes, values, and behaviors, particularly in

(continued)

TABLE 6–1. *(Continued)*

	Association, American Psychological Association, *Joint statement on the impact of entertainment violence on children*	children. Its effects are measurable and long-lasting."
2001	U.S. Surgeon General, *Youth Violence: A Report of the Surgeon General*	"A substantial body of research now indicates that exposure to media violence increases children's physically and verbally aggressive behavior in the short term (within hours to days of exposure). Media violence also increases aggressive attitudes and emotions, which are theoretically linked to aggressive and violent behavior. Findings from a smaller body of longitudinal studies suggest a small but statistically significant impact on aggression over many years." (p. 92)

The U.S. Army uses a combat simulator that resembles a Super Nintendo game called *Duck Hunt*, and the Marine Corps uses a modified version of the popular video game *Doom* to teach recruits how to shoot to kill (Grossman & DeGaetano, 1999). Many law enforcement agencies use *Fire Arms Training Simulator*, which is similar to the arcade video game *Time Crisis*. No studies have been conducted, however, to examine the effects of video shooting games on the marksmanship of youth.

Several experiments that randomly assigned participants to play either a violent or nonviolent video game found increased aggressive behavior after playing the violent game (Bartholow & Anderson, 2002; Irwin & Gross, 1995). Such studies have shown that players will have more aggressive thoughts, interpret ambiguous situations as more hostile, and respond more aggressively to perceived provocation by a peer (Anderson & Dill, 2000; Bushman & Anderson, 2002; Calvert & Tan, 1994; Kirsh, 1998). The effects of violence in the video game can be shown even when compared to nonviolent games that produce comparable physiological arousal, excitement, frustration, and enjoyment (Anderson et al., 2004).

A correlational study found that students at the University of Missouri-Columbia who played violent video games were more likely to report hitting or threatening someone in the past year, even after controlling for antisocial personality characteristics (Anderson and Dill, 2000). Another correlational study found that 8th and 9th grade students who played violent video games were more likely to engage in physical fights with peers (Gentile, Lynch, Linder, & Walsh, 2004).

Research on the effects of violent video games is still new, and lags well behind the decades of research on television violence. Nevertheless, such research is important because video games have grown astronomically in popularity. A national survey conducted by the Annenberg Public Policy Center at the University of Pennsylvania (Woodard & Gridina, 2000) found that more than 90 percent of children ages 2 to 17 play video and computer games and that two-thirds of homes have video game equipment. According to parent report, girls average about a half-hour per day playing video games, while boys average more than an hour per day. Although most parents (88%) supervise their children's television viewing, fewer than half of parents (48%) report supervising their children's time with video games.

WHAT DO THE SKEPTICS SAY?

Despite the broad consensus among scientific organizations and researchers, there remain plenty of skeptics who question the causal link between entertainment violence and human behavior. What do the skeptics say?

TABLE 6–2.
What Do the Skeptics Say?

Criticism	*Lots of kids enjoy entertainment violence without becoming violent.*
Response	Lots of people smoke without developing lung cancer, too. Ironically, the correlation between smoking and cancer is about the same as the correlation between media violence and aggression (Bushman & Anderson, 2001). Not everyone is affected to the same degree by entertainment violence, and even so, researchers do not contend that entertainment violence alone is sufficient to cause violent behavior. Violence is the product of multiple factors.
Criticism	*The research experiments are flawed because they do not show that entertainment violence produces real violent crime.*
Response	
	Admittedly, most studies investigate milder forms of aggressive behavior, including aggressive thoughts or feelings, rather than violent crime. After all, it would be unethical to conduct a scientifically rigorous experiment in which half of the participants were expected to commit a violent crime. What these critics fail to

(continued)

TABLE 6–2. *(Continued)*

---

acknowledge is that many scientific fields conduct studies in stages. For example, medical studies almost always begin with experimental tests on laboratory animals before advancing to tests on human beings. Where the expected outcome is violent crime rather than relief from illness, however, it is not possible to advance to the final stage. In the same way, cancer studies cannot expose people to suspected carcinogens in order to prove that they cause cancer. Nevertheless, several longitudinal studies have shown that the more a child is exposed to television violence the greater the likelihood that this child will commit a violent crime as an adult (Huesmann, Moise-Titus, Podolski, & Eron, 2003). These studies are not as rigorous as a true scientific experiment, but like similar nonexperimental, longitudinal research on carcinogens, the accumulated evidence across many studies can produce adequate proof. The conclusion that smoking causes cancer is now well accepted, even though no experimental study has ever been done with human beings to produce cancer from smoking.

Criticism   *Most studies find only a small effect of entertainment violence on behavior.*

Response   The judgment that an effect is "small" is based on an outdated and misleading standard for judging effect sizes in social science research (Rosenthal, 1990). Even so-called "small" effects can be important, particularly when they are applied on a large scale to millions of people. Many valuable medical treatments are based on small effects, too. For example, the ability of aspirin to reduce heart attacks is now a well-accepted finding, but the scientific effect size accounted for only about .1% of the variance (Rosenthal, 1990). Most social scientists would have dismissed this effect size as trivial and overlooked an important medical break-through, when in fact this small effect saves many lives when applied on a large scale.

WHY DON'T MORE PEOPLE KNOW ABOUT THE EFFECTS OF ENTERTAINMENT VIOLENCE ON CHILDREN?

Although the overwhelming majority of researchers who study the topic are convinced that media violence causes aggression, there is a vocal minority whose skepticism has been widely disseminated. The debate among researchers has been heated. In an article entitled, "The case against the case against media violence," University of Michigan professor of psychology and communication studies L. Rowell Huesmann and his graduate student, Laramie Taylor (Huesmann & Taylor, 2003, p. 112) presented a forceful rebuttal to the critics:

> The best-known social scientists who deny there are any effects . . . generally have never done any empirical research on the topic. However, they are glib and compelling writers, and their opinions cannot simply be dismissed. Furthermore, there is a large body of other intellectuals who deny that there are any effects. They range from the president of the Motion Pictures Producers Association (Jack Valenti) to the president of the Entertainment Software Assocation (Doug Lowenstein); from movie directors (e.g., Rob Reiner) to comic book producers (e.g., Gerard Jones); from science writers (e.g., Richard Rhodes) to booksellers (e.g., Chris Finan, president, American Booksellers Foundation).

Huesmann and Taylor specifically challenged the objectivity of the best-known skeptic, University of Toronto professor Jonathan Freedman, by pointing out that his writings were funded by the Motion Picture Association of America. They describe key criticisms made in his most recent book (Freedman, 2002) as "clearly false," such as his claim that "Virtually no research shows that media violence desensitizes people to violence," "There is virtually no research on changes in attitudes due to viewing violence," and "A majority of studies show no ill effects" (Huesmann & Taylor, 2003, p. 117).

Huesman and Taylor (2003) proposed two factors that may inspire rejection of television violence research. First, there are strong financial interests in entertainment violence in television, movies, music, books, comics, and video games. These entertainment industries may be just as motivated to dispute the scientific evidence linking entertainment violence to aggressive behavior as the tobacco industry was to dispute the evidence linking smoking to cancer. The second source of motivation may be the strong American commitment to freedom of speech and artistic expression. Research confirming the effect of media violence on human behavior could be perceived as providing a rationale for censorship.

At least one industry-sponsored study has been regarded as biased against finding that television violence affects children. NBC conducted a three-year study of the correlation between exposure to television violence and aggressive behavior in 2,400 elementary school children and 800 teenage boys (Milavsky, Kessler, Stipp, & Rubens, 1982). The initial results appeared to indicate a relationship between TV violence and aggressive behavior, but the researchers made a series of statistical adjustments that rendered the results equivocal. Other researchers (Turner, Hesse, & Peterson-Lewis, 1986) have argued that a proper analysis of the NBC data demonstrates a real effect.

News coverage of research on entertainment violence has long been a source of frustration to scholars. Over the years many news accounts have downplayed the scientific evidence linking media violence to aggressive behavior. For example, in 1993 *Time* published an article aptly summarized by its title, "The great TV violence hype" (142 (2), 66–67). In 1995, *Newsweek* printed a story (Leland, 1995) disputing the link between entertainment violence and the media, then refused to publish a rejoinder (Bushman & Anderson, 2001). Similarly, when *The New York Times* published an op-ed article (Rhodes, 2000) scornfully criticizing the scientific literature on entertainment violence, the editors refused to print a rebuttal, even one prepared by the scientists whose work was criticized in the article (Huesmann, & Eron, 2001).

Even in recent years, when the evidence was strong enough that the U.S. Surgeon General, the National Institute of Mental Health, the American Medical Association, and other organizations took unequivocal positions that entertainment violence caused children to become more aggressive, it seemed to many researchers that the news media reports became *more* skeptical and less willing to acknowledge the conclusive nature of the evidence.

Psychologists Brad Bushman and Craig Anderson decided to test their perception of news media bias by examining how news reports had changed over the years. They collected a sample of 636 news reports on the effects of media violence from 1950 to 2000 and had them coded by trained judges. Their results were published in *American Psychologist*, the leading journal of the American Psychological Association, in an article entitled, "Media violence and the American public: Scientific facts versus media misinformation." They found that since the 1970s, news articles have become progressively more skeptical and less likely to report that viewing violence causes an increase in aggression (Bushman & Anderson, 2001).

Why would the news media be reluctant to acknowledge the link between entertainment violence and children's aggression? There are several possible explanations. One possibility is that news reporters are simply trying to be fair, and in order to give a balanced report of a controversial issue, feel obligated to give equal weight to both sides of the argument. This explanation would not account for the increasingly negative emphasis of news stories as the weight of scientific opinion has grown stronger.

Another explanation is that news reporters identify with their colleagues in the entertainment business or that they regard this research as a threat to their own interests. The investment of the news media in violent events is aptly reflected in the news editor's cliché, "If it bleeds, it leads." News accounts of violent crimes, especially the series of school shootings in the late 1990s, have been criticized for sensational coverage that might stimulate copycat crimes. After the Columbine shooting, the news media quietly lessened the prominence and intensity of its news coverage for school shootings.

CAN WE REDUCE THE EFFECTS
OF ENTERTAINMENT VIOLENCE?

The most immediate step that parents can take to reduce the effects of entertainment violence is to limit their children's exposure to it (Gentile, 2003). Parents can supervise their children's television viewing, refuse to purchase violent video games, and monitor and restrict their exposure to other forms of violent entertainment. The goal of these actions is not to completely eliminate a child's exposure to entertainment violence—that would be an impossible task—but to reduce exposure and, at the same time, emphasize that entertainment violence is not a preferred form of recreation.

The entertainment industry has supported the notion of increased parental supervision by adopting the use of ratings for movies, music, and video games (Gentile, 2003). The industry has also—reluctantly—supported the use of V-chip technology that permits parents to screen home television viewing for violent content. The entertainment industry's support of these parental monitoring efforts must be placed in the context, however, of its massive efforts to market all three forms of violent entertainment to children. According to an extensive study by the Federal Trade Commission, the motion picture, music recording, and electronic game industries attempt to market the same products to children that they label as unsuitable for children. The situation is analogous to the tobacco industry agreeing that children should not be permitted to purchase cigarettes, but then developing advertising programs that target youth.

Beyond simple supervision, parents can influence how their children respond to entertainment violence and reduce its impact on their children's attitudes and values. Several studies have suggested that when parents actively discuss the violent programs that their children watch, the adverse effects of violence on children's attitudes and aggressiveness are diminished (Nathanson, 1999; Singer and Singer, 1986). This is a neglected area that deserves more study (Anderson et al., 2003).

Another promising approach is "media literacy," which is the ability to critically analyze and comprehend media presentations. Media education began with an emphasis on helping students to understand and resist the techniques used in advertising, but this approach can also be used to help dispel some of the misconceptions about violence that are generated by entertainment violence. For example, in the most comprehensive scientific assessment of television violence, the National Television Violence Study (1998) found that 61 percent of programs on television contain violence, which greatly overrepresents the frequency of violence in real life. Further, the study found that 51 percent of the violent interactions on television showed no pain to the victim, and only 16 percent of the violent programs depicted long-term negative consequences to violence. Among children's programs, only 6 percent showed long-term negative consequences. In other words, a child watching a violent program will see that the violence causes no pain in half the victims and almost no long-term negative consequences.

More than twenty years ago, Huesmann and colleagues (Huesmann, Eron, Klein, Brice, & Fischer, 1983) made two attempts to reduce the likelihood that elementary school children would emulate aggressive behavior they observed on television. In their first attempt, children were taught to analyze the realism of television programs, but this effort had no apparent effect on aggressive attitudes or behavior. In a second attempt, the children were engaged in a project to produce a videotape explaining why it is bad to imitate television violence. Children who participated in this project showed less aggression than a control group.

A more recent study at Oregon State University attempted to change the attitudes and behavior of more than 400 elementary school students by teaching them to be critical viewers of television violence (Rosenkoetter, Rosenkoetter, Ozretich, & Acock, 2004). The researchers in this study felt that previous attempts at media education were too brief to produce lasting changes, and as a result, they designed a series of 20-minute sessions that were held once or twice a week throughout the school year. In this program children learned to identify unrealistic violent events, such as a person who is shot but suffers no pain or injury. The classes repeated basic themes using multiple perspectives and brought in guests who could distinguish their own career experiences from the unrealistic portrayals of their field on television. One example was a police officer who explained to students that he had never in his career had occasion to shoot anyone. The researchers found that by the end of the year, the students were watching fewer violent television shows and were less aggressive on the playground and classroom, compared to students who did not participate.

From a broader perspective, entertainment violence can be regarded as a public health problem (Anderson et al., 2003). Repeated exposure to excessive violence in the entertainment media constitutes a kind of social toxin that raises the level of aggression in children and eventually contributes to societal crime and violence. A public health approach would mount a large-scale, multi-faceted public education campaign to educate parents and encourage them to limit their children's exposure to entertainment violence and to encourage healthier alternatives. Similar to efforts to combat drug abuse, there would be television commercials, programs in schools, and pamphlets in the offices of pediatricians. There would be routine education of teachers, physicians, nurses, child-care workers, and others who work with children. Agencies in both the public and private sector would participate. Over time, the public would develop a better understanding of and greater concern about the effects of entertainment violence, and parents would recognize the importance of being conscientious in supervising their children's recreational activities.

WHY HAVEN'T WE DONE MORE TO REDUCE
ENTERTAINMENT VIOLENCE?

In May 1999, only a few weeks after the Columbine shootings, the U.S. House Judiciary Committee (1999) held hearings on youth violence and culture. The Committee assembled an array of experts in various fields to speak on the causes of youth violence, with a particular emphasis on cultural factors such as movies, music, and video games. All of the speakers were seated at the same table, so that one might speak after the other in succession.

The person awarded the privilege of being the first to testify was Jack Valenti, President of the Motion Picture Association. Mr. Valenti spoke with great charm and persuasiveness. He began by sympathetically acknowledging that there was too much violence in the media, from his personal perspective, and promised the committee that responsible leaders in the industry were taking steps to reduce it. After this reassuring introduction, he forcefully spurned the view that violent movies or television programs could cause aggressive behavior and asserted that these artistic works simply reflected the high level of violence in American society. He pointed the finger to other causes of violence, then defended and praised the entertainment industry for its efforts to establish a rating system so that parents could identify movies and programs they did not want their children to watch. He concluded by asserting that responsibility for reducing violence lay with parents, not the entertainment industry, and that it was critical to our constitutional freedom and liberty that the writers and actors of the industry be protected from censorship. After this brief testimony, one congressman after another offered him thanks and gratitude for his remarks. Remarkably, Mr. Valenti then left the hearing without waiting to hear any of the other speakers. He was the only speaker to depart before the end of the session, although virtually every subsequent speaker had rejoinders and rebuttals to his comments. The hearing resulted in no legislative action.

There are obvious financial and political reasons why so little action has been taken to reduce the impact of entertainment violence on children, but it is important to consider whether there are not psychological reasons as well. If scientists discovered unequivocal evidence that a popular food consumed by millions of children every day contained a toxic substance, there would be a public outcry and call for protective action. This would likely overwhelm any lobbying effort by the food industry, although it seems unlikely that anyone in the industry would be foolish enough to contest the issue if there was clear evidence that the toxin was harming children.

It would not matter if most children had only a mild reaction, that only a small proportion of the children who consumed the food became gravely ill, or that only a tiny percentage of them died, if it could be shown definitively that the toxin in the food were the cause. It would not matter if there were other sources of this toxin, or that some children developed the same illness from different causes: Parents would act quickly to keep their children from eating this food. Lawyers would file class-action suits against the manufacturers, distributors, and retailers. Regulatory agencies would swiftly enact consumer safety measures. Why is there not the same reaction to the discovery that entertainment violence has a toxic effect on children?

One critical difference between a food toxin that makes the body ill and a social toxin that affects a person's behavior is that the causal pathway from social toxin to behavior is more complex and must pass through an intervening step: the person's decision to engage in aggressive or violent behavior. Physical illness does not require a decision; it is an involuntary outcome that is not under a person's control. (Of course this is not to deny that a person's mental attitude cannot have a profound effect on a physical illness, or that some behaviors are impulsive reactions with little prior reflection.) The layperson sees an important difference between a chain of causal events that leads to involuntary illness and causal events that affect a person's decision-making. The model of causality used in most social science research, especially research in the tradition of behaviorism, does not make this distinction because it does not include notions of free will or volition (Skinner, 1971).

The layperson's concept of causality when it comes to human behavior depends heavily on the notion of free will or volitional choice. So long as a person retains the ability to make a choice, the behavior is regarded as under the person's control and therefore not caused by some external force like a television program. In contrast, the social science research on entertainment violence makes no use of a concept of free will or volitional choice. If a randomly selected group of children is exposed to a violent cartoon and afterwards engages in more aggressive behavior than children assigned to watch a nonviolent cartoon, then it is concluded that the violent cartoon caused the aggressive behavior.

The social scientist's view of causality is appropriate for making predictions about group trends, but is less persuasive in explaining individual behavior, where notions of personal responsibility and individual choice are paramount. So while the social scientist could point out that Daniel was exposed to high levels of entertainment violence that desensitized him to violence, lowered his inhibitions, and increased his aggressiveness, a judge in a court of law would want to know whether Daniel acted voluntarily in attacking his grandmother and whether he knew what he was doing was wrong. Unless it could be shown that Daniel's exposure to entertainment violence resulted in a mental illness that caused him to act involuntarily or somehow prevented him from recognizing that it was wrong to kill his grandmother—considerations that are key components of an insanity defense—the judge would regard Daniel's entertainment experiences as irrelevant to the issue of his guilt or innocence. As a result, Daniel would be considered criminally responsible for his actions and convicted for murder. At best, Daniel's childhood experiences might be considered at sentencing as a reason to mitigate his punishment.

Daniel was sentenced to 40 years in prison for the murder of his grandmother. In recognition of his youth, the judge agreed that Daniel could spend the first years of his sentence in a juvenile institution before being transferred to an adult prison.

Although social science findings might be of limited value in determining the guilt or innocence of an individual criminal defendant, from a policymaker's perspective it is valuable to know that exposing children to entertainment violence will affect their judgment or reasoning and result in more aggressive behavior. From a parent's perspective, it is vital to understand the impact of television and video games on a child's attitudes and values.

7

Does Prevention Work?

Two groups of girls lived in adjacent apartment complexes. Most of them knew one another since elementary school, but now, in high school, they began to hang out exclusively with the girls from their own complex and to see each other as rivals. It started with good-natured jokes and mocking comments, such as putting down someone's hairstyle or clothing. Over a period of weeks, however, the tone of their exchanges became more serious and the insults escalated into vindictive rumors. One girl spread a rumor that her boyfriend was cheating on her. This lead to a counter-rumor that the other girl had an STD. The rumors then evolved into threatening remarks, such as "I'm gonna whip her good."

One night the girls confronted each other on a downtown street, and harsh words erupted into a brawl that was broken up by the police. One girl was cut with a knife, and her friends vowed revenge. The conflict expanded when friends of the girls felt compelled to choose sides, and some of the rivals' boyfriends began to exchange threats, as well. The boys introduced guns into the dispute, and a shooting incident at a late-night dance sparked public concern and brought official attention to the problem.

The conflict inevitably came into the school, where the rivals glared at each other in classes and made provocative remarks in the hallways. The school cafeteria became divided territory. As the tension increased, rumors of an impending clash caused fearful students to skip school, often with parent permission. Some students reportedly began carrying weapons in anticipation of the need to defend themselves. Teachers noticed that their students were distracted and irritable. Parents called to complain and demand that something be done to prevent a violent incident at school. The school administrators, in turn, were worried and unsure what to do.

Successful prevention is a largely invisible process. Consider the hypothetical example of a school counselor who mediates a dispute between two students who are angry and upset with each other and on the verge of fighting: If the school counselor is successful in helping the students to calm down and resolve their differences, there will be no fight and the matter will be forgotten. Because counseling is a confidential process that goes on behind closed doors, no one else may know that a conflict had been defused.

But consider what happens when counseling is not successful. If the following week the counselor sees two more students who are angry with each other, and these students end up getting into a fight, the results will not be overlooked. On the contrary, if the fight takes place in a public place such as a hallway or parking lot, everyone in the school will know about it. As a result of the fight, the principal will know about the counselor's failure, but not about other successes. This is the nature of violence prevention: successful prevention is largely invisible, but prevention failures are often public events visible to everyone. As a result, even highly effective prevention efforts can appear to be unsuccessful because of a few exceptions.

How can we know whether prevention works? The most common approach is to measure the frequency of violence before implementing the prevention program (baseline assessment) and then again after the prevention effort has been in effect (follow-up assessment). If there is a decline in violence from baseline to follow-up, the program appears to be effective. This seemingly straightforward before-and after approach is not conclusive, however, because the change in violence could be due to factors other than the prevention program.

Schools are constantly changing environments. Each year, for instance, there are new programs, new students, and new staff. Anytime a school implements a violence prevention program, there are likely to be other responses to the problem at the same time. The principal may decide to "get tough" with students who get into fights or teachers may decide to try a new approach to classroom discipline. The PTO may invite a series of speakers and attempt to increase parent involvement. And in the community, there may be changes in law enforcement, in social and mental health services programs, and in after-school recreational programs.

The only way to determine whether a prevention program is effective is to conduct a controlled study. In an ideal controlled study, a group of students—or better yet, a group of schools—is randomly assigned to the prevention program (the target group) or a control group. The control group either has no prevention program or an alternative program that is being compared with the original program, in which case the control group is called a comparison group. The researcher measures the baseline and follow-up levels of violence in both the target group and the control group, to see whether the change in the target group is larger than the change in the control group.

The assignment to the target group versus the control or comparison group should be random, e.g., the researcher flips a coin so that the decision is made by chance. If the researcher simply chooses the group assignment, there is a potential for bias that undermines the integrity of the study. For example, the researcher might choose schools with the most cooperative administrators to implement the prevention program and assign schools with the less cooperative administrators to the control group.

Conversely, if the researcher permitted the schools to decide whether they wanted to participate in the prevention program or the control group, the schools with the greatest motivation to change would be most likely to choose the prevention program. The aim of random assignment is to minimize differences between the target and control groups, so that the only consistent difference between the groups is that one has the prevention program and the other does not. In many cases, random assignment is not practical, so researchers use statistical techniques to examine the impact of any identified differences between groups. For example, a researcher might implement a prevention program in schools in disadvantaged neighborhoods, then compare them to schools located in more affluent neighborhoods. The researcher would use one or more statistical methods to determine how much of the difference between target and control schools is correlated with affluence and how much of the difference can be attributed to the use of the prevention program.

It should be apparent from this brief discussion of research design that it is not easy to carry out a rigorous study. Even if the researcher is successful in achieving random assignment of groups, there are more challenges. A school might not completely implement the prevention program or use it with consistency. For example, if a school is attempting to launch a bullying prevention program, all of the teachers must be willing to participate—which could mean changes in their ordinary ways of monitoring and supervising students. Counselors must be willing to take a different approach to bullying incidents. Inevitably, there are stresses and strains on staff: sometimes a program proves too difficult to implement, or other school priorities divert time and energy from the program to other matters. Every educational researcher has tales to tell of programs that could not be fully implemented or accurately tested because of practical problems and unexpected events.

The terminology used in prevention research is sometimes confusing. In this chapter, the term "prevention" is used generically to refer to all forms of intervention, including work with violent youth for whom the goal is to avert further acts of violence. Criminologists use the term *rehabilitation* to mean efforts to prevent offenders from committing further crimes, which is known as *recidivism*. On the other hand, the public health approach that has come to dominate the field of violence prevention distinguishes three levels of prevention: *primary* prevention that takes place before the disease or problem occurs, *secondary* prevention when the disease or problem is evident, but not yet severe, and *tertiary* prevention when the disease or problem is at an advanced stage (Caplan, 1964). The public health model is most clearly applicable to an infectious disease spreading through a population, but since violence is not a disease, the distinctions among types of prevention are less meaningful. Some kinds of violence, such as bullying, are pervasive and do not develop in progressive stages, while other forms of violence, like serious assault and homicide, are discrete events where concepts of secondary and tertiary prevention do not apply.

An alternative to the traditional public health model of prevention is to define preventive interventions based on the target population: *universal* interventions are delivered to the general population, *selective* interventions are targeted at those presumed to be most at risk, and *indicated* interventions are provided to those who already exhibit the problem (Munoz, Mrazek, & Haggerty, 1996). This model has been adopted as more appropriate to school violence prevention (Osher, Dwyer, & Jackson, 2004).

MYTH 10: Nothing works in preventing youth crime and violence.

FACT: Although early studies of prevention efforts supported the conclusion that "nothing works," more recent studies demonstrate that juvenile crime and violence, including violence in schools, can be prevented.

THE MYTH THAT "NOTHING WORKS"

For many years the prevailing view in criminology was that "nothing works" in preventing juvenile delinquency and violence (Cullen & Gendreau, 2001; Elliott, 1997). A classic study started in 1935 contributed to this pessimistic perception (McCord, 1992). The Cambridge-Somerville Youth Study was devised by Richard Clark Cabot, a retired Harvard medical professor whose contributions to medicine included work on the differential diagnosis of typhoid fever from malaria. Cabot, who wanted to apply standards for medical research to the field of delinquency prevention, was a controversial figure whose outspoken criticism of the diagnostic abilities of general practitioners prompted the Massachusetts Medical Society to consider expelling him (Deardoff, 1958). Cabot was deeply interested in the field of social work and became president of the National Conference on Social Work in 1931; he held the view that delinquent youth could be saved from criminal careers if someone could give them the friendship, guidance, and support they lacked from their families. Consequently, he planned a controlled study, innovative for its time, to demonstrate how social workers could transform the lives of delinquent boys (McCord, 1992).

In this pioneering study, a group of approximately 500 boys under the age of 12 were randomly assigned by coin toss to participate in treatment or serve in a control group not receiving the treatment. Treatment consisted of weekly meetings with a social worker who tried to build a close personal relationship with the boy and assist his family in whatever way seemed best. There was no formal treatment method; the social workers differed in their treatment approaches and success in establishing relationships with the boys. After ten years, the social workers had seen their boys an average of twice a month for five years. Although the unselected boys were assigned to the control group, their families were free to seek treatment services from some other source.

More than forty years later, when the boys were men with an average age of 47 years, researchers searched for all available records to determine what had happened to them. The men were classified as having an undesirable outcome if they were convicted of a major crime, died before age 35, or received a medical diagnosis of alcoholism, schizophrenia, or manic-depression. Surprisingly, 42 percent (105 of 253) of the boys who had received this treatment suffered an undesirable outcome in comparison to just 32 percent (81 of 253) of the untreated boys (McCord, 1992). Since some of the families may have been uncooperative with treatment, the researchers compared the cases in which the family was or was not cooperative. Dismayingly, the boys whose families had been cooperative with treatment were more likely to suffer a negative outcome than the boys who had been uncooperative, strongly suggesting that the treatment itself had been harmful.

The Cambridge-Somerville study seemed like proof that treatment for delinquent boys was ineffective, but what kind of treatment was it? There was no treatment protocol or standard method that was being tested; each social worker was left to devise his or her own approach. Moreover, meetings between the social workers and the youths were erratic, and the *average* contact was only twice per month—woefully inadequate to make a substantial impact on a delinquent boy and his family. Imagine an evaluation of a medical treatment in which neither the type of medication being tested or the dosage of medication to be used was standard, and each doctor used a different medication and different dose; how could one draw meaningful conclusions from such a study? Moreover, if boys were assigned to receive this inadequate treatment, it might prevent their families from seeking more effective services, which, ironically, were available to boys in the control group. From this perspective, the Cambridge-Somerville study was doomed from the outset.

Despite its shortcomings, the Cambridge-Somerville study was groundbreaking because it was one of the first systematic attempts to evaluate a delinquency prevention program (McCord, 1992). It set a standard for evaluating prevention programs. The underlying problem, however, was that there was no systematic program to evaluate. Unfortunately, many other studies suffered from the same shortcoming: the prevention programs were poorly specified, and even if adequately specified, might not have been carried out according to plan. For decades, assessment of most prevention programs came to similarly negative conclusions: Evaluation researchers pointed out repeatedly that rehabilitation or prevention programs were not clearly designed or carefully conducted, or both (Gottfredson & Gottfredson, 2001; Henggeler, Melton, Brondino, Scherer, & Hanley, 1997). This made it impossible to determine whether the disappointing results of these programs were due to the plan itself or its implementation Even the best approach will not work if it is not faithfully implemented.

In 1974, sociologist Robert Martinson of the City University of New York took a provocative stand on the question of whether prevention efforts were effective. He published a scathing critique of rehabilitative efforts with criminal offenders in general—and based on a review of 231 studies—concluded that most rehabilitation efforts had "no appreciable effect on recidivism." Although many supporters of prevention efforts rejected Martinson's views as overstated and asserted that programs would be more effective if they were properly carried out, these objections had little impact. Martinson's conclusions, and similar conclusions reached by others (e.g., Greenberg, 1977) were highly influential with policymakers, who interpreted them to mean that "nothing works" (Finckenauer, 1982; Petrosino, 2005).

The timing of Martinson's (1974) rejection of rehabilitation was unfortunate: Starting in 1973 violent crime began to rise in the United States and did not peak until the end of the decade (Reiss & Roth, 1993). An anxious public was drawn to "get tough" and "law and order" policies. Politicians soon learned that it was important to be seen as "tough on crime" and to belittle opponents as "soft on crime." The sentiment that "nothing works" fueled a movement away from rehabilitative approaches to both adult and juvenile offenders and replaced it with heavy emphasis on punishment and deterrence.

Decades later, researchers are now studying the social impact of Martinson's critique and the negative effect it had on rehabilitation policy in the United States (Petrosino, 2005; Sarre, 2001). Between 1975 and 1989, the United States imprisoned more people than ever before, with the result that the inmate population tripled and the average prison time served per violent crime also tripled (Reiss & Roth, 1993). What was the result of this threefold increase in incarceration? The United States was imprisoning more of its citizens than any other nation—but did punishment have the expected deterrent effect of lowering crime? According to the Panel on the Understanding and Causes of Violent Behavior established by the federal government's National Research Council (Reiss & Roth, 1993), the answer is unequivocally "No": Even though the United States tripled the number of people (mostly men) sent to prison and tripled the length of time served for violent crimes, crime did not fall. Deterrence on a massive scale did not work.[1] States that greatly increased their incarceration rates for criminal offenders did not achieve substantially different results from other states, and states with the most severe punishments—including the death penalty—did not experience lower crime rates.

If deterrence was ineffective, what could be done to prevent crime? Criminologists had become disenchanted with the idea that prevention efforts aimed at changing crime-prone individuals—such as psychotherapy and education— could be effective. Instead, they had adopted the view that crime was caused by social factors such as poverty, prejudice, and injustice that required changing the structure of society rather than the minds of individuals. Accordingly, it became an accepted practice in academia to reject any effort to prevent crime through programs aimed at changing individuals rather than society.

Explanations for crime that considered the individual's character or personality were dismissed as "mere psychology" (Wilson & Herrnstein, 1985). In part, this disavowal of psychological factors reflected disciplinary rivalry between psychologists and other social scientists such as sociologists, criminologists, and political scientists. Each group regarded its discipline as the most valid approach to understanding crime and violence, and generally ignored the research and writings of those in other fields.

In 1985 two Harvard professors, political scientist James Q. Wilson and psychologist Richard Herrnstein, broke through disciplinary barriers between social and psychological approaches when they coauthored a book on the causes of crime with the provocative title, *Crime & Human Nature* (Wilson & Herrnstein, 1985). In their analysis of research on crime, they attempted to reconcile conflicting theories and synthesize them into a single model. They pointed out that a lot of research on the psychological characteristics of criminal offenders was largely being overlooked in other disciplines. At the same time, they explained how social factors could be integrated with psychological factors to form a comprehensive model.

The Wilson and Herrnstein (1985) model began with the premise that criminal behavior is a choice made by an individual based on his or her evaluation of the likely consequences of this decision. Whereas most individuals

---

[1]Although the American experiment in massive incarceration had little or no deterrent effect on criminals, this is not to say that the threat of punishment does not deter the ordinary citizen. For most adults, the threat of any form of incarceration is sufficient deterrence, whether the punishment is one year in prison or twenty years. The more narrow question under study was whether *increasing* the length of incarceration would also increase the deterrent effect on crime-prone individuals, and the answer to this question was clearly negative.

conclude that the negative consequences of a criminal act outweigh the potential benefits, crime-prone individuals are those who characteristically give greater weight to the benefits than the costs of crime. Wilson and Herrnstein elaborated this model to explain how different combinations of psychological factors and social conditions can influence a person's decision-making process. For example, a crime-prone youth might have limited academic aptitude and poor reasoning that affect his or her evaluation of the negative consequences of crime, or he might be unusually impulsive and short-tempered, or someone with a decided preference for risk-taking and excitement. Such psychological factors would be most influential among young persons who live in social conditions that promote crime, such as poverty, high unemployment, easy access to weapons and drugs, a lack of parental supervision, etc. This view suggested that crime might be prevented in many different ways, although no single method could be expected to thwart all criminal behavior.

In the past two decades, hundreds of studies have been conducted on different methods of preventing crime and violence. These methods have come a long way from the 1930s, when it was deemed sufficient simply to send out social workers to be "supportive" of delinquent youth and their families. Today's approaches are more structured and goal-oriented, and there is more attention to seeing that a program adheres to its plan or design. Programs must have *treatment fidelity*, which means that the program is implemented as designed and there is monitoring to ensure that it continues to be carried out according to plan.

Researchers have repeatedly demonstrated that prevention programs that have treatment fidelity are much more effective than programs without such monitoring (Lipsey & Wilson, 2001). There are now thousands of studies that have evaluated hundreds of different kinds of prevention or rehabilitation approaches, and the accumulated weight of these studies demonstrates conclusively that some methods *do* work—and although no method can eliminate crime or violence, the pessimistic view that "nothing works" is clearly wrong (Petrosino, 2005; Sarre, 2001).

SCHOOL-BASED PROGRAMS CAN
PREVENT VIOLENCE

There is a large body of evidence that school violence can be prevented with carefully implemented interventions (Howard, Flora & Griffin, 1999; Lipsey & Wilson, 2001). In recent years a group of researchers at Vanderbilt University led by Mark Lipsey has taken on the formidable task of reviewing thousands of different studies of prevention and treatment programs. They used the statistical procedure of meta-analysis to combine results across studies to determine whether there are consistent patterns of findings (Lipsey & Wilson, 2001).

In one meta-analysis, Wilson, Lipsey, and Derzon (2003) identified 221 studies of school-based interventions that in some way attempted to reduce aggressive or disruptive behavior by students. The studies involved nearly 56,000 students and each included pre-post assessment of at least one form of aggressive behavior broadly defined to include fighting, bullying, assault, conduct disorder, and acting out. These researchers found a wide range in program effectiveness, but calculated an average effect size of .25 for well-implemented demonstration programs. An effect size of this magnitude would eliminate approximately half the incidents of fighting in a typical school year.

The most extensively studied programs are designed to improve students' social competence (Wilson, Lipsey, & Derzon, 2003). Social competence refers to the ability to interact with others in a socially appropriate manner and particularly to be able to deal with potentially difficult situations such as peer pressure to use drugs or engage in other delinquent behavior. A typical social competence program has lesson plans for instructors to teach students how to deal with peer pressure or resolve peer conflicts. Students are taught how to listen and respond respectfully to others. Often through role-playing and demonstration exercises, they learn communication skills such as how to deflect criticism and assert their opinions in a nonprovocative manner, and how to use these techniques in typical peer situations in which they must resolve a conflict or cope with disappointment.

Some programs include a cognitive-behavioral component in which students learn relaxation techniques, practice self-monitoring, or rehearse step-by-step procedures for thinking through problems. Cognitive-behavior therapy for persons of all ages is one of the most popular and widely used forms of psychotherapy in the United States (Barrett & Ollendick, 2004; Beck, 1995), and has been found to be effective in the treatment of conduct disorder and aggression in youth (Kazdin, Siegal, & Bass, 1992; Lochman, 1992).

What are the characteristics of the most effective programs? Not surprisingly, Wilson, Lipsey, and Derzon (2003) found that quality of program implementation was critical. Schools that experienced problems in fully establishing a program experienced less success, and programs that were employed as part of a demonstration project were more successful than programs that operated under routine conditions. Demonstration projects were probably more successful because there was more careful attention to program fidelity, i.e., making sure that the program is faithful to the standards and requirements of the original model. The evaluation of programs that were being used routinely showed relatively weaker effects, even when evaluated by outside researchers. This finding argues for greater attention to program fidelity in routine administration of school-based programs, particularly in light of studies on the quality of school-based prevention programs. In their survey of 3,691 such programs, Gottfredson and Gottfredson (2001) found that typical prevention efforts were not well integrated into normal school operations and that the school staff who implement these programs were in need of better training, support, and supervision.

Wilson, Lipsey, and Derzon (2003) found that violence prevention programs were effective at all age levels, and that most programs were equally effective with girls and boys, and with students of different ethnic backgrounds. Both high-risk and low-risk students benefited from prevention programs, although as is often found in such studies, there was greater improvement in high-risk populations, where there would be greater room for change.

Programs delivered by teachers were most effective, followed by programs delivered by researchers and then those delivered by laypersons. This makes sense, since teachers are experienced in managing groups of children and presenting information in a way they can understand. One of the problems that may plague ineffective prevention programs is that they are delivered by persons who are not adequately trained to work with groups of students. The prevention field is generally underfunded, and services are often delivered by volunteers or paraprofessionals.

SCHOOL-BASED PROGRAMS THAT WORK

Although there are hundreds of commercially available violence prevention programs for schools, most have not been rigorously tested and shown to be effective (Howard, Flora, & Griffin, 1999). The challenge for school authorities is to select programs that have been adequately tested; there is no education counterpart to the U.S. Food and Drugs Administration to assure that a drug or medical treatment is safe and effective before it is placed on the market. Fortunately, there are dozens of programs that have been found to be effective. Here are a few:

Conflict resolution training. Many school-based prevention programs center around a curriculum for teaching students how to resolve conflicts without resorting to violence. An excellent example is the Responding in Peaceful and Positive Ways (RIPP) program, which consists of 45-minute lessons taught to sixth grade students once a week for 25 weeks (Meyer, Farrell, Northup, Kung & Plybon, 2000). Students work in small groups to practice a series of steps for handling problem situations. They learn to stop and calm down before responding to a situation, to identify the problem and their feelings about it, and then to select from four nonviolent options: resolve, avoid, ignore, or defuse the conflict. Evaluations of RIPP have found lower rates of fighting and fewer in-school suspensions (Farrell & Meyer, 1997; Farrell, Meyer, & White, 2001).

Another example of a violence prevention curriculum is the PATHS program, which stands for Promoting Alternative Thinking Strategies (Kusché & Greenberg, 1994). PATHS is designed for all elementary grades and is taught by the classroom teacher three times per week in 20-minute sessions. There are 130 different lessons and recommendations for incorporating lessons into other subjects. PATHS has been implemented in more than 1,000 schools, and children who participate in PATHS show a wide range of positive effects, including decreased behavior problems and lower peer aggression (Greenberg, Kusché, Cook, & Quamma, 1995; Greenberg, Kusché, & Mihalic, 1998; Kusché & Greenberg, 1994).

One of the most widely used curricula is the Second Step program, which has lessons for students from preschool through ninth grade (Committee for Children, 2005). Second Step emphasizes teaching social skills that are often lacking in aggressive children, including empathy, impulse control, problem solving, and anger management. There are approximately 20 lessons, which vary in length from 20 to 50 minutes, for each grade level. Several studies have found increases in friendly behavior and positive interactions, and reductions in physical aggression and disruptive behavior in students who participated in the program (Grossman et al., 1997; McMahon, et al., 2000). It is estimated that 15,000 schools use the Second Step curriculum.

Peer mediation. Peer mediation can be regarded as a special form of conflict resolution training that teaches students to serve as mediators or "peacemakers" (Johnson & Johnson, 2004) for one another. Peer mediation programs are popular because they involve students directly in helping one another; in a typical peer mediation program, a cadre of students is trained to serve as mediators for the student body (Lupton-Smith, 2004). When two students have an argument or dispute, they bring their grievances to a pair of mediators who then guide them through a procedure designed to facilitate a discussion that will resolve the conflict. The mediators usually give each party an opportunity to speak, then guide them through steps that might include identifying common interests and points of agreement, exploring possible solutions, and finally, guiding them to make decisions and reach an agreement that resolves the dispute.

Peer mediation is not suitable for all forms for student conflict, particularly if one party is an aggressor who has seriously injured or bullied the other. Victims of bullying are often unable to negotiate with bullies on equal terms, so a mediation process may not be appropriate. On the other hand, most the everyday conflicts and disputes between students, which have not risen to the level of a bully-victim conflict, are reasonable candidates for mediation.

Research on peer mediation has lagged behind that on conflict resolution. Many early accounts of peer mediation made sweeping claims of effectiveness, such as "School mediation programs have proven themselves beneficial to students, the school community and the community as a whole" (Davis & Porter, 1985, p. 128) that were not supported by empirical studies. Publications touting the benefits of peer mediation often relied on anecdotal claims of effectiveness and testimonial statements by students, e.g., "I'm a better person" (Davis & Porter, 1985, p. 126). Such statements, while compelling from a marketing perspective, are viewed with suspicion by researchers who have been trained to regard anecdotal evidence as unreliable.

The reputation of peer mediation also suffered from early reviews of the evidence that concluded that peer-led programs were generally ineffective or even had detrimental effects (U.S. Department of Health and Human Services, 2001). However, negative effects may be due to the kind of training and supervision that peers receive; programs led by peers with conflict mediation training are superior to programs led by untrained peers (Johnson & Johnson, 1996). The flagship of peer mediation programs is the "Teaching Students to Be Peacemakers" program developed by David Johnson and Roger Johnson of the University of Minnesota (Johnson & Johnson, 2004). Unlike most other peer mediation programs, the Peacemakers program has been rigorously evaluated and found to be effective; a meta-analysis of 16 studies using the Peacemakers program in students from kindergarten through ninth grade found a broad range of positive effects (Johnson & Johnson, 2002). Students who received the training demonstrated knowledge of the negotiation procedures up to a year after training, applied the procedures accurately in conflict situations, and were more effective than untrained students in resolving conflicts. Perhaps most important, the number of discipline problems dropped by about 60 percent and referrals to the principal's office by about 90 percent (Johnson & Johnson, 2004).

COMMUNITY-BASED PROGRAMS THAT WORK

There are thousands of community-based programs designed to prevent youth violence and delinquency. These programs enroll millions every year, but in many cases staff are not well trained and the programs are poorly implemented. Research on community-based programs demonstrates that some programs *can* work, but this is no guarantee that the programs *will* work in every community.

Mentoring.   Mentoring is a popular approach supported by more than 4,500 organizations (Rhodes, 2002) and involving more than 5 million children and adolescents (McLearn, Colasanto, & Schoen, 1998). Mentoring is appealing because it is inexpensive and seems to require little more than an adult volunteer who can spend a few hours each week with a child.

How do we know that mentoring works? Many adults can look back on their childhood and recall a teacher, coach, or some other adult who took a special interest in them and inspired them. Anecdotal evidence like this, however, is selective and not necessarily representative of what happens on a larger scale. Research shows that mentoring can indeed have a positive impact on youth, but frequently mentoring is unsuccessful and, in some cases, has adverse effects.

Perhaps the first place to start in studying mentoring is to consider so-called natural mentoring: relationships that develop spontaneously between an adult and a youth who is not a family member. Researchers at the University of Illinois at Chicago (DuBois & Silverthorne, 2005) examined survey data from 3,187 adolescents who participated in the National Longitudinal Study of Adolescent Health. Mentors were defined as an adult other than parents or stepparents who "made an important positive difference in your life at any time since you were 14 years old" (DuBois & Silverthorne, 2005, p. 519). Using this broad and inclusive definition, the researchers found that approximately three-fourths (72%) of youths had a mentor. As might be expected, the largest category of mentors (40%) were family members such as an older sibling or grandparent. Among nonfamily members, the most common mentors for adolescents were teachers or guidance counselors (26%); others were coaches (5.6%), religious leaders (5.1%), the parents of friends (4.8%), coworkers (4.4%), employers (4.1%), and neighbors (1.3%).

The adolescents were interviewed again about 7 years later, when they were 18 to 26 years old. Researchers found that those who had mentors were more likely to complete high school and attend college, and less likely to have joined a gang or to have hurt someone in a fight in the past year. Mentoring was also associated with higher self-esteem and life satisfaction, but was not associated with reduced alcohol or drug use, or reduction in depressive or suicidal symptoms. Overall, the results were positive and support the idea that mentoring is beneficial; however, the results of correlational studies are never conclusive. The benefits attributed to mentoring could have been due to personal factors that happen to be associated with mentoring; for example, young people who have more appealing personalities or greater social skills might attract mentoring relationships and have greater success with school.

The evidence from studies of natural mentoring is at least consistent with the anecdotal experiences of many adults who remember their mentors fondly and believe that the relationship was helpful. But can we assume that successful mentoring relationships can be arranged by third parties? Can strangers become effective mentors, particularly for at-risk children or adolescents?

Studies of mentoring programs find that mentoring relationships are not easily created; simply assigning a well-meaning adult to spend time with a disadvantaged child will not guarantee success. Volunteers for mentoring programs often find that it is difficult to establish a relationship with their assigned youth, particularly if there are social, cultural, or racial differences that make communication and trust more difficult—or the mentor and child simply might not get along. Studies of mentoring programs have found that approximately half of mentor pairings fail to develop into ongoing relationships, often leaving both parties feeling disappointed and disillusioned (Freedman, 1993; Grossman & Rhodes, 2002; Morrow & Styles, 1995).

One of the first large-scale studies of mentoring was conducted by the Big Brothers/Big Sisters program in eight cities and involved 959 youth (Grossman & Tierney, 1998). This study had the virtue of being a controlled experiment in which youth were randomly assigned to a mentor (487 youth) or to a waiting list (472 youth), which meant they were in the control group. In this way it was possible to isolate the effects of mentoring. In addition, the adult volunteers received training and supervision on mentoring and met with their young persons three or four times a month for approximately one year. Over the course of 18 months, the researchers found that the Big Brothers/Big Sisters program resulted in a 46 percent reduction in drug use, a 32 percent reduction in hitting people, and a 52 percent reduction in truancy associated with mentoring.

The weakness of the Big Brothers/Big Sisters study was that the positive outcomes were based solely on the self-report of the mentored youths; there was no independent corroboration that mentored youth were less likely to use drugs, hit someone, or skip school. It is conceivable that the mentored youngsters reported more favorable outcomes in part because they knew such answers were expected of them, and it is also possible that youngsters who were awaiting mentors were more inclined to give responses reflecting need for a mentor.

Psychologists at the University of Missouri-Columbia conducted a meta-analysis of 55 studies that evaluated mentoring programs (DuBois, Holloway, Valentine, & Cooper, 2002). Overall, mentoring was modestly effective in most studies, producing small improvements in areas such as academic achievement, social and emotional adjustment, or employment success. There were not enough studies of adequate size and rigor, however, to determine what aspects of mentoring produced the most benefits.

Certain features of mentoring programs made them more successful, such as providing ongoing training and support for mentors, offering structured activities for mentors and youths, and setting expectations for frequency of contact. Programs that had greater parental involvement were also more successful, as well mentoring relationships that involved more frequent contact and a closer relationship between mentor and youths. Children from disadvantaged backgrounds and low socioeconomic status were most likely to benefit from mentoring programs, but those with personal vulnerabilities, such as a history of academic failure, were less likely to benefit. One finding that raised concern was that poorly implemented programs could produce negative outcomes such as poorer school attendance or lower grades.

Supervised recreational programs. The peak times for juvenile crime are during the hours immediately after school (Snyder, Sickmund and Poe-Yamagata, 1997); the level of juvenile offending at 3 p.m. on school days is more than three times greater than at noon or midnight. Contrary to public perception, problems ranging from drug use to teen pregnancy are also linked to afternoon hours (Riggs & Greenberg, 2004): more teens use illegal drugs, get into fights, steal, and engage in premarital sex during the hours after school than late at night. Based on these observations, afternoon basketball holds more promise than midnight basketball as a means of preventing delinquent behavior.

One reason for the high rate of problem behavior after school is that many children and adolescents are left unsupervised because their parents are at work. In American society, work hours do not correspond with school hours, which is a costly legacy from times when mothers were expected to be at home and fathers were not considered important to child care. A nationwide adjustment of school and work hours to permit at least one parent to be home when children finish the school day would undoubtedly have a substantial effect on juvenile crime.

Nevertheless, with millions of children left unsupervised every weekday afternoon, after-school programs are of great potential value and deserve serious consideration in prevention planning for any community. After-school programs have grown increasing popular in the past decade, and have been funded on a large scale by private foundations as well as the federal government, which spent nearly $1 billion on 21st Century Community Learning Centers in 2002 (Riggs & Greenberg, 2004). In fact, several controlled studies have found that well-supervised after-school recreational programs substantially reduce juvenile crime, drug use, and vandalism. For example, a Canadian study (Jones and Offord, 1989) of an intensive after-school program (using sports, music, dancing, and scouting) reported a 75 percent reduction in juvenile arrests, while arrests at a comparison site rose 67 percent.

Probably the best known after-school program is The Boys and Girls Clubs of America, which has over 3,700 affiliated clubs serving over 4.4 million children (Boys & Girls Clubs of America, 2005). The mission of the Boys and Girls Clubs is to provide supervised recreational and educational programs to at-risk youth. Specific programs vary from club to club depending on what is needed in the community, but usually include educational and counseling services in addition to recreational programs. A study of ten Boys and Girls

Clubs by the U.S. Office of Substance Abuse Prevention reported 22 percent lower levels of drug activity and increased levels of parent involvement (Schinke, Cole, and Orlandi, 1991). A rigorously designed three-year longitudinal study of 16 clubs in eight states (St. Pierre, Mark, Kaltreider, Aikin, 1997) also found reductions in alcohol and drug use, particularly in clubs that had active parent involvement.

The research support for after-school programs is promising, but far from convincing to many researchers (Riggs & Greenberg, 2004). Most studies are based on small samples of youths who voluntarily joined the program, so it is not clear whether they are representative of others in their neighborhoods; those who join an after-school program may be less inclined to delinquent behavior than others in their neighborhood. And while it is doubtful that a single type of after-school program would be effective for all youth, there has been little research on matching activities to individual needs.

The U.S. Department of Education (2003) conducted an evaluation of 49 elementary and middle school after-school programs—called 21st Century Community Learning Centers—by comparing them to control groups of schools without such programs. The study found that students made only small academic gains and demonstrated no improvement in safety and behavior. These disappointing findings, however, are clouded by problems in the research design (Riggs & Greenberg, 2004): Centers were evaluated after only one year of operation, so that start-up problems, staff training, and other challenges that might have reduced the program's effectiveness were not considered. Programs may have better results after the first year.

Moreover, it appears that some of the school divisions involved in the study set up alternative after-school programs in the control schools, which effectively sabotaged the study design (Riggs & Greenberg, 2004). Any gains made by students in the Learning Centers would be underestimated if they are compared to students in another after-school program rather than to students not in any form of after-school program. This is the sort of unexpected problem that can thwart researchers attempting to study real world conditions.

FAMILY-FOCUSED PROGRAMS THAT WORK

Prevention programs that focus on improving family functioning are usually conducted on a smaller scale than other prevention efforts, and also require more intensive effort over a period of months. Nevertheless, such programs have the potential to make lasting changes on children and adolescents who are most at risk for violent and delinquent behavior. In light of the high social and economic costs of violent crime, even a modestly successful program can be cost-effective.

Parent education. Parent education programs are based on the premise that parents can be taught to be more effective in managing their children's behavior, and that this improvement will divert a child from developing increasingly defiant and aggressive patterns of misbehavior that eventually result in delinquency and violence. Parents are taught principles of behavior management, such as using positive reinforcement to increase the child's appropriate behavior rather than punishment in response to undesired behavior. They are also taught to be more consistent by setting explicit goals and keeping records of their child's behavior and its consequences. Parent training can work, but a few lessons are not sufficient; effective programs extend their training over a period of months.

There is good research evidence that parent management training is effective with aggressive and disobedient children (Brestan and Eyberg, 1998; Cedar and Levant, 1990; Kazdin, 2005). Here are some of the best-validated approaches to parent education:

- Parent Management Training for Conduct Disordered Children is the most influential parent training model for antisocial children. Developed by Patterson et al. (1992) at the University of Oregon Social Learning Centre, the program teaches parents more effective methods of disciplining and managing their children.
- The Barkley Parent Training Program provides an explicit manual that is used widely to train parents of children with severe behavior problems (Barkley, 1997). The program teaches a 10-step model supported by regular consultation with a therapist.
- The Incredible Years Series, developed by Carolyn Webster-Stratton at the University of Washington, is a well-validated program that makes use of video vignettes to demonstrate positive parenting techniques (Webster-Stratton, 1999; Webster-Stratton & Hammond, 1997; Webster-Stratton, Mihalic, Fagan, Arnold, Taylor, & Tingley, 2001). In a series of randomized clinical trials, the parent program reduced misbehaviour both at home and at school.
- Family and Schools Together (FAST) is a comprehensive program that incorporates parent training and home visits along with school-based efforts to improve the social skills and academic performance of elementary school children (Conduct Problems Prevention Research Group, 1992; McDonald, Billingham, Conrad, Morgan, et al., 1997). FAST has been implemented in more than 26 states. Notably, the program has a high retention rate; 88 percent of the families that attend one multifamily session go on to complete the program. Evaluations have found decreases in children's aggressive and oppositional behavior, and improvements in the parent–child relationship.

- Strengthening Families Program: For Parents and Youth 10–14 (SFP 10–14) is a 7-week curriculum for groups of 10–12 families (Molgaard & Spoth, 2001; Molgaard, Spoth, & Redmond, 2000). The curriculum is designed primarily to prevent drug use by improving parenting skills. The program, which has been found to prevent drug use as well as reduce aggressive and hostile behavior, has been implemented in 500 school districts.
- Syracuse Family Development Research Program (FDRP) is a program aimed at parents of infants from low socioeconomic circumstances (Honig, 2002; Lally, Mangione, & Honig, 1989). A team of Home Visitors begins weekly visits with young mothers, often beginning in the last trimester of pregnancy, and continues until the child is five. The Home Visitors teach parents how to care for their infants and stimulate their cognitive development. A 15 year follow-up study found that females, but not males, performed better in school and received fewer grades lower than C than those who did not receive home visits. Most impressively, however, male youth had lower rates of juvenile delinquency and committed fewer crimes such as robbery and rape than control youth.

Family therapy.   Family therapy refers to a host of different treatment approaches that emphasize treating the whole family rather than individuals. The literature on family therapy is voluminous and focuses on psychiatric disorders and relationship problems.

Functional family therapy (FFT; Alexander & Parsons, 1982) is a form of family therapy that has been especially effective with delinquent youth. FFT usually extends over a 3-month period and involves 8 to 12 one-hour sessions for most cases and up to 30 sessions for more difficult cases. The treatment requires highly trained therapists who are certified in this approach, which makes use of cognitive and behavioral methods to improve family relationships and increase reciprocity and cooperation among family members. Outcome studies demonstrated that FFT improved family relationships and reduced recidivism among adolescents referred by juvenile court for offenses such as truancy, theft, and unmanageable behavior (Alexander, Barton, et al., 1998; Klein, Alexander, & Parsons, 1977).

Multisystemic therapy (MST; Family Services Research Center, 1995; Henggeler et al., 1998) is one of the most ambitious and intensive forms of family therapy, and boasts an impressive track record of success. In controlled outcome studies, MST has proven to be superior to standard treatments for chronic juvenile offenders, inner-city at-risk youth, child-abusive families, and other traditionally difficult populations.

MST contrasts markedly with the unspecified form of treatment provided in the Cambridge-Somerville Youth Project: whereas the Cambridge-Somerville social workers saw their boys approximately twice a month with a general goal of establishing a close and supportive relationship, the MST therapist attempts to make radical and immediate changes in family functioning by seeing the family in its home several times a week and identifying specific family problems or needs.

A hallmark of MST is that the therapist takes an active role as a problemsolver who works closely with parents to identify and remedy problems in a wide variety of areas, ranging from a child's school attendance to marital discord. Therapists make flexible use of family therapy, parent education, and cognitive-behavioral techniques. They work on improving family relationships, strengthening parental authority and effectiveness, and modifying children's behavior. This approach is carefully described in a treatment manual (Henggeler et al., 1998), and studies have shown that in order for treatment to be effective, the therapists must faithfully adhere to MST principles and procedures (Henggeler, Melton, Brondino, Scherer, & Hanley, 1997).

WILL IT ALWAYS WORK?

No strategy is effective for all youth or all settings, and every prevention program will have some who fail. Unfortunately, failure inevitably receives more attention than success, and can distort perceptions of program effectiveness. All programs are vulnerable to these misperceptions if they fail to routinely and rigorously document overall success rates. Programs that can reduce violent crime by even 10–20 percent are likely to be cost-effective, due to the high cost of juvenile crime for victims, communities, and the criminal justice system.

Finally, even the best validated program will not succeed if it is not adequately funded and faithfully implemented by competent staff. A new treatment program must be sufficiently explained in training manuals and guides, and supervised by qualified practitioners, that it can be replicated in a new setting. Staff training and general quality control have often been neglected in prevention settings. More generally, programs must demonstrate adequate treatment fidelity, i.e., they must faithfully conduct the treatment program as it was designed. All too often program developers have rushed to implement new treatment programs without adequate training and preparation, so that treatment failure is a result of poor implementation, not an inadequate treatment model (e.g., see Henggeler, Melton, Brondino, Scherer, and Hanley, 1997).

In 1997 the U.S. Department of Education sent a strongly worded letter to state school superintendents, stating,

"After ten years of providing support (in excess of $5 billion) for drug and violence prevention programs, states and communities, Congressional leaders, the Office of National Drug Control Policy (ONDCP) and the Department of

Education at very concerned that SDFS (Safe and Drug-Free Schools) funds are not being utilized at the school district level in the most effective manner possible. A recent study by the Department of Education on the effectiveness of common drug prevention programs showed that drug prevention programs (in the districts evaluated) had only a 'small effect' on preventing drug use. . . . In response to this study and others, we are proposing some significant changes in the way SDFS is administered at the local level." (cited in Atkinson, Deaton, Travis, & Wessel, 1999).

The following year Congress passed the Safe and Drug-Free Schools and Communities Act (SDFSCA), which marked a sea change in how schools could select and implement prevention programs by establishing its Principles of Effectiveness. These principles required schools using SDFSCA funds to choose programs based on scientific evidence of their effectiveness and to carry out systematic evaluations of the results of their programs. This forced school divisions to examine whether there was published research evidence in support of the programs they wanted to establish and to revise their applications for SDFSCA funds accordingly. To assist schools in identifying effective programs, the U.S. Department of Education convened a panel of experts that identified 42 acceptable programs (U.S. Department of Education, 2002).

It soon became apparent that programs could not be readily classified as effective or ineffective. Research to validate a program is a gradual process and evidence must be accumulated across multiple studies; studies using more rigorous designs must be given more weight than less rigorous studies. The most rigorous study design, termed an experimental design, randomly assigns youths to participate in the prevention program or a control group (or some other alternative to the prevention program). Such studies are rare, because they are difficult to arrange. More often, studies are not able to randomly assign students to one group or another, and instead rely on quasi-experimental designs in which the researcher picks an available comparison group, such as students from a different school in the same community. In some cases the researcher simply measures the participants before and after the program without the benefit of a comparison group.

There are many other factors to consider in evaluating the scientific support for a prevention program. The program might have impressive short term effects, for instance, but how long do they last? Few studies examine the long-term impact of prevention programs. How are effects measured? Programs may influence any number of different behavioral domains from underage drinking to violent crime, and disruptive behavior in the classroom to bullying and fighting. Moreover, the effectiveness of a program may differ for boys and girls and vary across age groups. Ethnicity and social-economic status also must be considered. If a program shows different effects for different groups or across different studies, how should its effectiveness be classified?

Ultimately, the U.S. Department of Education (2002) panel decided that only nine programs could be considered "exemplary," while 33 were deemed "promising" because the evidence supporting them was not strong enough. Not surprisingly, there is plenty of room for disagreement about what constitutes an effective program. In just a few years, a large number of organizations devised their own lists of effective programs, each using somewhat different criteria and standards. Government agencies such as the Office of Juvenile Justice and Delinquency Prevention (OJJDP), the Substance Abuse and Mental Health Services Administration (SAMHSA), and the Centers for Disease Control and Prevention (CDC), developed lists of effective programs, as did private organizations such as the American Policy Youth Forum. The Center for the Study and Prevention of Violence at the University of Colorado developed a "blueprint series" of publications devoted to model programs it deemed to be effective. In most cases, the organizations convened panels of experts who discussed and debated the literature before arriving at consensus.

The U.S. Surgeon General's report on youth violence (U.S. Department of Health and Human Services, 2001) identified seven approaches as "model" programs and 22 approaches as "promising." The report then examined how each program had been evaluated by six other organizations. There was a wide range of disagreement across organizations, even for programs with extensive research support. For example, Multisystemic Therapy was identified as a model program by the CDC, but not by OJJDP. Parent training with The Incredible Years Series was not recognized by the CDC, but was highlighted as a "blueprint program" by the Center for the Study and Prevention of Violence. No program made the list of every organization.

By 2003, the number of lists of effective programs had grown even larger, with the Institute of Medicine, the Hamilton Fish Institute, and other organizations weighing in with their choices. The Southwest Educational Development Laboratory (2005) identified 193 different programs that were named on one or more organizations' lists of scientifically based programs, and they counted 26 programs that were on least three lists.

To answer the question posed at the outset of this chapter: Yes, prevention works. In fact, there are a large number of programs that work, although they differ widely in what they attempt to do and how well they do it. Research to evaluate a program is difficult and reasonable experts may differ in what they regard as sufficient evidence to establish a program's validity. But if research can demonstrate that certain programs work, can it also demonstrate that some do not work? And what happens when a popular program is found to be ineffective? These questions will be addressed in the next chapter.

What happened to the two groups of girls embroiled in an escalating conflict? No single prevention program resolved the problem, but the combined efforts of several agencies working in collaboration produced impressive results.

As tension mounted in the community, school and court authorities brought in a team of professional mediators to work with the two groups of girls. The mediators met with the girls individually and convinced them to attend a day-long mediation session. During this session, the mediators facilitated a conversation in which each of the girls shared her perspective on what happened. In an unhurried atmosphere, the girls spent hours airing their grievances, unraveling rumors, and clarifying misunderstandings.

When each girl had told her story and expressed her feelings and concerns, the mediators advised the girls that they could devise their own plan for ending the feud. The mediators were careful not to take sides or make specific suggestions, so that solutions would be devised by the girls rather than imposed from an outside authority. In this way the girls decided to end their dispute and settled on terms for reconciliation.

After the successful mediation, many of the girls received additional services, including family therapy, individual counseling, and academic tutoring, according to their individual needs. To the surprise and relief of authorities, the girls ended their dispute and engaged in no further acts of aggression or violence toward one another. After two years, the agreement was still being honored, and some previous rivals had become friends.

8

What Doesn't Work?

When Jimmy was in the fifth grade, a police officer came to his classroom and taught a course on "saying no" to drugs and violence. Jimmy liked Officer Wilson and even thought that he might want to be a police officer one day. At the end of the course, Jimmy received a "Just Say No" t-shirt and a certificate. The next year, when he went to middle school, an older boy offered him a cigarette in the rest room and Jimmy turned it down.

But the "Just Say No" program was not designed to deal with the problems that Jimmy faced at home. His father drank heavily, and when he was drunk, he was angry and abusive. He beat Jimmy occasionally, but most of his anger was directed at his wife. As a result, by the time Jimmy was in the 9th grade, his parents had divorced and Jimmy and his mother had moved into an apartment. By this time, Officer Wilson's 5th grade lessons were long forgotten. Jimmy went to a new school and found a new group of friends, who convinced him that drinking beer was cool. When they started to drive in the 11th grade, the boys got together to drink every weekend. One of their favorite places to drink was a small park two miles outside town, and on Friday nights they liked to race their cars down the long curvy road through the deserted park. One night it had started to rain and the road was slick. Coming around a curve, Jimmy's car started to slide; he jerked the wheel too hard and lost control of the car, which went off the road and hit a tree. Jimmy died at the hospital.

Every year a few students are killed at school, but thousands die in automobile accidents. Perhaps because traffic accidents are so common, they do not evoke the same shock and concern as a school shooting—yet from a public health perspective, underage drinking is far more dangerous to young people (Bonnie & O'Connell, 2004). Dollars spent to prevent school shootings could save far more lives if they were spent to keep underage drinkers off the road.

Prevention programs often address both drug use and violence at though they were manifestations of the same problem or somehow amenable to the same solution. Drug use and violence are often seen together, but either can be present without the other and programs effective for one might not be effective for the other. Even so, the federal government's Safe and Drug-Free Schools and Communities Act combined drug prevention and violence prevention in one federal office, funded by a single program. For these reasons, both drug abuse and violence prevention programs will be considered here.

Underage drinkers—defined as drinkers under the age of 21—account for about one-fifth of alcohol consumption (Foster et al., 2003). According to student self-reports in the annual Monitoring The Future surveys, about half of 12th graders and just over a third of 10th graders report drinking alcohol in the past 30 days (Johnston, O'Malley, & Bachman, 2003). Drinking is especially dangerous for young drivers, who are involved in fatal crashes twice as frequently as adult drivers (National Highway Traffic Safety Administration, 2002). In 2003 alone, 6,409 persons ages 15 to 20 were killed in traffic accidents, including 2,283 deaths that were alcohol-related (Mothers Against Drunk Driving, 2005).

During the 1970s, 29 states experimented with lowering the drinking age to 18, but they later reversed course when alcohol-related automobile accidents soared in the 18- to 20-year-old age group. Although a legal prohibition does not prevent all underage drinking, reinstatement of the drinking age to 21 dramatically reduced the number of alcohol-related fatalities for persons between 18 and 21. This unintended social experiment demonstrated the seemingly invisible—but substantial—impact of prevention. The National Highway Safety Traffic Administration (NHSTA, 2005) calculated that approximately 900 lives were saved by minimum-drinking-age laws in 2002. Few prevention programs could claim this kind of success, yet like most prevention efforts, its impact is largely unnoticed because there are no specific victims one can identify as having been saved.

WHAT DOESN'T WORK?

Prevention research not only determines what works; it can also determine what does not work and is a waste of time and effort. In 1996, Congress passed a law requiring the Attorney General to provide an independent review of the effectiveness of state and local crime prevention programs and, specifically, to identify factors that would reduce youth violence. The National Institute of Justice selected a group of researchers from the University of Maryland's

Department of Criminology and Criminal Justice to conduct this review (Sherman, Gottfredson, MacKenzie, Eck, Reuter, and Bushway, 1997). In 1997, these researchers, led by criminologist Lawrence Sherman, released a mammoth 543-page report of their findings that shook the world of crime prevention and criminal justice.

Sherman's group concluded that some popular and widely used programs do not work. This was welcomed by the community of criminal justice researchers as a whole—who had reached similar conclusions—but met with a great deal of resistance from advocates of programs that were identified as ineffective. Nearly a decade later, many of these programs continue to be in widespread use with millions of children and adolescents, despite strong scientific evidence that they are worthless—and in some cases, harmful—to the youth who participate in them.

The Maryland researchers set up a rigorous set of standards for the quality of scientific studies of crime prevention and then painstakingly evaluated hundreds of studies to identify those that met these standards. Researchers then synthesized evidence from the best available studies and reached conclusions about what worked and what did not work in preventing crime. In some cases it was not possible to say whether a program worked because it had not been rigorously tested, but many well-known programs (see table) were tested and found to be ineffective. This chapter will review four of the most popular and widely used prevention methods that do not work.

Prevention Programs That Do Not Work

- Correctional boot camps
- Drug Abuse Resistance Education (D.A.R.E.)
- "Scared Straight" programs
- School uniforms

CORRECTIONAL BOOT CAMPS

Many military veterans recall boot camp as an arduous yet formative experience that marked their transition from adolescence to adulthood, so the idea of sending juvenile offenders to a camp where they must work hard and learn to respect and obey authority seems sensible. But no program, however appealing, can claim success without empirical testing. The youth who are sent to correctional boot camps differ in many ways from the broader population that enters military training, and the nature and purpose of their training differ in important ways as well. These differences cannot be overlooked. Also,

the graduates of correctional boot camp usually return to the same circumstances that contributed to their delinquency, whereas many military veterans
return to a more affluent community with decidedly more favorable prospects.

Correctional boot camps for juvenile offenders became popular in the 1990s,
and by 2000 the Koch Crime Institute (2000) could identify at least 40 juvenile boot camps in the United States. Boot camps vary widely in the types of
educational and therapeutic services they offer, but generally they share an
emphasis on paramilitary discipline, regimentation, and physical training.

MYTH 11: Boot camps reform juvenile offenders.

FACT: The available evidence demonstrates that boot camps do not
reform juvenile offenders, and some camps appear to increase rather
than decrease the criminal behavior of their graduates (Peters, Thomas,
& Zamberlan, 1997).

In 1992, the U.S. Office of Juvenile Justice and Delinquency Prevention
(OJJDP) funded the development of three juvenile boot camps (in Cleveland,
Ohio; Denver, Colorado; and Mobile, Alabama) for the purpose of evaluating
the effectiveness of this approach (Peters, Thomas, & Zamberlan, 1997). In
each locality, juvenile offenders were adjudicated by the court and then randomly assigned to either attend the boot camp or complete their original sentence (usually some combination of confinement and probation). The boot
camps were followed by an aftercare program that lasted at least 6 to 9 months
and included educational, vocational, and counseling services.

A comprehensive evaluation of the boot camp experiment raised serious
concerns about the quality of the programs and their effects (Peters, Thomas,
& Zamberlan, 1997). On the positive side, most of the juveniles successfully
completed the boot camp programs, and most of them made substantial gains
in academic achievement, as measured by higher test scores, and were able to
return to school or enroll in a GED program when they graduated to aftercare.

More important, however, was the evaluation of criminal recidivism, defined as a court-adjudicated new offense occurring after release from the program. For two of the boot camps, the rate of recidivism for attendees was
comparable to the rate for the control group. In Denver, 39 percent of the
boot camp youth versus 36 percent of the control group youth committed a
new offense during the follow-up period. In Mobile, 28 percent of the boot
camp youth versus 31 percent of the control group youth recidivated.

The most troubling finding of the study, however, was that 72 percent of
the youth who attended the boot camp in Cleveland recidivated, in compar-

ison to 50 percent of the youth in the control group. At all three sites, recidivism occurred more quickly in the youth who attended boot camps than in the control group. For example, reoffending youth in the Cleveland program were charged with a new offense an average of 176 days after their release, whereas reoffending youth in the control were charged with a new offense after an average of 205 days.

Although these studies discredited the boot camp model—and boot camps are omitted from government lists of effective programs (U.S. Department of Education, 2001; U.S. Department of Health and Human Services, 1999)— proponents might argue that these three camps were not well-run and so did not constitute a fair test. The federal evaluation found that all three boot camps suffered from administrative and logistical problems, such as high staff turnover, uncertainty over lines of authority and responsibility, and problems with their physical facilities (Peters, Thomas, & Zamberlan, 1997). Although all three programs were able to adequately implement the boot camp phase of their program, all had difficulties with their aftercare programs in integrating youth back into their families, schools, and neighborhoods. The Denver program shut down in 1994, while the Mobile program failed in its first year and then was restarted with a new model. The Cleveland program relocated twice within its first year.

Another reason that boot camps do not work is that treatment programs that bring together groups of delinquent youth may inadvertently increase their propensity for antisocial behavior (Dishion, McCord, & Poulin, 1999). When delinquent youth are brought together in group settings they tend to reinforce and support one another's antisocial attitudes and aggressive behaviors. This observation has led many authorities to question the value of group treatment approaches with delinquent youth, which they describe as having an iatrogenic effect, meaning that the treatment itself is harmful (for a contrasting view, see Mager, Milich, Harris, & Howard, 2005).

Apart from these three evaluations, there is a conspicuous lack of evidence in support of juvenile boot camps. The available research on boot camps for young adults produced mixed results. A study of eight adult boot camps found that they improved the attitudes of participants, but had no effect on recidivism (MacKenzie, 1994). Other evaluations of individual programs also reached negative conclusions. An evaluation of the Regimented Inmate Diversion project of the Los Angeles County Sheriff's Department, for instance, described it as "A boot camp that didn't work" (Austin, Jones, & Bolyard, 1996).

In reviewing the overall status of boot camps, a Department of Justice official concluded frankly that "One of the major driving forces contributing to the proliferation of boot camps has been the significant level of political interest in establishing them, ranging from the local politician to the highest levels of Federal Government" (Hayeslip, 1996, p. 2). Further, he noted that

"The political popularity of boot camps rests in part on the strong appeal created by the media" (p. 3).

DRUG ABUSE RESISTANCE EDUCATION

D.A.R.E. is undoubtedly the most popular and widely used prevention program in American schools. D.A.R.E. began in 1983 as a collaborative effort between the Los Angeles Police Department and the Los Angeles Unified School District. In 22 years, it has expanded to include more than 80 percent of the nation's school districts, as well as 54 other nations; D.A.R.E. estimates that 26 million U.S. school children participate (D.A.R.E., 2005). The original core curriculum was designed as a drug prevention curriculum for uniformed police officers to teach to students in their last (5th or 6th) grade of elementary school, although there are D.A.R.E. programs for other grade levels that are less widely used. D.A.R.E. is both a drug and violence prevention program, and it is intended to prevent children from using alcohol, tobacco, and other illegal drugs.

MYTH 12: D.A.R.E. reduces student drug use and violence.

FACT: Although D.A.R.E. is a popular and well-regarded program that generates positive attitudes and favorable reviews from its participants, rigorous, large-scale controlled studies have repeatedly found that D.A.R.E. does not reduce student drug use or violence (Perry et al., 2003; Ringwalt et al., 1994; Rosenbaum & Hanson, 1998).

Early studies, which suggested that D.A.R.E. might be effective, suffered from limitations that clouded the validity of their conclusions (West & O'Neal, 2004). First, much of the evidence supporting D.A.R.E. was based on studies that were conducted by agencies or groups affiliated with D.A.R.E. and were not published in refereed journals. To be accepted as scientifically rigorous, studies should be conducted by independent researchers and then the results of those studies should be subject to independent peer review by other researchers.

Another limitation was that many of the early D.A.R.E. evaluations relied on surveys of participant attitudes and beliefs that were collected at the conclusion of the D.A.R.E. curriculum, when such attitudes and beliefs are most likely to favor the goals of the curriculum and the expectations of its instructors (West & O'Neal, 2004). Recent D.A.R.E. students might claim that they are not using drugs or getting into fights, but this is not sufficiently convincing evidence. Long-term follow-up studies are necessary to demonstrate whether a program has a lasting impact and actually reduces adolescent drug use and violence.

In 1994, Ringwalt and colleagues (Ringwalt et al., 1994) released an evaluation of the D.A.R.E. program based on a meta-analysis of eight methodologically rigorous studies that involved 9,300 students and 215 schools. All eight studies assessed students before and after completion of the core D.A.R.E. curriculum and included control groups of students who had participated in D.A.R.E.. The results demonstrated that D.A.R.E. was most effective at increasing knowledge about drug use and enhancing social skills, with slight improvements in attitudes toward police and self-esteem. *Attitudes* about drug and alcohol improved, but *use* did not decline. These results helped generate a storm of criticism and often contentious debate concerning the merits of D.A.R.E..

In defense of D.A.R.E., one limitation of most outcomes studies was that they examined drug and alcohol use shortly after completion of D.A.R.E., when students are 11 or 12 years old and the baseline rates of drug use are so low that the effects of D.A.R.E. might not be evident. To overcome this limitation, Rosenbaum and Hanson (1998) reported results of a six-year longitudinal study of 1,798 students from 36 schools. This methodologically rigorous study employed randomized control groups and corrected for many statistical and methodological problems of previous studies. There were expectations that this study would salvage D.A.R.E.'s reputation and demonstrate conclusively that it was effective. Instead, the study found that D.A.R.E. did not reduce drug use—and that in suburban schools, D.A.R.E. was associated with a 3–5 percent *increase* in drug use. It seemed that in communities where drug use was not already prevalent, the D.A.R.E. program might actually raise interest in drug experimentation rather than decrease it.

The Minnesota D.A.R.E. Plus project. Another explanation for D.A.R.E.'s ineffectiveness could be that since the program was delivered in elementary school—before most children are confronted with the opportunity to use drugs—it might be more effective in higher grades when students are dealing with peer pressure and other influences that lead to drug use and violence. Accordingly, 24 schools in Minnesota participated in a study of a revised D.A.R.E. program for 7th grade students (Perry et al., 2003; Komro, Perry, Veblen-Mortenson, Stigler, Bosma, Munson, & Farbakhsh, 2004). The 7th grade program included ten sessions on character and citizenship, as well as specific skills for resisting peer pressure to use drugs and strategies for avoiding potentially violent situations. The study was conducted by researchers at the University of Minnesota School of Public Health with funding from the National Institute on Drug Abuse.

The Minnesota D.A.R.E. program also investigated an augmentation of the standard D.A.R.E. curriculum called "D.A.R.E. Plus." (Plus stands for "Play and learn under supervision"). The rationale for D.A.R.E. Plus was that the most effective prevention programs attempted to influence children beyond the classroom through activities in their homes and neighborhoods. Accordingly, the D.A.R.E. Plus component included after-school activities and the creation of neighborhood action teams lead by adult volunteers. The neighborhood action teams planned constructive activities such as a bullying prevention seminar, community forums, and neighborhood cleanups.

The 24 schools were randomly assigned to one of three conditions: (1) the standard 10-session classroom curriculum; (2) the D.A.R.E. Plus program, which included the standard curriculum; and (3) a wait-list control group, in which schools waited one year before implementing any D.A.R.E. programs so that their 7th grade students could serve as a control group. The programs were evaluated by having students complete self-report surveys at the end of the 7th grade and then again at the end of the 8th grade. A total of 4,976 students completed baseline and follow-up surveys.

In 2003, the Minnesota researchers reported that the standard D.A.R.E. curriculum had no effect on 7th graders in reducing tobacco, alcohol, or other drug use (Perry et al., 2003). The D.A.R.E. Plus program did show small, but statistically significant, reductions in tobacco, alcohol, and drug use for boys, although not for girls. The scales showing the reductions were self-report scales that measured "behavior and intentions" combined, rather than behavior alone, so it is not certain that there were reductions in tobacco, alcohol, or drug use.

Next, the Minnesota researchers reported the effects of the program on self-reported physical violence, verbal aggression, weapon carrying, and victimization (Komro, Perry, Veblen-Moretenson et al., 2004). These results were also largely disappointing. For boys and girls, the standard D.A.R.E. curriculum produced no differences on any of the four violence-related outcomes in comparison to the control group of students who did not participate in D.A.R.E.. Among boys, there was a slight decrease in self-reported violence among those who participated in D.A.R.E. Plus compared to the control group. Among girls, neither the standard D.A.R.E. curriculum nor the D.A.R.E. Plus program produced statistically significant differences from the control group. The authors pointed out that their study was the first independent evaluation of the D.A.R.E. curriculum for middle or junior high school students, and that their results cast doubt on the effectiveness of the D.A.R.E. curriculum.

The D.A.R.E. controversy. Police officers often find teaching young people to be a rewarding experience that builds positive relationships. Their personal observations and informal feedback from students often give them a strong impression that the program is worthwhile and effective. It is no wonder that D.A.R.E. officers tend to be firm believers in their program, but this kind of experience, however compelling, is no substitute for objective evidence from independent studies. The clash between the personal experiences of D.A.R.E. officers and the results of scholarly investigations have produced more than a decade of sometimes rancorous debate over the effectiveness of D.A.R.E.

Public policy organizations such as Drug Policy Alliance have adopted carefully worded positions against D.A.R.E., as reflected in their fact sheet citing authorities who report D.A.R.E. to be costly and ineffective (Kalishman, 2003). The University of Colorado's Center for the Study and Prevention of Violence (1998) describes D.A.R.E. as a program with "no deterrent effect," but diplomatically praises D.A.R.E. for efforts to revise its program.

Other organizations have gone further, with open attacks on D.A.R.E. The Family Council on Drug Awareness (2005) described D.A.R.E. as "an abused school program" and "fundamentally dishonest." Its website contains a series of articles criticizing D.A.R.E. and recapping news stories of D.A.R.E. officers who have been arrested or accused of corruption, misuse of funds, drug use, and other offenses. The Drug Reform Coordination Network, an organization that opposes the "drug war" and what it regards as excessive incarceration of drug offenders, regularly publishes the names of communities and police departments that have stopped supporting. D.A.R.E.

D.A.R.E. has responded aggressively to criticism. For example, when a ten-year follow-up study by the University of Kentucky, funded by the National Institutes of Health, found D.A.R.E. to be ineffective in reducing drug use (Lynam, et al., 1999), the Director of D.A.R.E. America, Glenn Levant, was quoted as calling the study "bogus" (Law Enforcement News, 1999) and "an academic fraud" (Pugh, 1999). Levant charged that critics are biased against D.A.R.E. because they have a financial interest in prevention programs that compete with D.A.R.E., "I truly believe they are setting out to find ways to attack our programs and are misusing science to do it. The bottom line is that they don't want police officers to do the work, because they want it for themselves" (Miller, 2001).

In another case, D.A.R.E. reviewed an advance copy of an article for the *Washington Post* and pressured *Post* editors to make changes to the article without the knowledge of the article's author (Cunningham, 1994). The revised article omitted material critical of D.A.R.E. and contained erroneous information provided by D.A.R.E. that the *Post* subsequently retracted (*Washington Post*, February 4, 1994).

One of the more remarkable wrinkles in the D.A.R.E. debate began with a blistering attack on D.A.R.E. by freelance writer Stephen Glass in articles published in *The New Republic* (Glass, 1997) and *Rolling Stone* (Glass, 1998). Glass went much further than other critics and boldly contended that D.A.R.E. operated as a criminal organization bilking the public of millions of dollars in support of a fraudulent and ineffective program. Glass further asserted that D.A.R.E. conducted a massive effort to suppress negative research findings and that D.A.R.E. supporters threatened researchers with bodily harm, vandalized their cars, and attempted to smear their reputations with false accusations. When Glass was found to have fabricated an unrelated article about computer hackers, an investigation of all his writings determined that he had systematically invented quotations and events that never occurred in at least 27 stories, including both D.A.R.E. articles.

D.A.R.E. filed a 10 million dollar libel suit against Glass and a $50 million suit against *Rolling Stone*. The suit against *Rolling Stone* was dismissed because Glass was writing as a freelance contributor and the magazine editors were unaware of his fabrications. D.A.R.E. appealed to a higher court, but its appeal was denied. The suit against Glass, however, was settled for an undisclosed amount of money and terms that required him to send a public letter of apology to D.A.R.E. The letter, published on the D.A.R.E. Web site, acknowledges that he discounted evidence in support of D.A.R.E. and fabricated incidents in order to write a sensational story.

CONTINUING HOPE FOR D.A.R.E.

Despite the strident defense of its effectiveness, D.A.R.E. officials have accepted the need to revamp and improve its program. The head of D.A.R.E.'s scientific advisory panel, Herbert Kleber of the National Center on Addiction and Substance Abuse at Columbia University, stated, "Our feeling was, after looking at the prevention movement, we were not having enough of an impact. There was a marked rise in drug use. Our job was to answer the question, how can we make it better?" (Zernike, 2001). Even D.A.R.E. America director Levant admitted, "There's quite a bit we can do to make it better and we realize that. I'm not saying it was effective, but it was state of the art when we launched it. Now it's time for science to improve upon what we're doing" (Zernike, 2001).

If D.A.R.E. does not work, can any educational program prevent drug use? Studies have found that schools that devise their own alternatives to D.A.R.E. are not effective either, and may have the unintended effect of *increasing* drug use (Rosenbaum & Hanson, 1998). There is, however, evidence that some drug education programs are effective: Interactive programs that emphasize interpersonal skills to counter peer pressure and use a participatory teaching approach are more effective than programs that rely on moral persuasion, fear arousal, or self-esteem building (Gottfredson, 1997; Ringwalt et al., 1994). Life Skills Training (Botvin, 1998; Botvin, Baker, Dusenbury, Botvin, & Diaz, 1995) is one of the most effective and well-documented drug education programs. Unlike D.A.R.E., Life Skills Training, for example, is presented by teachers to 6th or 7th graders, with 15 sessions during the first year and booster sessions the following two years. The program emphasizes self-management and social skills, as well as strategies for dealing with peer pressure to use drugs. Outcomes averaged from a dozen studies document that Life Skills Training reduces tobacco, alcohol, and marijuana use by 50–75 percent, and that treatment effects were still evident six years later.

Despite the substantial evidence against the D.A.R.E. program, it remains politically popular and is supported at the highest levels. In 2005, President Bush continued a presidential tradition by declaring April 14 National D.A.R.E. Day (http://www.dare.com/home/tertiary/default1b34.asp). Presidential recognition of D.A.R.E. would seem to be inconsistent, however, with the Department of Education's Principles of Effectiveness that require schools to use programs that are supported by scientific research.

SCARED STRAIGHT PROGRAMS

Most individuals are appropriately intimidated by the prospect of incarceration. The threat of being arrested and sent to jail or prison is a sufficiently powerful deterrent for the average citizen to make the idea of stealing a car or robbing someone unthinkable. So it seems reasonable that adolescents who break the law may not have fully appreciated the consequences.

MYTH 13: Delinquent youth can be "scared straight."

FACT: Scared straight programs have no beneficial effect and, on the contrary, may even *increase* delinquent behavior (Petrosino, Turpin-Petrosino, & Buehler, 2003).

One of the earliest and most influential "scared straight" programs was the "Juvenile Awareness Project" of New Jersey's Rahway State Prison (Finckenauer, 1982). Professor James Finckenauer of Rutgers University conducted an in-depth examination of the program and its seminal role in the national scared straight movement. His account reveals how an appealing idea was promoted and exaggerated through a process he termed a "panacea phenomenon," in which the public—as well as criminal justice and law enforcement officials—adopt the unwavering belief that a simple approach is curative despite all evidence to the contrary.

In 1976, Rahway officials began bringing youth into the maximum security prison to meet with inmates who called themselves "The Lifers' Group." At first, the Lifers took a low-key approach and simply explained to their young visitors what prison was like and why they should avoid the same fate that befell them. Over time, however, their methods evolved from counseling to what they termed "shock therapy" that was designed to frighten and intimidate the youths. The program became popular with criminal justice officials and law enforcement officers, and local newspapers began to report extraordinary success rates for the project. For example, the Newark *Star Ledger* reported that 2,921 juveniles had visited the prison and fewer than 10 percent subsequently got into trouble (cited in Finckenauer, 1982). A professional publication, *Police Chief* (July 1977, cited in Finckenauer, 1982) quoted an official who claimed that only one of 155 juveniles was arrested following their visit to Rahway. Such claims of success were largely speculative and based on anecdotal information, not on a systematic, controlled study. Moreover, because many of the youths were not delinquent to begin with, there was no reason to expect a high arrest rate in a period of months following a visit to the prison.

A major turning point occurred in January 1978, when an article touting the program appeared in *Reader's Digest*, which sells 30 million copies in twelve languages (Finckenauer, 1982). The article depicted the dramatic effect of a prison visit on nine teenage boys who had been in trouble with the law and were given an opportunity to see what lay in store for them if they did not change their ways. At the end of the visit, all of the youths were stunned, and the youngest threw his arms around the juvenile officer who had brought them to the prison and exclaimed, "Don't ever let them take me back there!"

Filmmaker Arnold Shapiro read the *Reader's Digest* story and decided to make a documentary, *Scared Straight!*, about the Rahway program. This sensationally popular documentary helped convince the public that delinquent youth could be reformed if only they realized what prison was like. In this documentary, 17 New Jersey teenagers spent three hours in Rahway while the Lifers gave them a crude, in-your-face account of prison life, jeering and cursing at them and describing the graphic details of anal rape. The film showed the youths visibly transformed from cocky, tough-talking delinquents to frightened and penitent schoolboys. Despite its obscene language, the film was aired uncensored on national television in 1979 to tremendous public and critical acclaim. The film won an Oscar and eight Emmys for its director, who described the success of his film:

> I had no idea when I created and produced *Scared Straight!* that it would turn out to be one of the most award-winning and enduring documentaries of the 20th Century. The impact that it had upon kids and adults was unparalleled in any film I've made in more than 30 years of producing. *Scared Straight!* literally saved lives, turned lives around, and prevented many young people from entering a life of crime. I am honored to have had the opportunity to make this documentary and to know what a positive influence it has been in so many people's lives. (Docurama.com, 2005)

In the 1999 sequel *Scared Straight! 20 Years Later*, Shapiro interviewed the boys as adults and reported that 15 out of the 17 juvenile delinquents went on to become "productive members of society." The sequel concluded with testimony from two social workers who claimed that 80 percent of the teens they work with are inspired to turn their lives around by a scared straight approach.

But could it simply be a matter of scaring these boys into changing their lives? If so, the scared straight approach would be the most efficient and cost-effective form of prevention ever devised. A Maryland program was touted as costing only one dollar per participant (Petrosino, Turpin-Petrosino, & Buehler, 2003). One would expect a great deal of interest in trying this approach. Scared straight programs were implemented in at least 30 jurisdictions across the United States and in Australia, Canada, Germany, Norway, and the United Kingdom. Studies evaluating the effect of the scared straight approach on subsequent criminal offending were conducted in California, Illinois, Kansas, Maryland, Michigan, Mississippi, New Jersey, Texas, and Virginia.

What did these studies find? A group of scholars affiliated with Harvard University and Bridgewater State College (Petrosino, Turpin-Petrosino, & Buehler, 2003) identified nine especially rigorous studies of the scared straight approach. In each study a group of youths was randomly (or alternately) selected to visit a correctional institution or to serve as comparison subjects in a no-treatment control group. A total of 946 youths (or young adults) participated in these studies. The results demonstrate the discrepancy between observer perception and objective outcomes. The young participants, their parents, and their teachers all expressed positive reactions to the program, but the objective evidence was that the programs did not reduce subsequent criminal behavior. In each study, either there were no statistically significant differences between the prevention group and the control group or, on the contrary, the youth who participated in the scared straight program engaged in *more* criminal offending than those in the control group. As the researchers concluded, " . . . on average these programs result in an increase in criminality in the experimental group when compared to a no-treatment control.

According to these experiments, doing nothing would have been better than exposing the juveniles to the program" (Petrosino, Turpin-Petrosino, & Buehler, 2003, p. 53).

In fact, study findings were so consistently negative that by 1993 researchers had ceased studying scared straight programs; as far as scholars are concerned, the question has been answered and the issue is dead. Nevertheless, the scared straight idea continues to have popular appeal. For example, a well-meaning father in Pittsburgh was so upset that his 13-year old son had gotten in trouble at school that he decided to implement his own scared straight approach (Stack, 2005). He dropped the boy off at a local juvenile detention center, where he knew some of the guards. The guards took their mission seriously, and started by ordering the boy to submit to a strip search. When the boy refused, four guards stripped him by force, in the process bruising him and tearing his clothing. The boy was given a detention center uniform and made to scrub a toilet. Later, he was paraded in front of older teens at the center, who enthusiastically taunted him and called him "new meat." After an hour, the boy was released, and when he told his mother what had happened, the incident came to the attention of authorities (Associated Press, 2005). The guards were suspended from their jobs and charged with false imprisonment and assault. The boy's father was charged with conspiracy.

School uniforms. In 1987, Cherry Hill Elementary in Baltimore received national attention when its students voluntarily began wearing school uniforms. Parents supported the program as a way to cut clothing costs and reduce social pressures in their low- to middle-income community (Million, 1996). The school principal observed that school discipline problems declined, attendance improved, and test scores increased. But were these changes due to school uniforms? Were uniforms the cause of so many positive changes or merely evidence of the underlying motivation and determination of parents, students, and teachers resolved to improve their school? School staff and parents believed that school uniforms were responsible for improvements in students' behavior, and that is what the press reported. Over the next few years, other schools reported similar results, generating a widely-held view that school uniforms improve student behavior.

MYTH 14: School uniforms improve student behavior.

FACT: Students do not behave more appropriately in schools with uniform policies (Brunsma, 2002, 2004; Brunsma & Rockquemore, 1998).

Spurred by the apparent success of voluntary programs, California's Long Beach Unified School District in 1994 implemented one of the nation's first mandatory school uniform policies for all 60,000 elementary and middle school students. This was the nation's largest concerted attempt to improve student behavior through school uniforms. Professor Sue Stanley of California State University, Long Beach conducted a highly influential evaluation of this new policy. Because uniforms were required in every school, there was no readily available control group, and so the study (Stanley, 1996) simply compared the levels of discipline problems reported in school records during the year prior to the new policy with the year when the school uniform policy was in place. Across 60 schools, Stanley found that school suspensions declined 28 percent in elementary schools and 36 percent in middle schools, fighting and assault with a deadly weapon both decreased by 50 percent, and vandalism by 18 percent.

To her credit, Dr. Stanley cautioned that these reductions were not necessarily due to the school uniform policy, since the schools made a number of simultaneous efforts to improve student behavior. It is quite possible that some combination of changes made by the school division had an impact, but that school uniforms were given credit because they represented the clearest and most visible change. In addition, the decline in behavior problems may have been part of a national or regional trend that had nothing to do with school policies. Nevertheless, these remarkable improvements in a large urban school division excited school administrators across the country and stimulated many other schools to adopt similar policies. It seemed that school uniforms "worked" and others were eager to try them. Even President Clinton, in his 1996 State of the Union Address, endorsed the concept of school uniforms as a way to improve student behavior and reduce gang violence (Brunsma, 2004).

What is appealing about school uniforms? In schools that are concerned about gangs, a school uniform policy prohibits the wearing of gang colors and gives administrators a rationale for acting against gang members who defy the policy. In schools where students are robbed of designer jackets and expensive athletic shoes, school uniforms eliminate such temptations to crime. In communities where socioeconomic status is expressed through differences in clothing and becomes a source of peer conflict, school uniforms create a more level playing field. Regardless of setting, school uniforms are thought to encourage more polite and civil behavior among students and to focus their attention on schoolwork.

David Brunsma was a sociology graduate student at the University of Notre Dame studying for his comprehensive examination in the sociology of education when he learned that Clinton had endorsed the use of school uniforms (Brunsma, 2004). As a Catholic attending a Catholic university, Brunsma was taken aback by the implication that the academic success of students in

Catholic schools might be attributed to their widespread use of school uniforms. The idea that school uniforms might be a solution to school violence struck him as "A classic sociological clash between common sense and social scientific reasoning. An age-old battle between anecdote and evidence, between fear and reason" (p. xix). He and a classmate decided to undertake a study that would compare schools that had school uniform policies with those that did not.

Brunsma's study (Brunsma & Rockquemore, 1998), which launched his career as a sociologist and a leading expert on school uniforms, examined data collected by the U.S. Department of Education in its National Educational Longitudinal Study of 1988. This government project tracked the academic achievement of a nationally representative sample of students from the 8th grade into the 10th grade. Brunsma and Rockquemore (1998) found that the 8th graders who attended schools with uniform policies did not differ in school attendance or attitudes toward school from students in schools without such policies. Students who wore uniforms did not behave more appropriately. They did not report less substance use. And in fact, school uniform policies actually had a small *negative* effect on academic achievement. In other words, uniform policies had no apparent beneficial effects.

Despite the negative evidence, school administrators were attracted to the idea of school uniform policies as a means of improving student behavior and reducing violence. Many schools established uniform policies in the face of vocal opposition from parents, and in some cases, became embroiled in legal battles when they attempted to enforce the new dress codes. Brunsma (2004) observed that school divisions often were not interested in research findings that contradicted their plans for school uniforms and he frequently found his findings dismissed or distorted in news stories that focused on the glowing reports of success by others.

Brunsma (2004) completed additional studies in Pennsylvania schools and again found no support for uniform policies. Brunsma then conducted a review of all available studies of school uniforms (Brunsma, 2002) and found that eight studies examined attitudes and perceptions toward school uniforms rather than the actual effects of school uniforms on student behavior or academic performance. For example, a collaborative study conducted by the clothing company Land's End and the National Association of Elementary School Principals (cited in Brunsma, 2004) surveyed 755 school principals. This study found that 84 percent of principals believed that uniforms improved the school's image in the community, 79 percent believed that they improved classroom discipline, and 62 percent believed they improved student safety at school. Such beliefs might be welcome news to a clothing company that sells school uniforms, but they would not constitute scientific evidence that uniforms do have these beneficial effects. When asked how they determined the effects of a school uniform policy, the most frequent response was that they simply relied on teacher and student comments.

Brunsma (2004) attempted to gain more information about the principal survey from Land's End, but was unsuccessful. Instead, he found that Land's End, a subsidiary of Sears, created its school uniform division in 1997, and in 2003 spent approximately $3 million marketing school uniforms to public schools. When he inquired about research on school uniforms, he was told that "all studies show that uniforms help" (p. 190).

Brunsma knew that the officials at Land's End were not correct when they claimed that all studies supported the use of school uniforms. Few studies have even attempted to examine the actual effects of school uniforms on student attitudes, behavior, or academic performance. These studies vary in scope and quality, and most—lacking control groups—simply compare schools before and after adopting a school uniform policy (Brunsma, 2002). Such before-and-after studies do not consider the impact of other changes in school policy and practices that accompanied the use of school uniforms, so that even if they find improvements (which is generally not the case), they cannot be confidently attributed to the use of uniforms. Even so, the available studies do not support the use of school uniforms; to the contrary, they suggest that uniforms are of little or no value as a means of improving student behavior, attendance, or academic performance. For example, the Educational Testing Service (2000) conducted a large-scale study of students in eighth through twelfth grade to determine what kinds of school policies were associated with lower levels of disruptive behavior and violence by students. Students with school uniforms did not differ significantly on any measures of disciplinary infractions or drug use from students in schools without uniforms.

CONCLUSION

Many school administrators believe that school uniforms improved their students' behavior. Similarly, many corrections officials believe that juvenile boot camps will reduce criminal recidivism, many police officers believe that D.A.R.E. will prevent drug use, and many social workers believe that scared straight programs will deter delinquents. These may be the sincere beliefs of dedicated public servants, but subjective impressions such as these are not reliable. It is natural to see positive results from a program by noticing signs of improvement while overlooking or discounting contrary evidence. It is human nature to look for trends and to perceive that a causal relationship exists when one event follows another, but the human brain is not designed to analyze large quantities of statistical data or to compute correlation coefficients from memory. Although it may be true that "seeing is believing," it is too easy to see statistical trends where none exist.

Even if an observer accurately perceives that a problem has decreased, the statistical trend toward improvement could be due to many factors, such as the motivation and determination of the school staff, and not necessarily the prevention program. There also may be improvements in student behavior that simply reflect trends that would have occurred without the prevention program or any effort to make a change. Most delinquents stop engaging in illegal behavior as they grow older and more mature, a well-established phenomenon called desistance (Mulvey et al., 2004). This means that *any* program following a group of adolescent delinquents into adulthood would find an eventual decrease in illegal behavior among most of the youths, and so could claim to be successful. And so well-meaning professionals that rely on their personal observations are likely to continue believing in the effectiveness of boot camps, D.A.R.E., scared straight programs, and school uniforms. Without controlled studies using objective data, however, we cannot know what works and what doesn't.

9

How Can We Deal with Student Threats?

A 7th grade student named Steve is riding the school bus one morning when the bus driver overhears him tell another student, "I'm gonna kill Bill." Bill is an older boy who rides the same bus. The bus driver informs the principal. What should the principal do?

One of the legacies of the school shootings of the 1990s was that school officials became acutely concerned with student threats of violence. Investigations of the Columbine shooting revealed that the two boys, Dylan Klebold and Eric Harris, had made threats for at least a year (Columbine Review Commission, 2001). Columbine students recalled that the two boys repeatedly talked about shooting people and setting off bombs. They obtained an arsenal of firearms with the help of a girl who had turned eighteen and so was old enough to make purchases for them. They experimented with constructing and setting off bombs and they went on "rebel missions" in which they committed acts of vandalism in their neighborhood. They threatened revenge against students they disliked and posted angry, threatening statements on a Web site. One family became so concerned about the threats against their son that they contacted the police (Merritt & Brown, 2002). The boys also communicated their anger and violent intentions to school staff: In a creative writing assignment one of them wrote in gruesome detail about torturing and killing a bully who had teased him. They made repeated references to committing acts of violence in videos and plays.

The Secret Service and FBI studies of school shootings confirmed that the threatening behavior of Klebold and Harris at Columbine High School was not atypical of other cases (O'Toole, 2000; Vossekuil, Fein, Reddy, Borum, &

Modzeleski, 2002). On the contrary, most of the student assailants made threatening statements before they acted but the statements were largely ignored.

Following the Columbine shooting, schools experienced a frightening upsurge in threats of violence. Students across the country compiled hit lists of people they disliked and called in false bomb threats to disrupt their schools; some schools closed for summer vacation early that year, because there were so many violent threats. The upsurge in threats was no coincidence; the students were inspired and stimulated by the lurid news coverage of school shootings. These threats were almost all pranks or exaggerated expressions of anger by students who did not intend to carry them out, but how could one tell whether a threat was genuine? Every school principal's nightmare was that his or her school would be the next Columbine. Clearly, schools would have to deal with the problem of student threats; the policy that soared to the forefront was called "zero tolerance."

ZERO TOLERANCE

If Steve attended a school with a strict zero tolerance policy for threats of violence, the consequences would be severe. When Steve admitted making the statement, "I'm gonna kill Bill," the principal needed no further information and immediately suspended him for 365 days. Steve's parents complained that the punishment was too harsh, and that Steve did not really intend to harm Bill, but the principal replied that it did not matter what Steve intended to do, he had no choice but to follow the school board policy and suspend him.

"Zero tolerance" refers to the policy of automatic punishment for any violation of a rule, regardless of the circumstances or nature of the violation. Zero tolerance first gained national attention as a drug enforcement policy in 1988 when President Reagan's attorney general, Edwin Meese, ordered customs officials to seize the vehicles and property of anyone crossing the border with even trace amounts of drugs (Skiba & Knesting, 2001). Although zero tolerance policies are also used to punish students for bringing drugs to school—including medications and such items as cough drops and Midol—the focus of this chapter will be on zero tolerance for weapons and threats of violence.

When first introduced, the term "zero tolerance" had a *get tough* quality that appealed to the public and quickly entered the domain of political rhetoric. School divisions in some states began to adopt zero tolerance polices as early as 1989, but the practice became a national policy in 1994 when, under the Clinton administration, the Gun-Free Schools Act mandated a one-year suspension for any student found to have brought a firearm to school. Thus, zero tolerance was in place prior to the widely publicized school shootings that occurred a few years later, but after these shootings, the policy was dramatically broadened.

MYTH 15: Zero tolerance policies make schools safer.

FACT: There have been no scientific studies of zero tolerance policies (Skiba & Knesting, 2001). There are plenty of cases, however, in which zero tolerance policies resulted in excessive punishment of students for behavior that was not dangerous to others.

Although the federal law permitted local school divisions to modify expulsions on a case-by-case basis—in other words, to consider mitigating circumstances and impose a lesser punishment when it seemed appropriate—this provision was frequently overlooked or superseded in practice by using automatic expulsion for all infractions (Skiba & Noam, 2001). Schools gravitated toward simply expelling students who were found with any kind of firearm at school. School boards and, in some cases, entire states, adopted the most extreme form of zero tolerance, where punishment is always expulsion (usually defined as suspension from school for at least 365 days). In Ohio, schools were required to have a zero tolerance policy that made no exceptions (Tebo, 2000).

Why have a policy that makes no exceptions? Beyond the political appeal of taking a "get tough" stance on student misbehavior, there are practical reasons why zero tolerance is an attractive policy. Making decisions about the punishment of students is difficult for school principals, who spend a great deal of time making decisions about the appropriate consequences for student misbehavior. Regardless of the severity of the punishment they choose, they are inevitably criticized for being too harsh or too lenient. If they punish one student and not another, it appears that they are being unfair. If they apply a certain punishment on one occasion, they are expected to apply it in all similar occasions.

Principals may be criticized by parents, teachers and, in the worst cases, their administrative superiors: the superintendent and school board. In many cases, parents have legal recourse to appeal a school principal's decision and can demand a hearing before an administrative officer or the school board. If they are not satisfied with the outcome, they can challenge the decision in court: Every large community has attorneys with expertise in the practice of school law, and they can place the school principal's decision-making under intense scrutiny.

Why is zero tolerance so appealing? A zero tolerance policy removes the element of judgment that makes school administrators vulnerable to criticism. It removes the pressure of defending their actions and justifying why they decided to punish a student, and it eliminates the charge that they are inconsistent or unfair in punishing some students and not others.

Zero tolerance is even more attractive to administrators because it eliminates their need to make subjective judgments about the meaning or intent of a student's behavior. If the student violated the rule, the consequences are automatic and no judgment is needed. The pursuit of a zero tolerance policy that sends a stern message and requires no administrative judgment became a slippery slope that led steadily further away from the original focus on firearms.

The first step beyond firearms was to include weapons that looked and functioned like firearms, such as BB guns and pellet guns. Even though the federal law specifically excludes BB guns and other pellet guns from the definition of a firearm, school divisions routinely applied the same policy of automatic expulsion to students found with them. And while an explosive device, such as a grenade or pipe bomb, can be readily identified as a prohibited firearm, what about students who bring firecrackers, smoke bombs, or caps for toy guns to school? Zero tolerance policies apply the same punishment to a student who intends to blow up his classroom as the student who sets off a firecracker on the playground. One Colorado school even expelled a seventh-grade student for one year for playing with a friend's miniature laser pointer, which the school labeled a "firearm facsimile" (Rutherford Institute, 2003).

Many schools applied zero tolerance to toy guns and cap guns, reasoning that they could be used to frighten or intimidate. In cases scattered around the country, children were subject to zero tolerance consequences for bringing toy guns to school, even if by accident. Seattle schools received national attention for their zero tolerance policy, which mandated unconditional expulsion for students who brought even a toy gun to school. In one case, a ten-year-old boy was expelled from elementary school because he had a 1-inch plastic toy pistol that was an accessory to his G.I. Joe action figure (*Seattle Times*, January 8, 1997).

The Seattle boy discovered he had accidentally left the tiny toy in his pocket when he checked to see if he had his lunch money. Another student saw the toy gun and asked about it. According to a school spokesperson, the boy displayed the gun "in a manner that was not appropriate." Clearly, a 1-inch piece of plastic is not a dangerous weapon; the rigid application of zero tolerance, however, mandated that the principal expel the boy without considering the circumstances. The school spokesperson defended the principal's action by noting that "the district has a zero tolerance policy on weapons, and it is mute on size."

After Seattle initiated its harsh policy, the Washington state legislature sensibly modified its zero tolerance law to allow school divisions to expel students for possession of toy weapons only if they were used with "malice," meaning "evil intent, wish, or design to vex, annoy, or injure another person" (*Seattle Times*, October 7, 1998). Nevertheless, Seattle continued to expel students for bringing toy weapons to school under any circumstances. In one case, a sixth-grade student was expelled when a squirt gun fell out of his backpack. The boy's family hired an attorney to challenge the expulsion, which was reduced to a suspension. He returned to school three weeks later.

Seattle school authorities subsequently acknowledged that there were at least twelve cases in which students were expelled from school for incidents involving toys rather than real weapons. The Seattle superintendent vigorously defended the district policy, contending, "You cannot equivocate on this issue. And I personally will not back down on this issue. . . . No guns of any type. No weapons. Don't even think about bringing them" (*Seattle Times*, October 7, 1998).

Despite changes in the state law and newspaper editorials admonishing school officials to use common sense in applying zero tolerance policies (*Seattle Times*, May 29, 2001), expulsions in Washington continued. In 2004, Spokane school authorities suspended three boys for bringing miniature toy guns from their G.I. Joe action figures (*The Spokesman-Review*, January 28, 2004). One boy had taken the toys to school because he was going to play with them at an overnight birthday party. One of the toy guns was sticking out of the boy's backpack, however, and the boy and two friends began to play with the toys at the school lunch table, where one of the boys playfully pointed one of them at other students. The students were suspended for violation of the school district's policy against threats, which defines a threat as "any statement, written or spoken, or action which creates a reasonable fear of bodily harm" (*World Net Daily*, January 29, 2004). The question is whether a minature toy gun can create a reasonable fear of bodily harm: Is it reasonable to fear an eight-year-old pointing a three-inch plastic toy?

While some toy guns look so much like real guns that they can be frightening, what about objects that are clearly not guns? In a widely publicized case, Jonesboro, Arkansas school authorities suspended a first-grader for pointing a breaded chicken finger at a teacher and going "pow-pow" (*Associated Press*, February 11, 2001). And in several other cases, school authorities suspended students for simply pointing their fingers like a gun (Rutherford Institute, 2003). A New Jersey third grader was arrested and held in police custody for four hours because he pointed an L-shaped piece of paper at his classmates in a game of "cops and robbers." After two court appearances, the criminal charges were dismissed. The boy has since been treated for emotional distress, and attorneys have filed suit on charges of false arrest, malicious prosecution, and violations of free speech rights (Rutherford Institute, 2003).

Zero tolerance also expanded beyond the realm of firearms to knives. Under zero tolerance, there is no distinction between a knife that is used as a weapon and a knife used for benign purposes. The result was that students were subject to the same harsh consequences whether they brought a butter knife or a switchblade to school. Across the country, students were suspended from school for bringing such items as a plastic knife, a kitchen knife, a nail clipper, and a manicure kit (Rutherford Institute, 2003).

A Michigan honors student was recommended for expulsion because he attended his prom wearing a Scottish bagpiper's outfit that included a 3.5 inch ceremonial knife that is attached to a bagpiper's right sock (Institute for Children, Youth, & Families, 2003). The case generated national media coverage, support from the American Civil Liberties Union, and demonstrations by indignant bagpipers. Ultimately, the student avoided formal expulsion by agreeing to take college classes for a semester before returning to school.

In several cases, students were found to have knives in their cars, often left there by accident. For example, an 18-year-old female National Merit Scholar from Florida was arrested and jailed, suspended from school, and barred from attending graduation because there was a kitchen knife in her car. The knife had likely fallen out of a box when the family was moving a few days before.

Any kind of sharp object or projectile, no matter how innocuous, can be construed as a dangerous weapon under zero tolerance. A five-year-old in California was expelled after he found a razor blade at his bus stop, carried it to school, and dutifully gave it to his teacher; a seventeen-year-old in Chicago was arrested and subsequently expelled for shooting a paper clip with a rubber band (Skiba & Peterson, 1999). Consider how such incidents would have been handled by school administrators prior to the emergence of zero tolerance and the pervasive fear of school shootings: A child who turned in a razor blade would have been praised for being conscientious, and the student who shot a paper clip with a rubber band would have been admonished—and perhaps required to stay after school—but not arrested or expelled. Although there has been no systematic research to identify how many such cases have occurred, it is evident from news media accounts that excessive punishment of students for trivial misbehavior is widespread and ongoing, despite the publicity and ridicule such cases have elicited.

Inevitably, zero tolerance was applied to statements as well as weapons. A few weeks after the 2001 school shooting in Santee, California, a New Jersey prosecutor urged local school officials to adopt a zero tolerance policy for any kind of student threat, even if made in jest (Zernike, 2001). The school board followed his recommendation and mandated suspension for any student who made any kind of threatening statement. Within six weeks, the schools had suspended over 50 students, most of them children in kindergarten to third grade. The police department prepared files on each of these students and, in some cases, interviewed them without parental permission.

What kinds of threats did the New Jersey students make? A 10-year-old girl was upset that the teacher would not give her permission to go to the bathroom; after the girl wet her pants, she whimpered, "I could kill her!" Other students were suspended for making similar angry statements that did not reflect a genuine intention to harm or kill someone. One student made an angry threat to retaliate after being pushed on the playground. He was punished; the student who pushed him was not. Faced with so many cases and outraged parents, the school board reversed its policy and returned decision-making authority to school principals.

The central problem with zero tolerance policies is that all threats of violence are treated as equally dangerous and deserving of the same consequences (Tebo, 2000). Such policies provide no latitude for school authorities to consider the seriousness of the threat or degree of risk posed by the student's behavior. Criticism of zero tolerance is widespread, and spans the political spectrum from the liberal American Civil Liberties Union to the conservative Rutherford Institute, both of which have supported lawsuits challenging zero tolerance practices.

The Rutherford Institute (2003) opposes zero tolerance policies because they limit free speech, punish students without due process rights, and deprive them of access to public education. In most cases, however, courts and appeal boards have upheld the school's right to punish students for zero tolerance violations and have denied lawsuits seeking redress.

- An Oregon fourth-grader was suspended from school for singing a parody of the "Barney & Friends" song that made threatening references to others. The Rutherford Institute sought to have the suspension reversed, but it was upheld (*Douglas Mansfield v. Salem-Keizer Public School District*).
- A South Carolina tenth grader was expelled for one semester when he accidentally brought a Swiss Amy knife on an ROTC field trip. He had left the knife in his pants pocket while working in the yard the previous day and there was no evidence that the student threatened anyone or had any intent to use the knife. School authorities modified the school's weapons policy, but refused to overturn the expulsion or expunge the student's record (*Jayson Gilbert v. School District 5*).
- Four New Jersey kindergarten boys were suspended for three days for playing "Cops and Robbers" on their school playground. One of the boys and his family filed suit for emotional trauma to the child and asked to have the suspension expunged from his record. The case was dismissed in the U.S. district court for New Jersey and then by the Third Circuit Court of Appeals. In appealing the case to the U.S. Supreme Court, John Whitehead, president of The Rutherford Institute, asserted, "When public school authorities claim first graders playing 'Cops and Robbers'

on the playground are engaged in 'threatening' and 'dangerous' activity, one wonders whether it is the children or the adults who can't tell the difference between fantasy and reality. The right to freely express oneself is a fundamental right protected by the First Amendment—whether one is eight or eighty" (Rutherford Institute, 2003).

In 2001, the American Bar Association passed a resolution condemning zero tolerance:

> [T]he ABA opposes, in principle, "zero tolerance" policies that have a discriminatory effect, or mandate either expulsion or referral of students to juvenile or criminal court, without regard to the circumstances or nature of the offense or the student's history.

The ABA position highlights another frequently raised concern about zero tolerance policies, which is an apparent discriminatory effect. Minority students, particularly African-Americans, are disproportionately affected by zero tolerance policies (Browne, Losen, & Wald, 2001). Although racial disparities in school discipline existed prior to the emergence of zero tolerance, the more severe consequences for even minor misbehavior make the problem worse.

A report by the Advancement Project and The Civil Rights Project of Harvard University (2000) recounted the example of five African-American males, ages 17–18, who began throwing peanuts at one another on a Mississippi school bus. When one of the peanuts struck the bus driver, she pulled over and called the police. The students were arrested and charged with felony assault. The charges were eventually dismissed, but the boys lost their bus privileges. Lacking transportation to travel 30 miles to their school in a poor rural county, they all dropped out of school. The report concluded, "Zero Tolerance has become a philosophy that has permeated our schools; it employs a brutally strict disciplinary model that embraces harsh punishment over education" (p. 3).

Proponents of zero tolerance claim that a strict policy is needed to send a clear message to students and deter them from dangerous behavior. But is there any evidence that zero tolerance makes schools safer? In their review of research on school safety, Skiba and Knesting (2001) reported "zero evidence" for zero tolerance; a basic problem is that there are no controlled studies that have directly examined this policy, despite its widespread adoption. In the absence of systematic research, advocates of zero tolerance can claim success no matter what outcome occurs (Skiba & Knesting, 2001). If schools with zero tolerance report an increase in school expulsions, school authorities can claim that they are cracking down and removing dangerous students from school.

Conversely, if schools experience a decline in expulsions, school authorities can claim that the policy has been effective in deterring students from bringing weapons to school.

The underlying methodological problem with disciplinary statistics is that school expulsions are not a valid indicator of the effectiveness of zero tolerance. In order to evaluate the effectiveness of zero tolerance, researchers must measure the level of violence and disruptive behavior in schools. Measures of school safety must be independent of the practice or approach that is being evaluated; otherwise, the process becomes an exercise in circular reasoning. Just as you cannot determine the curative power of a medication by tracking how often it is administered in a community, you cannot judge the effectiveness of zero tolerance by counting how many students are expelled.

The best way to examine the effectiveness of zero tolerance is to compare the levels of violent and disruptive behavior in schools with and without zero tolerance policies. Ideally, schools should be randomly assigned to use zero tolerance or some alternative approach, so that a true experiment can be conducted; otherwise, the schools that have chosen to use zero tolerance may differ systematically from schools that do not employ this approach.

Understandably, such studies have not been done. In addition to the cost and complexity of such a study, which would require dozens if not hundreds of schools in order to conduct meaningful statistical analyses, it would be difficult to convince school authorities to adopt discipline policies that they might not otherwise support. Consider some of the problems that arise in conducting an experiment in real world situations: If some principals who endorsed the practice of zero tolerance were asked to refrain from using it and adopt an alternative approach, and other principals who opposed zero tolerance were asked to begin using it, it would not be a fair test of either approach. (The same would be true of the teachers in those schools who are usually the first to observe and report a student's misbehavior, which makes the assignment process even more complex and problematic.) Neither group of schools could be expected to fully and wholeheartedly carry out a policy not endorsed by their administrators (and faculty).

Random assignment is considered essential for conducting scientifically rigorous studies, but in studies of human behavior, one cannot simply assign persons to behave in certain ways. In a medical study one can administer medication to some patients and not others, but in educational research, the research subjects are inextricably part of the treatment or intervention that is being studied. Educational research subjects react to being studied and in this way they introduce new uncontrolled variables that can confound the experiment. This problem plagues the study of any school policy or program; not surprisingly, progress in educational research is slow.

PROFILING

If Steve, the seventh grader who made a threatening statement, attended a school using a profiling approach rather than zero tolerance, there would be a different process leading to a different outcome. In this scenario, after Steve admitted making the statement, "I'm gonna kill Bill," the principal would want to determine whether Steve fit the profile of a dangerous student. Steve told the principal that he was angry at Bill because Bill picked on him all the time, but he had no intention of killing anyone. Steve went on to say that he had no friends at school and that he did not want to go to school anyway. The principal consulted an official list of warning signs for violence that had items such as, "low school interest and poor academic performance," "social withdrawal," "excessive feelings of isolation and being alone," "excessive feelings of rejection," "feelings of being picked on and persecuted," and "uncontrolled anger" (Dwyer, Osher, & Warger, 1998). The principal concluded that Steve fit the profile of a dangerous student and moved him to an alternative school.

Along with the expansion of zero tolerance, another response to the school shootings has been the effort to *profile* seemingly dangerous students before they engage in violence. Profiling is an appealing concept that appears to make sense: Draw up a list of the characteristics of dangerous students so that they can be identified before they commit an act of violence.

MYTH 16. Psychological profiling can prevent school violence.

FACT: The conclusion of the FBI's own criminal profiling unit was that psychological profiling was not an appropriate approach to prevent school violence (O'Toole, 2000). A subsequent report by the U.S. Secret Service and Department of Education reached the same conclusion (Fein, Vossekuil, Pollack, Borum, Modzeleski, & Reddy, 2002). Checklists and warning signs used to profile students tend to identify far too many nonviolent students as violent (Sewell & Mendelsohn, 2000).

In July 1999, just a few months after the Columbine shooting, the FBI's National Center for the Analysis of Violent Crime convened a conference on school shootings. The NCAVC includes the Behavioral Sciences Unit, a group renowned as the nation's leading experts on criminal profiling and popularized in television shows and movies such as *Silence of the Lambs*. The FBI's leading experts on profiling spent a week with experts (including the author) in education, psychology, psychiatry, and other fields. The conference was held outside Leesburg, Virginia, at the Xerox training center, which is a sprawling complex of ultra-modern buildings including dormitories, high-tech meeting rooms, and dining facilities so that the conference attendees could spend the entire week immersed in study with minimum outside distractions. The secluded location made it possible to hold the conference under tight security, and the press was not allowed to attend.

Each day the meetings began with a series of presentations by experts in different fields, raising critical issues that were discussed and debated by the audience of several hundred. In addition, the FBI brought in staff from schools such as Columbine and Jonesboro's Westside Middle School, where school shootings had taken place, so that attendees could hear firsthand accounts of what happened. For many of these speakers, it was a painful, but cathartic, experience to describe the traumatic events that they had experienced. In the afternoons, attendees were divided into small groups to tackle specific questions and seek viable violence prevention strategies.

Starting on the first day, experts debated profiling and whether it could be applied to school shootings. The FBI experts' conclusions were provocative and unexpected: The nation's leading authorities on profiling might be expected to endorse the use of their own method, but on the contrary, they agreed that profiling was not appropriate in the case of school shootings:

> One response to the pressure for action may be an effort to identify the next shooter by developing a "profile" of the typical school shooter. This may sound like a reasonable preventive measure, but in practice, trying to draw up a catalogue or "checklist" of warning signs to detect a potential shooter can be shortsighted, even dangerous. Such lists, publicized by the media, can end up unfairly labeling many nonviolent students as potentially dangerous or even lethal. In fact, a great many adolescents who will never commit violent acts will show some of the behaviors or personality traits included on the list. (O'Toole, 2000, pp. 2–3)

Why did the FBI reach this unexpected conclusion? Traditionally, criminal profiling is *retrospective*, i.e., investigators seek to determine who committed a crime. However, the sort of profiling necessary to prevent a school shooting would be *prospective*, which is a profoundly different procedure. Whereas conventional, retrospective profiling begins with a crime scene investigation and follows a deductive process of identifying and eliminating suspects, prospective profiling has no crime scene and is an inductive process of inferring who might commit a crime. The traditional profiler always knows that someone committed a crime and it is a matter of finding out who, but the prospective profiler is saddled with the far more speculative task of finding someone who *may* commit a crime.

The hazards of prospective profiling were illustrated with an account of a school shooting in which a student wore a black trench coat to conceal a shotgun. The idea of wearing a black trench coat in a school shooting dates at least as far back as a popular 1995 movie, *Basketball Diaries*, in which the young Leonardo DiCaprio starred as a high school basketball player who became involved in drugs and crime. In a macabre slow-motion dream sequence in this movie, DiCaprio burst into a classroom wearing a black trench coat. Screaming in rage, he pulled a shotgun from the trench coat and shot his teacher and several students who had teased him and, in a bizarre twist, his friends in the class laughed and cheered him on. This sparked the imagination of youths responsible for more than one school shooting.

In the minds of anxious school administrators, wearing a black trench coat seemed to be an indication of impending violence, and any student wearing a black trench coat was viewed with suspicion. Some school divisions went so far as to ban all trench coats.

But are black trench coats dangerous? There are many reasons to wear a trench coat that have nothing to do with DiCaprio's movie or plans to commit a school shooting. The FBI's experts ridiculed the idea that dangerous youths could be so easily identified, and pointed out that for every case of a school shooting involving a student in a black trench coat, there were thousands of nonviolent students across the nation who wore similar attire. Wearing a black trench coat appears to be the modern equivalent of wearing a black hat in the cowboy movies of an earlier generation.

Statistically, trench coats are worthless as a sign of violence because the accuracy rate would be less than one in a thousand. Furthermore, linking trench coats to violence would stigmatize countless innocent students. The problem is not unlike the practice of racial profiling, in which some police officers are quick to stop an African-American driver on suspicion of illegal activity.

Warning signs.   Despite the questionable nature of profiling, many governmental agencies and professional organizations devised lists of "warning signs" to identify potentially violent students (American Psychological Association, 1999; Dwyer, Osher, & Warger, 1998; National School Safety Center, 1998; Sewell & Mendelsohn, 2000). Warning signs are basically characteristics used to construct a profile.

As could be expected, the criteria in the warning signs checklists cast an overly broad net in identifying potentially violent youth. The sixteen warning signs in the federal government's guide (Dwyer, Osher, & Warger, 1998) included such items as "history of discipline problems," "drug use and alcohol use," "feelings of being picked on and persecuted," and "excessive feelings of rejection." The American Psychological Association's (1999) "warning signs" pamphlet sounded an ominous note with the statement, "If you see these immediate warning signs, violence is a serious possibility." The list of "immediate warning signs" included "increase in risk-taking behavior," "increase in use of drugs or alcohol," "significant vandalism or property damage," and "loss of temper on a daily basis." Most school authorities could identify students in their schools who appear to meet these signs, yet fail to pose a threat for violence.

Similarly, the National School Safety Center (1998) developed a 20-item "Checklist of characteristics of youth who have caused school-associated violent deaths." This checklist included items as general as "has been previously truant, suspended, or expelled from school," "has little or no supervision from parents or a caring adult," and "tends to blame others for difficulties she or he causes." The items on such checklists may well describe the small group of youths who committed school shootings, but this does not make them useful, specific indicators of violence. Because the occurrence (base rate) of severe violence is low, checklists of student characteristics will invariably lead to the false-positive identification of a large number of students who will not be violent (Sewell & Mendelsohn, 2000).

The lists of warning signs contain items that warrant concern; for example, alcohol and drug use is a well-known correlate of delinquency and violence, and losing one's temper on a daily basis or committing acts of vandalism are behaviors that merit intervention. The previously mentioned federal list of warning signs (Dwyer, Osher, & Warger, 1998) is part of a larger document that presents an action guide for schools. The action guide contains thoughtful advice and recommendations for school authorities, and gives many examples of strategies, interventions, and programs designed to prevent student violence.

The authors of the federal warning signs report recognized the potential problems of a warning signs approach. They cautioned, "Unfortunately, *there is a real danger that early warning signs will be misinterpreted*" (p. 7, Dwyer, Osher, & Warger, 1998). These authors urged school authorities to refrain from using the warning signs as a basis for punishing students or excluding them from school. They expressed concern that the warning signs could be used without regard to the student's situational or developmental context. They cautioned against acting on the basis of stereotypes or overreacting to a single sign.

THREAT ASSESSMENT

If Steve attended a school using a threat assessment approach, the principal would want to determine what Steve meant by his threatening statement and whether it constituted a serious threat or merely an expression of anger. The principal interviewed Steve about the alleged threat, and when Steve admitted making the threat, the principal asked a series of questions about Steve's intent, including how and why he would carry out the threat. The principal found out that Steve was angry with Bill for teasing him and used the phrase "kill Bill" from a movie title as a way to "tease him back." The principal interviewed Bill and several students to corroborate Bill's statements. The students reported that Bill teased younger students on the bus and often picked on Steve. Finally, the principal considered that Steve's record contained no history of aggressive behavior and was seen as well-behaved by his teachers. The principal disciplined Steve for his inappropriate language and had him apologize to Bill. Then he met with Bill to address his behavior toward Steve and other students.

A threat assessment approach offers the principal flexibility in deciding how to deal with Steve and focuses more directly on the critical issue of what Steve meant by his statement. If Steve does not intend to harm Bill, but is making an inappropriate remark out of anger or frustration, he can be disciplined, but not treated as though he were a dangerous student. By attempting to resolve the underlying problem that generated the threat, this approach results in a course of action that is less punitive and disruptive to Steve's education than either zero tolerance or profiling approaches would be. In many respects, threat assessment is not new, but rather the kind of common-sense approach that most school administrators would take if not influenced by the specter of Columbine and other school shootings.

MYTH 17: It is impossible to prevent school shootings.

FACT: Although school shootings are so shocking and surprising that they may seem unpredictable, many school shootings have been prevented, and examination of these cases can be useful in identifying means to prevent other shootings. The FBI and Secret Services studies of school shootings (O'Toole, 2000; Vossekuil, Fein, Reddy, Borum, & Modzeleski, 2002) identified threat assessment as a potentially effective method of preventing students from carrying out targeted acts of violence.

A key finding from the FBI study of school shootings was that in almost every case, the student shooter communicated his intentions to peers days or weeks in advance of the crime. Had these intentions been reported to authorities, it would have been possible to prevent the shootings. In support of this conclusion, the FBI found other cases in which school shootings were prevented because students did report a classmate's threats to authorities. These observations led FBI researchers to conclude that schools should be trained to identify and evaluate student threats in a prompt and systematic manner.

The FBI report cautioned that "all threats are not created equal" (O'Toole, 2000, p. 5) and that each threat must be carefully investigated to determine what danger, if any, the student poses to others. Students who make threats differ in their motivation and capacity, as well as in their intention, to carry out a violent act. For this reason, the FBI recommended that schools adopt a threat assessment approach.

What is threat assessment? Threat assessment is an approach to violence prevention originally developed by the U.S. Secret Service and based on studies of persons who attacked or threatened to attack public officials (Fein, Vossekuil, & Holden, 1995; Fein & Vossekuil, 1999). Although the public is familiar with the visible security that the Secret Service provides to the President, the Secret Service devotes just as much effort behind the scenes to evaluating persons who might pose a threat to the President or other protected officials. Threat assessment has evolved into a standard approach to analyze a variety of dangerous situations, such as threats of workplace violence (Fein & Vossekuil, 1998). In 2002, a joint report of the U.S. Secret Service and Department of Education recommended that schools train threat assessment teams in order to respond to student threats of violence (Fein, Vossekuil, Pollack, Borum, Modzeleski, & Reddy, 2002).

A threat assessment is conducted when a person (or persons) threatens to commit a violent act or engages in behavior that appears to threaten violence. This kind of threatened violence is termed "targeted violence." Threat assessment is a process of evaluating the threat, and the circumstances surrounding the threat, to uncover any facts or evidence that indicate the threat is likely to be carried out.

Threat assessment is ultimately concerned with whether someone *poses* a threat, not whether he or she has *made* a threat. Anyone can make a threat, but relatively few will engage in the planning and preparation necessary to carry out the threat. Threat assessment attempts to identify persons who pose a threat, which means that they have the intent and means to carry out the threat. Moreover, threat assessment does not conclude when a person is determined to pose a threat; rather, threat assessment aims to determine how serious the threat is and what should be done to prevent its being carried out.

How can schools conduct threat assessments? The FBI report (O'Toole, 2000), as well as the Secret Service and Department of Education joint report (Fein, Vossekuil, Pollack, Borum, Modzeleski, & Reddy, 2002), provided compelling reasons for schools to adopt a threat assessment model. Nevertheless, the reports' recommendations were essentially untested. Could the threat assessment approach used in law enforcement be adapted for schools? How would a school-based threat assessment team operate, and what would be the results? Under the author's direction, the Virginia Youth Violence Project of the Curry School of Education at the University of Virginia sought to answer these questions.

We established a work group of educators from two school divisions (Cornell, Sheras, Kaplan, Levy-Elkon, McConville, McKnight, & Posey, 2005). The two school divisions contained a socioeconomically and ethnically diverse population of 16,400 students enrolled in four high schools, six middle schools, 22 elementary schools, and three alternative schools. The work group studied how school principals typically handled threats in these 35 schools and attempted to identify common-sense practices and procedures that would be consistent with FBI and Secret Service recommendations. Over a period of two months, the group reached consensus on a set of guidelines for school-based teams to follow in responding to student threats.

Threat assessment teams were trained in each school. The teams, which were headed by the principal or assistant principal, included a school counselor, school psychologist, and school resource officer, and were trained to follow a seven-step decision tree (Cornell & Sheras, 2005; see Figure 9–1). The initial stages of a threat assessment are typically handled by the team leader and can often be easily resolved. In more complex or ambiguous cases, the principal may bring in additional team members. The seven steps will be reviewed briefly here.

At *step one*, the leader of the threat assessment team interviews the student who made the threat, using a standard set of questions. The principal also interviews the recipient of the threat and any witnesses. The principal is not concerned simply with what the student said or did, but the context in which the threat was made and what the student intended by making the threat.

At *step two*, the principal must make an important distinction between threats that are serious, in the sense that they pose a continuing risk or danger to others, and those that are not serious, because they are readily resolved and do not pose a continuing risk. Threats that are not serious or are readily resolved are termed *transient* threats. Serious threats are called *substantive* threats. Transient threats are defined as behaviors that can be readily identified as expressions of anger or frustration (or perhaps inappropriate attempts at humor), but which dissipate quickly when the student has time to reflect on the meaning of what he or she has said. The most important feature of a transient threat is that the student does not have a sustained intention to harm someone.

If the threat is judged to be transient, it is resolved quickly at *step three* without engaging the full team in a comprehensive threat assessment. The principal may require the student to apologize or explain to those affected by

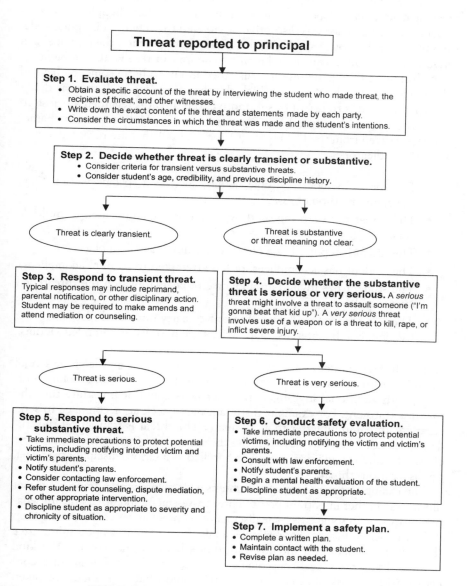

FIGURE 9–1.   Threat assessment decision tree.

threat, or take other action to make amends for the student's behavior. The principal may also respond with a reprimand or other disciplinary consequence if the behavior was disruptive or violated the school's discipline code. If a transient threat was sparked by an argument or conflict, the principal can involve other team members in helping to address or resolve the problem.

Substantive threats represent a sustained intent to harm someone beyond the immediate incident during which the threat was made. If there is doubt whether a threat is transient or substantive, the threat is regarded as substantive. One way to identify a threat as substantive is to look for certain characteristics derived from the FBI report (O'Toole, 2000) that are regarded as presumptive indicators:

- The threat includes plausible details, such as a specific victim, time, place, and method of assault;
- The threat has been repeated over time or communicated to multiple persons;
- The threat is reported as a plan, or planning has taken place;
- The student has accomplices, or has attempted to recruit accomplices;
- The student has invited an audience of peers to watch the threatened event; and
- There is physical evidence of intent to carry out the threat, such as a weapon, bomb materials, map, written plan, or list of intended victims.

Although the presence of any one of these characteristics may lead the school administrator to presume the threat is substantive, none is an absolute indicator; with additional investigation, other facts could demonstrate that the threat is transient. For example, a student might seek an accomplice to send an angry, threatening letter to a classmate. The threat is transient if the student does not intend to carry out the threat, but only means to frighten the classmate. Such an incident would be handled as a serious disciplinary matter, not as a serious threat.

The example of a student who frightens a classmate with a transient threat illustrates another important point: Threat assessment and discipline are separate processes. In some cases, the disciplinary consequences can be severe even if the threat is transient. For example, a false bomb threat is not a substantive threat if the student only intends to disrupt school, but nonetheless this kind of threat has serious legal consequences. In general, threat assessment is concerned with the risk of future harm to others and what steps should be taken to prevent the threat from being carried out, whereas discipline is concerned with punishing a student for his or her actions. Threat incidents usually require a response that combines threat assessment and discipline.

Threat assessment teams must always consider the context of the threat and make reasoned judgments based on all available information. The team should consider the student's age and capabilities, mental stability, prior history of violent behavior, and other relevant factors. The guidelines assist the team in its investigation, but do not provide a prescription or formula.

If the threat is determined to be a substantive threat, the principal skips step three and proceeds to step four. At *step four,* the substantive threat is determined to be *serious* or *very serious.* The distinction between serious and very serious threats is based on the intended severity of injury. A *serious* threat is a threat to assault, strike, or beat up someone. A *very serious* threat is a threat to kill, sexually assault, or severely injure someone. A threat involving the use of a weapon is generally considered a threat to severely injure someone.

In the case of a serious substantive threat, the team moves to step five. At *step five,* school authorities are obliged to act to protect potential victims. These protective actions depend on the circumstances of the threat, as well as any information that indicates how soon and where the threat might be carried out. Immediate protective actions include cautioning the student about the consequences of carrying out the threat and providing supervision so that the student cannot carry it out at school. A team member should contact the student's parents, so that the parents can assume responsibility for supervising the student outside school. The parents may be summoned to school so that the student does not leave school without supervision.

The level of supervision should be consistent with the nature and seriousness of the threat. For example, a visibly angry student who threatens to beat up a classmate should be confined to an office or classroom under continuous adult supervision. The school resource officer could meet with this student in order to gauge the seriousness of the situation and remind the student that his or her actions could have serious consequences. Often, a student will calm down and can be permitted to return to class, but only on the condition that the student not have any contact with the classmate. As a precaution, the student might be kept from a class attended by the classmate, and the student might be required to report to the office prior to school dismissal, rather than being released to ride the same bus as the classmate. Serious threats are resolved at step five.

Very serious threats require the most extensive action by the team. The team skips step five and moves to steps six and seven. At *step six,* the school administrator takes immediate action to assure that the threat is not carried out. The student should be detained in the principal's office until his or her parents have arrived. In addition, the law enforcement officer on the team must determine whether the student has violated the law, and if so, what law enforcement action should be taken. A student who threatens someone with a weapon, or is found to be in possession of a weapon, is likely to be arrested.

The team must notify the intended victim, and if the victim is a student, the victim's parents. The school psychologist should begin a mental health evaluation of the student as soon as possible, with the initial goal of assessing the student's mental state and need for immediate mental health services. The student should be suspended from school, pending a complete assessment of the threat and determination of the most appropriate school placement.

At *step seven*, the team completes a safety evaluation that integrates findings from all available sources of information in a written safety plan. The safety plan is designed both to protect potential victims and to address the student's educational needs. The plan includes mental health and counseling recommendations, findings from the law enforcement investigation, and disciplinary consequences. At this point, the principal decides whether the student can return to school or should be placed in an alternative setting. If the student is permitted to return to school, the plan describes the conditions that must be met and the procedures in place to monitor the student when he or she returns.

How did student threat assessment work? Over the course of one school year, the 35 schools dealt with 188 student threats. The majority (70%) of threats were transient threats. Of the remaining 30 percent that were substantive threats, 22 percent (42 cases) were serious substantive threats, and just 8 percent (15 cases) were very serious substantive threats that required a more comprehensive evaluation.

Threats were made by students at all grade levels, from kindergarten through 12th grade (see Figure 9–2). In elementary schools, threats were most frequent in 3rd and 4th grades. At this age level, many students are starting

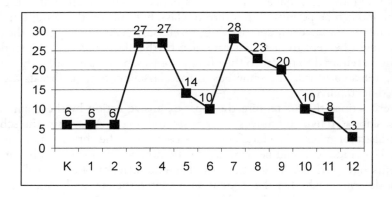

FIGURE 9–2.   Threats reported at each grade level.

to develop social groups and become engaged in rivalries for who would be "best friends" with whom. In some cases, these rivalries generated arguments and threatening statements. In a typical case, a fourth-grade girl wrote a letter making fun of a rival, and then, in reply, received a letter that contained some kind of threat. When her mother discovered the letter in her backpack, she contacted the principal and a threat assessment ensued. As might be expected, the overwhelming majority (85%) of the 86 threats in elementary students were determined to be transient, and could be resolved through counseling.

Middle schools (grades 6–8) experienced the highest rate of threats, particularly among the 7th and 8th grades. The 60 threats by middle school students were almost equally divided between transient (58%) and substantive (42%) cases; many involved an argument or conflict between students that escalated into a threat to fight or assault someone. Studies (Nansel et al., 2001) have reported that bullying is most prevalent in middle school grades, and bullying often involves threatening behavior by a bully. In some cases, however, the victim of bullying made a provocative threat in retaliation (e.g., "I'm going to shoot him if he doesn't leave me alone").

In high school there were more threats in the ninth grade than any other grade; this is not surprising, since ninth graders generally commit more disciplinary violations than the other students. Threats probably declined during the high school years in part because students became more mature and because they tended to be less likely to disclose threats to school authorities. The 42 high school threats were divided between transient (55%) and substantive (45%) cases.

What did the students threaten to do? As shown in Figure 9–3, most common was a threat to hit or beat up someone (77 cases, 41%). In addition, there were 27 threats to kill, 24 threats to shoot, and 18 threats to cut or stab. There were 32 cases in which the threat was vague or nonspecific ("I'm going to get you"), and 10 miscellaneous threats, such as setting fires or detonating bombs. All types of threats were seen at all school levels, although threats to kill and threats to shoot actually occurred more frequently in elementary school than in middle and high school combined.

What were the disciplinary consequences for threats?   A threat assessment approach gives school authorities more flexibility in choosing the disciplinary consequences for students who make threats. Students who make serious threats can be appropriately disciplined with serious consequences, but students whose threats are not serious can receive less serious consequences.

Under a zero tolerance policy, many students would have been expelled from school for making threats to kill or injure someone. Using threat assess-

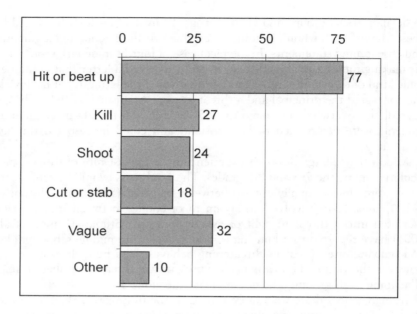

FIGURE 9–3.   Types of student threats.

ment guidelines, only three of the 188 threat cases resulted in expulsion from school:

- a 6th-grader who picked up a pair of scissors and threatened to stab a classmate;
- an 8th-grader who threatened to shoot a classmate;
- a 9th-grader who threatened to stab another student and was found to have a knife in her locker.

In each case, the student was expelled because of an accumulation of disciplinary violations prior to the threat; these three students had a combined total of 53 disciplinary infractions for the school year.

Suspension was the most common disciplinary consequence for a threat. Half (94 cases) of the students who made threats were given a short-term suspension. Some of these suspensions were in-school suspensions, meaning that the student spent the day in a suspension classroom, while in other cases the student was suspended from coming to school. The modal suspension (32 cases) was 1 day, with a range of one to ten days.

Twelve students were placed in an alternative educational setting, largely because they had a record of persistent behavior problems. These students had an average of 9.8 disciplinary infractions for the school year prior to their threat.

Only six students were arrested after making a threat. In each case, the school resource officer judged that the student's behavior warranted an arrest. Three of the arrests were made after the student made a false bomb threat. Two students were arrested because they assaulted a school staff member and had to be restrained. The final case involved the 9th-grade girl (noted above) who had a knife in her locker and had a history of assault.

What happened after the threat assessment? At the end of the school year, principals were interviewed to obtain follow-up information on each of their cases. The first and most important question was whether the students carried out their threats. In three cases, the principal was not sure whether a student's threat to hit another student was carried out, but in all other cases, the principals reported that the threat was not carried out. This suggests that threat assessment is a safe and effective procedure.

Principals were also asked about the student's relationship with the threat recipient after the threat was resolved. They were asked to judge whether the relationship had improved, remained about the same, or worsened. In 62 cases the principal did not feel sufficiently informed to make a judgment, but in the remaining 126 cases, the principals reported that in about one-third of cases the relationship had improved, and in nearly two-thirds (63%) the relationships were about the same; in only six cases (5%) was it worse.

Finally, principals were asked to assess the student's overall behavior after the threat. They rated 43 percent of the students as demonstrating improved behavior during the remainder of the school year, 39 percent as about the same, and only 18 percent as worse in their behavior. An independent review of school records found that many of the students continued to have discipline problems. More than half (53%) of the students had a subsequent disciplinary violation of some kind, and 16 percent had a disciplinary violation that involved violent or aggressive behavior such as hitting someone or getting into a fight.

It seems likely that the process of threat assessment contributed to the positive outcomes found in these schools, but this claim must be made with a caveat: this was a field-test study and not an experimental comparison between different approaches to student threats. The study was designed to demonstrate the viability of threat assessment as a new and previously untried procedure, but it did not have a comparison group to assess how threats would have been resolved using another method. A formal comparison with one or more alternative methods would be an appropriate next step, now that the threat assessment model has been devised and field-tested.

10

What Do Our Schools Need?

Larry's behavior problems were evident in kindergarten, when his teacher identified him as immature, inattentive, and often disruptive. His mother took a different view; she felt that Larry was frequently bullied by larger boys and that the school was not doing enough to control their behavior. Over the next few years, Larry frequently failed to do his work and made poor grades, and was retained. Several times the school recommended that Larry be considered for special education services, but his mother refused to allow him to be evaluated.

In middle school, Larry's behavior declined markedly: He laughed and talked to himself, and he avoided contact with other students. He walked with a slow, shuffling gait that made other students laugh. He avoided going into the cafeteria and secretly ate his lunch in the restroom. After Larry was caught making prank phone calls to the school, his mother finally relented and permitted a psychological evaluation. The psychologist found that Larry had above-average intelligence, but suffered from severe anxiety and low self-esteem, and he recommended that Larry be classified as seriously emotional disturbed. Reluctantly, Larry's mother permitted him to be placed in a special education classroom, but she declined to seek additional mental health treatment for him. By this point Larry's problems had grown much more severe, and he needed more than what his special education classes could provide.

During his high school years, Larry began drinking beer and wine because he found it made him feel less anxious. He also began to skip classes and roam the halls. The principal would sometimes find him hiding in a restroom or standing in a corner of the stairwell, rocking back and forth. Larry became obsessed with a female teacher and one day he forcibly attempted to kiss her on the cheek. The principal called the police and had Larry charged with assault and battery, then had him transferred to an alternative school. Larry blamed the principal and, for months, talked about shooting him—but no one took his statements seriously, because Larry often said things that were foolish or did not make sense.

At home, Larry's behavior became increasingly bizarre; he voiced the belief that he was somehow turning into a famous singer or television actor, and he became paranoid that his family was trying to poison him. After an incident in which he became violent and threatened his family, Larry was hospitalized, where he was diagnosed with alcohol abuse and schizophrenia, a severe mental disorder characterized by delusions and hallucinations. Larry was prescribed medication, but refused to take it.

One day Larry unexpectedly returned to his former high school armed with a pistol. He roamed through the halls until the principal came to confront him. Larry shot and killed the principal, then hid under a bush outside the school, where the police found and arrested him.

The answer to the question, "What do our schools need?" depends largely on one's perspective of what schools are supposed to accomplish. If schools are expected to teach the three R's and nothing more, then it may seem plausible that schools only need teachers, books, and a few other essential materials to teach students basic academic subjects. Violence prevention programs, the mental health services of school psychologists and counselors, and individualized educational programs (IEPs) for students with special needs would be superfluous. But what about students like Larry? How can schools teach students who have serious mental health problems? Although few students have problems as severe as Larry's, there are millions of students who experience stressful events and have psychological difficulties that affect their ability to learn. This chapter will address the inextricable connection between students' social and emotional development and their ability to learn. It will be argued that schools must broaden their perspective and their mission to accomplish the goal of educating all students and preparing them to function productively in society (Greenberg et al., 2003).

The idea that schools need to "get back to basics" and focus simply on instruction in academic subjects reflects a naive view of schools and students. Although there is plenty of scholarly debate on the purposes of American public education (Goodlad & McMannon, 1997), there is general agreement that schools are expected to prepare students to be good citizens—capable of working and functioning in modern society—and this invests schools with a mandate and responsibility that extends well beyond reading, writing, and arithmetic (Greenberg et al., 2003).

Standards for public education are set by each state, based on the values and outcomes endorsed by their legislatures. For example, in Pennsylvania, state law defines a broad purpose for public education (§ 4.11):

> (b) Public education prepares students for adult life by attending to their intellectual and developmental needs and challenging them to achieve at their highest level possible. In conjunction with families and other community institutions,

public education prepares students to become self-directed, life-long learners and responsible, involved citizens.

(c) Together with parents, families and community institutions, public education provides opportunities for students to: (1) Acquire knowledge and skills. (2) Develop integrity. (3) Process information. (4) Think critically. (5) Work independently. (6) Collaborate with others. (7) Adapt to change.

Pennsylvania's description of the purpose of public education presents goals that most states share, and to attain these goals schools must address the social and emotional adjustment of their students. Another example is Virginia, where public schools are required to provide "character education" to students. According to state law (§§ 22.1–208.01), "The purpose of the character education program shall be to instill in students civic virtues and personal character traits so as to improve the learning environment, promote student achievement, reduce disciplinary problems, and develop civic-minded students of high character."

Even if the only mission of schools were to teach core academic subjects, teachers would find that students are not equally prepared to learn, do not learn at the same rate, and cannot be taught using the same methods. In earlier times, students who could not keep up, or who did not behave, could be dismissed from school and left to find an occupation that matched their limited skills. In contrast, today's schools are expected to educate all students, a mission that is the core principle of the 2002 reauthorization of the Elementary and Secondary Education Act (Pub. L. 107–110), popularly known as the No Child Left Behind Act.

The nostalgic image of a single teacher instructing students from all grades in a one-room schoolhouse has another side, which is that many students *were* left behind by such schools, for reasons of race or disability. Many other students left school because their families needed them to work. In 1947, when the government began to collect educational attainment data, only about one-third of the U.S. adult population over age 24 had achieved a high school education (U.S. Census Bureau, 2004). Even as recently as 1970, fewer than half of the adult population (over age 24) had completed high school. Today, 85 percent of adults have completed high school, and most of those who have not completed high school are either immigrants or senior citizens. Clearly, schools are educating a much larger proportion of the population than in previous generations, and it is important to recognize that this tremendous accomplishment has required a reshaping of the purpose and goals of American education.

The notion that all students are entitled to public education is not explicit in the U.S. constitution and is a surprisingly recent development. Until the 1970s, students could be prevented from entering public schools if they were judged unable to benefit from the instruction that was available. Millions of students with handicaps, particularly mental retardation, were excluded because they were deemed unqualified for public education (Jacob & Hartshorne, 2003). This orientation changed radically in the early 1970s, when federal courts decided for the first time that states had an obligation to provide a public education to all students (e.g., *Pennsylvania Association for Retarded Children* v. *Commonwealth of Pennsylvania*, 334 F. Supp. 1257 = [D.C. E. D. Pa. 1971], 343 F. Supp. 279 [D.C. E. D. Pa. 1972]).

In 1975, Congress passed the Education of All Handicapped Children Act (Pub. L. 94–142) "to assure that all handicapped children have available to them . . . a free appropriate education which emphasizes special education and related services designed to meet their unique needs." With this legislation, signed by President Ford, the landscape of public education changed from a public service that was available to those students who were willing and able to participate to a legal entitlement that public schools were obligated to fulfill. President G. H. Bush signed an expansion of this law in 1990, the Individuals with Disabilities Education Act (IDEA), which was subsequently amended and reauthorized under President Clinton in 1997 and President G. H. W. Bush in 2004. The legislative history is significant because it demonstrates the sustained and bipartisan nature of support for this view of public education as a right that must be provided to all persons, regardless of their background or handicap status and, therefore, their capacity to learn.

These laws instituted a basic change in the scope of public education. Now public schools had to assume the Herculean challenge of educating *all* students, regardless of their capabilities and despite the cost or difficulty involved. Moreover, the academic failure of any student could no longer be considered an indication that the student was not suitable or capable; instead, a student's academic shortcomings were considered to indicate a failure by the school to provide a free and appropriate education. Although the educational reform movement that underlies high-stakes testing and the "No Child Left Behind Act" is often framed as holding schools *accountable*, accountability implies responsibility. Responsibility for school achievement is in essence shifted from student to school by the notion that schools are accountable for the academic achievement of all students.

The significance of the shift in responsibility for school achievement was compounded when the definition of a handicap (later termed a disability) was extended beyond physical limitations to include emotional and behavioral disorders: Children with serious behavior problems could, if so designated by federally regulated school procedures, be regarded as suffering from a psychological disturbance that was equivalent in legal status to a physical handicap (Hallahan & Kauffman, 2003; Jacob & Hartshorne, 2003). Schools could not discriminate against a student for a psychological disturbance any more than they could discriminate against a student who was unable to walk. Schools must be willing to accommodate this student's special learning needs, just as they would a student who was classified as suffering from mental retardation or any other disability.

THE NEEDS OF TODAY'S STUDENTS

If schools are designed to meet the educational needs of their students, it follows that what schools need is directly linked to what students need. Today's students represent a much larger and more diverse population than previous generations (Greenberg et al., 2003). Schools no longer enjoy the luxury of limiting instruction to a comparatively homogenous group of healthy, capable, and mostly Caucasian students; they must meet the needs of all students. Teachers cannot assume a common background and shared set of experiences and values in their students.

MYTH 18: Minorities constitute a small proportion of the student population.

FACTS: There are more than 73 million children (49.4 million ages 6–17) in the United States. Only 60 percent of U.S. children are White, non-Hispanic; the remaining 40 percent include 19 percent who are Hispanic, 16 percent Black, 4 percent Asian, and 4 percent from other races. Moreover, 19 percent of school-age children—nearly one in five—speak a language other than English at home and 5 percent have difficulty speaking English (Federal Interagency Forum on Child and Family Statistics, 2005).

MYTH 19: American children are raised in two-parent families with adequate food, housing, and income.

FACTS: Teachers cannot assume that all of their students will have two parents at home, and a substantial number of these students will live in poverty, many with inadequate housing, health care, and diet. Consider these facts:

- 17 percent of children live in families with incomes below the poverty level ($18,810 annual income for a family of four); the poverty rate soars to 42 percent among families headed by a female with no spouse.

- Only about two-thirds (68%) of children live with two parents; just 35 percent of Black children live with two parents.
- 35 percent of children born in 2003 were to unmarried women.
- 37 percent of U.S. households with children were classified as having insecure or inadequate housing and 18 percent of children were classified as living in food-insecure conditions. On a typical school day, over 16 million children participate in the free-or-reduced school lunch program (Food Research and Action Center, 2005).

The numbers of children who live in single-parent families do not tell the full story. Although many single parents manage to provide healthy, happy homes for their children, single-parent families are at increased risk for poverty, inadequate health care and housing, and other difficulties. In many cases, children experience the separation and divorce of their parents, and may be troubled by ongoing parental conflict that has an impact on their academic and social adjustment. In other cases, children may have lost a parent due to illness or accident, often with serious emotional consequences for the child (Dowdney, 2000). And still other children may be separated from a parent who is incarcerated; in 1999, approximately 1.5 million children had a parent in a state or federal prison, not including parents temporarily incarcerated in jails (Mumola, 2000).

MYTH 20: Few students have serious mental disorders.

FACTS: In thinking about the typical American school, it is easy to imagine classrooms of capable, eager students, when in fact many students experience serious emotional and behavioral problems that impair their ability to learn. The Surgeon General's conference on the mental health of children (U.S. Public Health Service, 2000) concluded that one in ten children and adolescents suffer from a mental disorder severe enough to cause some level of impairment (Burns, et al., 1995; Shaffer, et al., 1996). Yet, in any given year, only about one in five of such children receive specialty mental health services (Burns, et al., 1995), while the majority go untreated. Of course, these children continue to attend school, where their poor school performance and behavior problems result in poor grades and disciplinary violations.

MENTAL HEALTH NEEDS

What kind of mental disorders do children experience? The American Psychiatric Association's diagnostic manual (DSM-IV-TR, American Psychiatric Association, 2000) lists over two dozen disorders "usually first diagnosed in infancy, childhood or adolescence" (p. 13), including mental retardation, multiple types of learning disorders and communication disorders, pervasive developmental disorders such as autism and Asperger's disorder, attention deficit hyperactivity disorder (ADHD), and conduct disorder. There are many other disorders that can be found in the adult section, but which also occur frequently in children and adolescents, such as anxiety disorders, depressive disorders, and substance abuse. Because there are too many disorders to cover adequately, this section will concentrate on some of the most commonly diagnosed disorders that, for some students, lead them to engage in aggressive or violent behavior.

Depression is one of the most common mental disorders in children and adolescents, but can be difficult to distinguish from normal feelings of sadness or disappointment. Prolonged symptoms of depression can indicate a Major Depressive Disorder (MDD) that results in serious impairment. The lifetime prevalence of MDD in 15- to 18-year-olds is about 14 percent, and another 11 percent have minor depressions (Kessler & Walters, 1998). Aggressive behavior is a natural and common response to depression in children and adolescents, who may lash out at others because of their distress and frustration (Weisbrot & Ettinger, 2002).

Suicide is a complication of depression that warrants special attention, since it is the third leading cause of death among youth, after accidents and homicide (Commission on Adolescent Suicide Prevention, 2005). The rate of suicide among children ages 5 to 14 is .84 per 100,000, which is double the rate of other industrialized nations (Centers for Disease Control and Prevention, 1997b). The rate of suicide soars tenfold after age 14, to a level of 8.2 deaths per 100,000 persons ages 15 to 19 (National Institute of Mental Health, 2003). Suicide rates underestimate the prevalence of the problem, since there are 8 to 25 attempted suicides for every death. Even these figures underestimate the extent of the problem for schools, since anytime a student discloses thoughts of suicide, or feelings that life is not worth living, school officials must respond by evaluating the student's intentions, contacting parents, and in many cases, making arrangements for follow-up services in the community.

According to the Surgeon General's report on mental health (U.S. Department of Health and Human Services, 1999), *anxiety disorders* can be found in approximately 13 percent of children, and can include diagnoses such as social phobia, panic disorder, and post-traumatic stress disorder. Although most children with anxiety disorders are not aggressive, in some cases children who are troubled by anxiety, especially if their anxiety is the result of experiencing some violent event, respond by acting out aggressively. Anxious children are also vulnerable to becoming the targets of teasing and bullying by others.

Any student potentially could experience depression or anxiety in response to a stressful event or situation and might need support or assistance at school. Consider the high frequency of some common sources of stress and trauma, based on 2003 statistics:

- Approximately 906,000 children were confirmed victims of child abuse and neglect, a rate of 12.4 per 1,000 children (National Clearinghouse on Child Abuse and Neglect Information, 2005). Approximately 1,500 children died from abuse and neglect.
- Approximately 220,000 children ages 14 and younger were injured, and 1,591 were killed, in motor vehicle accidents (National Center for Injury Prevention and Control, 2005).
- Fire departments responded to 402,000 home fires, which included 3,145 fatalities and 14,075 injuries to adults and children (Karter, 2004).

There are other important mental disorders that affect children's school adjustment. For example, *Attention Deficit Hyperactivity Disorder* (ADHD) is a well-known, albeit controversial, disorder that can be diagnosed in 3 to 5 percent of school-age children (National Institutes of Health, 1998). Students with ADHD receive special education services under the federal category of "other health impairment" (Hallahan & Kauffman, 2003). Children with ADHD characteristically engage in impulsive and reckless behavior, often irritate and provoke others, and are at risk for aggressive behavior problems and substance abuse.

Conduct disorder is the diagnosis most commonly assigned to children and adolescents who engage in a persistent pattern of aggressive or delinquent behavior. The prevalence of conduct disorder ranges from 1 to 4 percent of 9- to-17-year-olds (U.S. Department of Health and Human Services, 1999). The federal criteria for identifying a student as eligible for special education services exclude children who are "socially maladjusted" unless they also have an "emotional disturbance" (34 C. F. R. § 300.7), so that students with conduct disorder are unlikely to qualify unless they also have a condition such as ADHD or an anxiety disorder.

Youth *substance abuse* is a major national concern because it is associated with so many negative outcomes, including violent and antisocial behavior, motor vehicle accidents, medical complications and illnesses, teen pregnancy, sexually transmitted diseases, school failure, suicide, and the development of other mental disorders (Dickinson & Crowe, 1997). The complexity of the substance abuse problem is beyond the scope of this chapter, other than to emphasize that it is an issue that schools cannot avoid and must address (Wagner, Tubman, & Gil, 2004). Although estimates of the prevalence of adolescent substance abuse rely heavily on anonymous self-report surveys of uncertain accuracy, studies consistently report high rates of underage drinking and use of illegal substances. The 2001 National Household Survey on Drug Abuse found that 10.8 percent of youth aged 12 to 17 had used an illicit drug (not including alcohol) at least once in the month before being interviewed (Spiess, 2003). The high rate of substance abuse among adolescents is well-documented in studies of motor vehicle accidents among young drivers, school suspensions and expulsions for drug possession, and drug test results among juvenile offenders (Bonnie & O'Connell, 2004; Dickinson & Crowe, 1997).

Schizophrenia is one of the most serious and debilitating mental disorders, with a lifetime prevalence of one percent of the population. Schizophrenia is characterized by periods of psychosis when the individual may experience hallucinations or delusions, and engage in bizarre and inappropriate behavior. Although schizophrenia usually does not emerge in full form until late adolescence or early adulthood, there are often prodromal symptoms in childhood and adolescence that include concentration and attention problems, anxiety, aggression, lack of motivation, mood problems, and social withdrawal (Commission on Adolescent Schizophrenia, 2005).

Autism and *Asperger's disorder* are classified as pervasive developmental disorders because they involve a profound impairment in normal social and intellectual development (Hallahan & Kauffman, 2003). Children with autism are often unresponsive to social cues and show little interest in other people, have poor speech and communication skills, and may exhibit ritualistic or rigidly stereotyped behavior. When frustrated or frightened, they may respond aggressively. Children with less severe symptoms may be diagnosed with Asperger's disorder. Approximately .2 percent of the child population are diagnosed with a pervasive developmental disorder.

Finally, *mental retardation* is diagnosed in children who exhibit markedly below average intellectual functioning along with impairment in adaptive skills such as communication and self-care (Hallahan & Kauffman, 2003). The prevalence of mental retardation in the school-age population is about 1 to 1.5 percent, and includes a wide range from children who can be taught to read and eventually hold a job to those who will function at a preschool level throughout their lives. Aggressive behavior is sometimes seen in students with mental retardation, generally because of their low tolerance for frustration and limited social skills.

All public schools can expect to have some students with serious mental disorders, and large public schools can expect to have students with *all* of these mental disorders. Based on the Surgeon General's report that approximately

1 in 10 adolescents suffer from a mental health disorder that is severe enough to impair their daily functioning, the average high school of 800 students (National Center for Education Statistics, 2002) will have approximately 80 psychologically impaired students. This means that, on an average day, the student body of a large public high school will likely include: students who are depressed and in some cases, suicidal; students who have debilitating anxiety; students who are hyperactive and impulsive; students who are aggressive and antisocial; students with substance abuse problems, some of whom may be intoxicated; and students with mental retardation. In some schools, there will also be students with an autistic disorder and students with schizophrenia.

Even among students who do not have serious mental disorders, there will be those who have recently experienced a stressful or traumatic event that will affect their emotional well-being and ability to function in school—a temporary condition termed an "adjustment disorder." In every school there will be students whose parents are getting a divorce or who struggle with family discord and violence at home. There will be students who have been physically or sexually abused, or who have been the victim of some other violent crime outside of school. There will be students who are troubled by the loss of a family member or close friend due to illness or accident. There are students who are coping with physical illnesses and injuries.

How will schools meet the educational needs of all of these students with so many different problems that affect their ability to learn? Schools cannot rely on mental health services in the community or the private sector because there are too few services available, they may be too expensive or not covered by health insurance, and some parents will refuse to seek help for their children (Evans et al., 2005; U.S. Department of Health & Human Services, 1999). Fewer than half of adolescents with serious mental disorders will be seen by a mental health professional in an average year (Romer & McIntosh, 2005).

Currently, schools deal with the mental health needs and problems of students through a patchwork of professional staff and services (Romer & McIntosh, 2005). About three quarters of schools have guidance counselors, and although counselors can spend some time addressing student mental health issues, their responsibilities are heavily devoted to course scheduling, achievement testing, assisting students with college and job applications, and other administrative matters. School psychologists are present on at least a part-time basis in about two-thirds of schools, but much of their time is committed to administering psychological tests to determine student eligibility for special education, and little or no time may be available for counseling. About 40 percent of schools have part- or full-time social workers who serve as a liaison with parents and coordinate care with outside agencies. In many schools the social and emotional problems of students go unrecognized, or if they are identified, there are not sufficient staff available to assist them. With limited staff, attention must be focused on the most acute and serious problems; this leaves no time for preventive efforts that could help students with their problems and concerns before they become more serious.

In 2002, President Bush established the President's New Freedom Commission on Mental Health for the purpose of identifying policies that would improve mental health services for adults and children. Over the next year, the 22 commissioners established 15 subcommittees that studied specific topics, consulted with professional organizations and agencies, held public hearings and solicited input from 2,500 individuals, and turned out a series of reports. Not surprisingly, the commission characterized the nation's mental health system as an inefficient and poorly coordinated maze of programs and made numerous recommendations for improvement. Many of these recommendations covered familiar ground: to reduce the stigma of mental illness that prevents people from seeking help, provide services to the poor and other underserved groups, and make better use of technological advances in health care and new, research-validated treatments.

Perhaps the most unexpected and provocative recommendations concerned the expanded role of schools in providing mental health services. As the New Freedom report observed, "Schools are where children spend most of each day. While schools are concerned primarily with education, mental health is essential to learning as well as to social and emotional development. Because of this important interplay between emotional health and school success, schools must be partners in the mental health care of our children" (New Freedom Commission on Mental Health, 2003, p. 58). The commission recommended that mental health programs be integrated into the mission of all schools and play a key role in the nation's health care system. Schools would provide a range of services, with efforts to promote positive, healthy development in all children along with programs to identify and intervene with children with mental disorders.

Perhaps the most controversial aspect of these recommendations was the proposal to institute mental health screening programs that would identify students who show indications of emerging problems that could respond to early intervention. A mental health assessment necessarily includes consideration of a child's family relationships and functioning both at school and at home, which raises concerns about family privacy and confidentiality. However, such concerns seem more ominous in the abstract than in practice. It is possible to screen students for stress, anxiety, depression, anger, and other general warning signs in a limited, confidential manner—without asking more intrusive questions about family relationships—and then to follow up by contacting parents in cases that seem to merit further inquiry. Such programs can be voluntary and based on parent consent; there are already model programs in dozens of states (New Freedom Commission on Mental Health, 2003).

The movement to integrate mental health services into schools is well advanced, and the commission report can be regarded as a call to expand, improve, and make more systematic the efforts that are already underway. For example, there are more than 1,500 school-based health centers that address mental as well as general medical health concerns (Center for Health and Health Care in Schools, 2003). Another example is student assistance programs (SAPs), which are analogous to employee assistance programs and began in 1987 with a primary focus on substance abuse, but grew to address other mental health concerns as well. By 2000, approximately one-third of states and over half of school divisions required SAPs in all schools (Brener, Martindale, & Weist, 2001). As Adelman and Taylor (2000) of the UCLA Center for Mental Health in Schools pointed out, "It is not a new insight that mental health and psychosocial problems must be addressed if schools are to function satisfactorily and if students are to learn and perform effectively" (p. 171).

THE SPECIAL EDUCATION
SERVICES MANDATE

The requirement that schools take responsibility for the academic success of all students—a mandate endorsed and extended by the No Child Left Behind Act—places a double burden on schools, because in order to assure their academic success, schools must consider the mental health problems that affect achievement and behavior in school. Schools are not *mandated* to provide mental health services to all students, but if a student is identified as in need of special education services, the school is obligated to develop an Individualized Education Program (IEP) and provide whatever services are necessary to meet the student's educational needs—at no cost to the family (Kauffman & Hallahan, 2005).

Special education services are expensive. Special education classrooms usually have fewer students and more staff than general education classrooms. Special education teachers often have aides to assist them, particularly in classrooms where students have disruptive behavior disorders and require close supervision. There are other costs, too: Special education programs require different books and curriculum materials, and their students must receive periodic psychological and educational evaluations to monitor progress and determine whether their educational needs are being met. If a student needs counseling, speech therapy, special transportation, or some other service that is specified in the student's IEP, the school must provide it. If a student requires residential placement in a special facility—and the public school cannot provide adequate instruction in any less restrictive way—the public school can be required to pay for it, even if the cost runs into tens or hundreds of thousands of dollars per year. The per-pupil cost of educating a student in special education is typically double or triple the cost of educating other students. When Congress passed the Education for All Handicapped Children Act in 1975, the federal government was to pay 40 percent of the additional expense, but in practice the federal share of the cost has never approached this amount (Kauffman & Hallahan, 2005).

The legal mandate to provide a free and appropriate education to students with psychological disabilities is a laudable standard, but it has the unintended effect of imposing a dilemma on school authorities. When schools recognize and pay for services to meet the needs of one student, they decrease the funds available for services to other students. Anytime a teacher or a counselor recognizes that a student is experiencing emotional or behavioral difficulties, there is a possibility that the student could be found eligible for special education services—in which case the school assumes responsibility for the cost of those services. These cost obligations create a disincentive for schools to identify and respond to the mental health needs of their students, and the criteria for determining whether a student is eligible for special education services are subject to much debate. Every school superintendent carefully monitors special education expenses, knowing that they have the potential to expand and consume a large portion of the school division's budget.

THE QUALITY AND VARIETY OF SCHOOL VIOLENCE PREVENTION PROGRAMS

Special education services are fundamental to helping all students achieve academic success, and frequently include IEPs to reduce aggressive and disruptive behavior—but school violence has more than one cause and is not remedied by a single solution. The issue of school violence crosses governmental boundaries between education and law enforcement, juvenile justice, mental health, public health, and other domains. Consider that the federal government has responded to the problem of school violence by supporting more than 123 different programs (U.S. Department of Health and Human Services, 2000). Although the federal government is frequently criticized for being too large and bureaucratic, the range and diversity of federal programs illustrate the complexity of issues that must addressed, and it would be unreasonable to expect one program to do it all.

A quick review of some of the federally supported programs demonstrates the multifaceted nature of the school violence problem. First, there are programs to assess the incidence of school violence, such as the Youth Risk Behavior Surveillance System and the School Crime Supplement to the National Crime Victimization Survey. Reliable and valid information on the nature and scope of violence in schools is essential to identify priorities and develop reasonable policies and practices.

Second, there are efforts to evaluate many of the national violence prevention programs that are found in schools throughout the nation, such as the School Resource Officer program, the 21st Century Community Learning Centers program, and the Safe Schools/Healthy Students Initiative. Literally millions of students are affected by these programs, and it is critical to know whether they succeed in improving school security and student safety.

The federal School Safety Technology Program is charged with addressing school security needs by developing improved methods of school surveillance and weapons detection. School security has become a large enterprise that has led schools to hire law enforcement officers and security officers, purchase metal detectors, cameras, and other components of security systems, and train staff in emergency and crisis response procedures (Trump, 2000). School administrators must be well informed about the legal and practical aspects of security, ranging from conducting student searches and responding to bomb threats, to recognizing drug dealing and gang activity (Trump, 1998).

The National Institute of Mental Health funds dozens of programs that examine the effectiveness of youth violence prevention programs that bridge family and school, such as the Families and Schools Together (FAST) Track Program, which is a controlled study being conducted in four states, the Linking the Interests of Families and Teachers (LIFT) program, which is a 10-week program for families whose children are deemed at risk for conduct problems and delinquency, and the Multisystemic Therapy (MST) program that was discussed in Chapter 7. The success of these kinds of programs offers hope that families can make substantial changes in how they raise their children and divert them from a pathway that can lead to violence.

There are several large-scale research programs designed to identify risk and protective factors associated with juvenile delinquency and violence. The National Center for Injury Prevention and Control, for instance, is studying the factors that promote weapon carrying among adolescents, and the National Institute of Child Health and Human Development is conducting a national longitudinal study of adolescent health that includes measures of family, peer, school and community influences.

There are numerous service programs that target specific populations with special needs and concerns; for example, the Center for Mental Health Services has a project to reduce violence against gay, lesbian, and bisexual youth, another to increase the resiliency of Asian-American and Pacific Islander youth, and yet another to reduce mental health stress for teachers. The Office of Public and Indian Housing has programs for youth living in public housing, and the Department of Labor has a program to find jobs for youth offenders and gang members. The problems in coordinating so many different programs are well-known and probably unavoidable, since they represent specialized interests and concerns that might not otherwise be represented in a single homogenous program (U.S. Department of Health and Human Services, 2000).

RECOMMENDATIONS

American education is undergoing a sustained period of change as schools evolve toward the goal of educating all children, recognizing that the 73 million children in the United States present a vast array of abilities and disabilities, cultural, social, and familial backgrounds, and learning needs. Although there are many useful programs already in place, there are some overarching needs that can be summarized here:

> **Recommendation 1: Continue to improve the quality of school-based violence prevention programs.**

In 1997, researchers with North Carolina's Research Triangle Institute (Silvia, Thorne, & Tashjian, 1997) released a report evaluating how schools made use of more than $5 billion from the federal Safe and Drug-Free Schools program over a ten-year period. The study found that school officials tended to ignore research on drug prevention, and that many effective programs were under-used in favor of programs that were of dubious effectiveness. As mentioned in Chapter 8, the U.S. Department of Education responded to these findings by sending a letter (cited in Atkinson et al., 1999, p. 8) to state school superintendents throughout the country, admonishing them that "funds are not being utilized at the school district level in the most effective manner possible" and advising them that "we are proposing some significant changes in the way SDFS is administered at the local level."

The following year, the U.S. Department of Education (1998) issued a new set of regulations for the use of funds from the Safe and Drug-Free Schools and Communities Act. These regulations, termed the Principles of Effectiveness, required schools to adhere to four standards in their drug and violence prevention programs:

1. Base programs on objective data about the drug and violence problems in their school or community.
2. Establish measurable goals and objectives for their programs and design program activities to meet these goals and objectives.

3. Implement programs that are based on research showing they are effective in reducing drug use or violence.
4. Evaluate their programs to examine their effectiveness and use the evaluation results to improve their programs.

The Principles of Effectiveness represent a tremendous step forward in improving the quality of prevention efforts in schools, but—nearly a decade later—it is questionable how well schools are adhering to them: Are they assessing the level of violence in schools with objective measures, or are they using unreliable methods that generate inflated results? Are they continuing to ignore research identifying effective prevention programs and opting for ineffective programs? Are they evaluating the effectiveness of their efforts and using the results to improve their programs?

The standards established by the Principles of Effectiveness seem reasonable, but they are not easily attained. There is no revolutionary change or bold new approach that will move American schools into an age in which all of their violence prevention efforts are effective; instead, much of the work that needs to be done is technical and laborious, and improvements come in small increments. The three main areas in which schools need to make improvements are: (1) better measurement of student violence, (2) routine and rigorous evaluation of program effects, and (3) a commitment to use effective programs and turn away from programs that are not effective.

Better measurement. In order for schools to fully embrace and follow the Principles of Effectiveness, they need reliable and valid measures of drug and violence problems. Most schools, however, rely on student self-report surveys, such as the Youth Risk Behavior Survey, that have questionable accuracy. Although student self-report surveys are widely used in educational and psychological research, there has been relatively little research on their accuracy. Researchers have been content to accept the results at face value—even as they acknowledge their limitations.

As discussed in Chapters 4 and 5, survey questions can be improved by elimination of overly broad questions that produce inflated results. For example, on some surveys, reports of large numbers of students carrying a weapon in the past 30 days can be inflated because students may have carried a gun while hunting or a knife while camping. On other surveys, rates of bullying can be inflated because the questions do not distinguish bullying from playful teasing or horseplay among peers.

Even a small proportion of students can skew survey results by exaggerating their claims of weapon carrying, fighting, and drug use. More rigorous and painstaking methodological research on school surveys is needed. What kinds of questions are most likely to produce exaggerated responses, for instance, and how well can we detect exaggerations from the pattern of responses? Extensive work of this type has been carried out successfully with psychological tests to measure symptoms of mental disorder, particularly in the evaluation of criminal defendants and others who might feign mental illness (Rogers, 1997). There is also an extensive body of research on the construction of opinion surveys for adults that could be brought to bear on student surveys (Weisberg, Krosnick, & Bowen, 1996).

In addition, there is a need to examine how students respond to self-report surveys and how well they understand the questions. One study suggested that when teachers are not trained to administer surveys in a standardized manner, and do not prepare the students to take the survey seriously, the results show much higher levels of extreme and inconsistent responses (Cross & Newman-Gonchar, 2004). Anyone who has administered classroom surveys knows how much the atmosphere in the classroom can influence how students respond to a task such as completing a survey. There should be more attention to preparing teachers to administer surveys and more instruction for students to make sure they understand survey questions and follow directions.

Even with improvements in student surveys, schools cannot rely on them as their sole source of information and should make greater use of interviews, peer reports, teacher observations, and official school discipline records. The process of gathering data from multiple sources that converge to give a more accurate and complete assessment is termed triangulation (Greene & Caracelli, 1997). Triangulated assessment recognizes that one form of measurement may have strengths that compensate for weaknesses of the other; for example, many incidents of bullying are known to students but not observed by teachers—but, on the other hand, teachers have a more mature perspective when judging the seriousness and chronicity of a student's bullying behavior. The combination of methods helps educators to construct a more complete picture of the nature and scope of aggressive behavior problems in their schools.

Routine and rigorous program evaluation. The addition of any new program is a strain on the limited time and energy of school personnel. Teachers have a full day of classroom teaching, then spend their afternoons and evenings grading papers and preparing lesson plans. The typical school principal is already overburdened with a 50–70 hour work week, not including time spent attending extracurricular activities (Los Angeles Unified School District Personnel Commission, 2003; National Association of Elementary School Principals, 2005). The additional challenge of adding a new program understandably leaves scant time and energy to consider how to evaluate it. As a result, many school programs are initiated with little or no provision to evaluate them according to the standards set by the Principles of Effectiveness.

Nearly every educational researcher has received calls for help from frantic school administrators who want assistance with the evaluation of a new program. In a typical situation, the school administrator calls in the spring to request assistance in evaluating a program that was implemented the previous fall. Since the program was funded by the Safe and Drug-Free Schools program, it is necessary to submit a year-end report documenting its effectiveness. Could the researcher come to the school and conduct a quick evaluation to document how well the program is working? The problem, of course, is that it is not possible to rigorously evaluate a program after it has been in effect. All too often, a program evaluation under such circumstances consists of a quick survey of staff perceptions of whether the program seems to be working, along with a detailed description of project activities, but no hard data to indicate whether the program is truly effective.

Good program evaluation is not just an examination of outcomes; more properly, it begins with the quality or fidelity of program implementation. When a prevention effort does not produce good results, it is important to determine whether the program was properly implemented before concluding that the underlying approach is not valid. University of Maryland researchers Denise and Gary Gottfredson (Gottfredson & Gottfredson, 2002) examined the quality of 3,691 school-based programs designed to prevent violent or problem behavior by students. Most of the prevention efforts fell short of the standards and practices established for that approach. For example, most curriculum-based programs failed to teach all of the lessons specified for that program. A study of Botvin's Life Skills Training program in 56 schools (Botvin et al., 1990) found that the percentage of material covered in the prevention curriculum ranged from 27 to 97 percent, with an average of just 68 percent. Not surprisingly, programs that were more completely delivered were more likely to produce positive effects.

Other prevention efforts studied by Gottfredson and Gottfredson (2002) routinely delivered the services in fewer sessions or for a shorter period of time than was recommended for that approach. Such limitations might be compared to a study testing the effectiveness of a new medication: If a hospital failed to give the new medication in an adequate dose or for a long enough period of time, it would be impossible to conclude whether or not it worked. Similarly, schools are often unable to reach valid conclusions about the effectiveness of their programs. Schools must be able to determine whether: (1) they have adequately delivered the program as it was designed; (2) the measures used to assess outcome are reliable and valid; and, only when both criteria have been met, is it possible to determine the program's effectiveness.

Program evaluation is a familiar requirement in educational settings, but it is not well-respected; unless there are adequate resources to plan and conduct evaluations, starting at the outset of the program and not hurriedly added at the end, the requirement is meaningless. Furthermore, rigorous standards for program evaluation have not become a routine and accepted part of school functioning, so that it has become accepted practice to rely on token efforts to describe a program and offer general observations and case examples as a substitute for more objective evidence. There is a substantial body of knowledge on the basic requirements for successfully implementing school-based prevention programs, most of it gleaned from the painful experience of failed efforts (Elias, Zins, Graczyk, & Weissberg, 2003; Kam, Greenberg, & Walls, 2003).

Effective programs. The ultimate goal of the Principles of Effectiveness is to assure that schools use programs that actually reduce student violence and drug use. As the New Freedom Commission (2005, p. 3) observed, "Far too often, treatments and services that are based on rigorous clinical research languish for years rather than being used effectively at the earliest opportunity." As described in Chapter 8, there is already an extensive array of effective programs for students at every grade level; there must be a more concerted effort and commitment from federal, state, and local authorities to support the use of these programs. There is also a need to show that programs that work under the advantageous conditions of a supervised and well-staffed research project can be implemented with comparable results under the more varied, and less advantageous, conditions that most schools must confront (Greenberg, 2004).

In order for schools to commit time and resources to effective programs, they must discontinue programs that are not effective. Yet nearly a decade after their establishment, schools continue to use programs that have unknown effectiveness. Worse, they persist in using programs such as D.A.R.E., that have been found repeatedly to be ineffective. A basic problem is that political considerations make it difficult for a school division to discontinue a popular program, especially one that has strong ties to law enforcement. Decisions to curtail a D.A.R.E. program, for instance, can be politically unpopular and likely to raise a storm of criticism: when Salt Lake City announced plans to stop their D.A.R.E. program, Mayor Ross Anderson came under intense political pressure and confessed to *The New York Times* (September 16, 2000) that the decision had been "a net political loss" for him.

D.A.R.E.'s history illustrates how political popularity can outweigh scientific evidence. D.A.R.E. has been determined to be ineffective in reports by the Surgeon General (U.S. Department of Health and Human Services, 2001), the General Accounting Office (Kanoff, 2003), and numerous independent studies that involved thousands of schools (Lynam et al., 1999; Perry et al., 2003; Ringwalt et al., 1994; Rosenbaum and Hanson 1998; Sherman, Gottfredson, MacKenzie, Eck, Reuter, and Bushway, 1997). D.A.R.E. remains conspicuously absent from lists of effective programs established by the U.S. Department of Education (2002), the Office of Juvenile Justice and Delinquency

Prevention (Howell, 1995), the Substance Abuse and Mental Health Services Administration (2005), the Centers for Disease Control and Prevention (Thornton et al., 2000), and other agencies. Nevertheless, D.A.R.E. remains the most widely used prevention program in schools, and each year the President declares a National D.A.R.E. day. The challenge for politicians (of all parties) is to support the value of involving law enforcement officers in the public schools, without sacrificing the integrity of commitment to effective programs, particularly when the stakes are as high as the reduction of drug abuse and violence.

> **Recommendation 2: Provide schools with the staff and other resources they need to respond to the mental health problems of their students.**

Schools cannot be the sole source of mental health services for their students. Even so, they must have adequate staff to respond to mental health crises and other urgent problems that occur in schools. They must also be able to provide on-site services to those students who can benefit from counseling and support while at school, as well as identify students who need additional treatment outside of school settings. Currently, few schools have enough staff to assume these responsibilities, and the result is that students with serious problems, such as Jeff Wiese and the other cases described in this book—as well as other troubled students who will not commit a violent act, but who suffer nonetheless—are either overlooked or given minimal attention.

According to a national survey commissioned by the Annenberg Public Policy Center (Romer & McIntosh, 2005), only about half (47%) of U.S. schools offer counseling for conditions such as anxiety and depression, and only one-third (34%) will counsel a student who has been a victim of physical or sexual abuse. Barely half (53%) have a full-time mental health professional (psychologist, counselor, or social worker) whose main job is to deal with student mental health issues. Most schools rely on part-time staff or staff members who are assigned to cover multiple schools. A single school psychologist who must work in two or more schools obviously has little opportunity to become sufficiently familiar with the student body, to develop working relationships with teachers, and to establish trust with students in need of counseling. Moreover, most school mental health professionals have other responsibilities that limit their time to counsel students. A majority (76%) spend less than half of their time counseling or working directly with students who have mental health problems, and about half (47%) spend less than 10 hours per week.

Recommendation 3: Make bullying prevention a national goal in public schools.

Although bullying prevention is but one form of violence prevention, bullying is a problem that occurs at all grade levels and intersects with many important dimensions of a child's social and emotional development. Bullying is a vital issue because bullying has serious and lasting consequences for victims, and students who bully others are at risk for continued aggressive and antisocial behavior (Olweus, Limber, & Mihalic, 1999). Fortunately, bullying prevention has already gained substantial momentum toward becoming a national concern, as reflected in the growth of bullying prevention programs and the increasing numbers of states that have mandated bully prevention efforts (Limber & Small, 2003).

As described in Chapter 5, there must be improvements in our ability to define and measure bullying, and further research to identify effective prevention methods. One useful approach may be to infuse bullying prevention efforts with strategies and methods that have been proven to be effective in working with aggressive youth, such as conflict resolution, problem-solving, and other social and interpersonal skills. Similarly, counseling for bullying can make use of cognitive-behavioral methods that are effective in teaching students anger control, empathy, and ability to get along with others.

Recommendation 4: Limit children's access to guns.

Children with access to guns pose a serious risk to public safety. When homicides by juveniles tripled during the 1980s, 100 percent of the increase in deaths was due to guns. This does not mean that guns are the sole cause of violence, but that this factor is a critical link in the chain of causal events that lead to juvenile murder: Without access to guns, juveniles are far less dangerous, and the risk of lethal outcomes is drastically reduced.

The single most important barrier to limiting children's access to firearms in the United States is the fear that gun safety measures would impose unnecessary and unconstitutional restrictions on the right to bear arms. Any proposed policy or change in law must withstand the scrutiny of a powerful lobby; however, programs like Boston's Operation Ceasefire demonstrated that a coordinated law enforcement effort that worked to reduce juvenile access to handguns can have a substantial effect on reducing juvenile violence and homicide. Similar efforts in other cities appear to have had beneficial effects. More research is needed to identify additional ways to discourage juvenile access to firearms.

Recommendation 5: Amend the Gun-Free Schools Act.

The major provisions of the Gun-Free Schools Act were carried forward in the No Child Left Behind Act. These provisions should be amended to clarify that expulsion is only necessary in cases that pose a serious threat to the safety of others; students should not be expelled for playful or accidental behavior. Since two of the federal government's law enforcement agencies and the U.S. Department of Education have recommended that schools use a threat assessment model in responding to student threats (Fein, Vossekuil, Pollack, Borum, Modzeleski, & Reddy, 2002; O'Toole, 2000), there should be federal funding for development, training, and evaluation of threat assessment methods in schools.

Recommendation 6: Avoid sensational news coverage of school violence.

After the Columbine shootings, students across the country engaged in copycat behaviors such as calling in bomb threats and preparing hit lists. One month after Columbine, 37 percent of American teenagers reported copycat threats at their own school, and 20 percent had experienced a copycat-related evacuation (Gallup, 1999). Investigations revealed that the students who carried out other shootings had also been influenced by news media coverage of prior incidents. For example, Kip Kinkel's friend Tim McCown recalled that Kip was keenly aware of the school shootings in Pearl, Paducah, and Jonesboro. "He reacted to the other school shootings, their shortcomings, almost like, how they failed. He talked about how—not that he'd do it that exact way, like, go to school and shoot people, but if he was going to go out, he'd try to take as many people out with him." (Kirk, Navasky, & O'Connor, 2000). The two Columbine assailants voiced similar aspirations to exceed the body count of previous school shootings (Columbine Review Commission, 2001).

The news media sensibly limited its coverage of school shootings after it became evident how much their coverage of the Columbine attack stimulated false bomb threats around the country, and this restraint probably helped contribute to the eventual drop-off in such incidents. News coverage that sensationalizes violence, dramatizes the pain and suffering of victims, and promotes fear in the general public is likely to capture the imagination of troubled students and inspire them to commit similar acts. If the news media would voluntarily restrain its coverage, it might reduce the amount of copycat behavior that follows.

> ## Recommendation 7: Make universal parent education a public health mission.

As extensive research in early childhood education has demonstrated, children must come to school prepared to learn or risk falling behind and failing during their elementary school years (Barnett & Hustedt, 2003, 2005). If schools are to educate all children, they must begin by helping all parents understand what their child needs and how they can help their child prepare for school. Public health initiatives that deliver parent education in early childhood have demonstrated remarkable effectiveness, even showing reductions in crime and violence when the children reach adulthood (U.S. Department of Health and Human Services, 2001). The knowledge and skills of parenting are too important to be neglected or trusted to instinct.

Parent education should include traditional topics such as children's health care needs and effective discipline techniques, but it should also help parents understand how the media influence children's attitudes, values, and behavior. Previous generations could not have imagined the level of violence that children routinely are exposed to in videos, writings, and songs, or that their children can sit in their bedrooms and converse with strangers anywhere in the world. This means that parents must monitor and supervise their children in ways that did not even exist a decade ago.

It follows that a society concerned with the well-being of all children should make parent education a public health mission and a valued component of public education. Courses in parenting should be a standard part of the high school curriculum, with additional courses offered to all adults who have children.

LIMITATIONS AND FUTURE DIRECTIONS

There are important aspects of school violence that are not covered in this book. Most notably, this book does not address minority and multicultural issues. Minority populations are underserved by our mental health system (New Freedom Commission, 2003) and often underachieve in school relative to nonminority students (Kao & Thompson, 2003). Closely related to the minority achievement gap is the problem that minority students are often subjected to disproportionate levels of discipline (Weinstein, Gregory, & Stambler, 2004). Zero tolerance policies appear to have exacerbated racial disparities in rates of suspension and expulsion (Advancement Project and the Harvard Civil Rights Project, 2000). These issues require more attention and analysis than this book can provide.

Another problem that deserves more attention are schools that are plagued by high rates of gang activity and violence. Although this book emphasizes the comparative safety and low rate of violence in most schools, this does not mean there are not schools with serious problems. All schools have fundamental and essential security needs (Trump, 1998, 2000), but all schools do not have the same needs, and some require greater safety and security measures than others.

A final important subject for further study and development is the emerging model of comprehensive services designed to promote a safe and supportive school environment (Osher, Dwyer, & Jackson, 2004). Violence prevention in schools is best imbedded in a pyramid model that contains three levels of services (Dwyer & Osher, 2000; Osher, Dwyer, & Jackson, 2004; Sprague & Walker, 2000). At the base of the pyramid are schoolwide programs that serve all students by helping to maintain a disciplined, caring, and supportive environment. At the middle level are programs for students identified as being at risk for behavioral difficulties, and at the top level are services for a small group of students who require individualized interventions. This trichotomy corresponds to the universal, selective, and targeted interventions described by Sprague and Walker (2000). The pyramid in Figure 10–1 depicts a model for dealing with students who are at risk for violence (Cornell & Sheras, 2005), and is intended to be consistent with more general intervention models (Dwyer & Osher, 2000; Sprague & Walker, 2000).

The foundation for a safe school rests on the creation of a caring community where students feel safe and secure. Safety and security derive from two conditions: (1) an orderly, predictable environment where school staff provide consistent, reliable supervision and discipline; and (2) a school climate where students feel connected to the school and supported by their teachers and other school staff. This combination of discipline and support is essential, and requires an organized, schoolwide approach that is endorsed and practiced by all school staff. Positive Behavior Support (PBS) is one approach that aims to create a stable, predictable, and supportive environment for students through behavioral interventions and systems change (Mayer, 1995; Sugai et al., 2000). PBS stresses that students should be taught social and communication

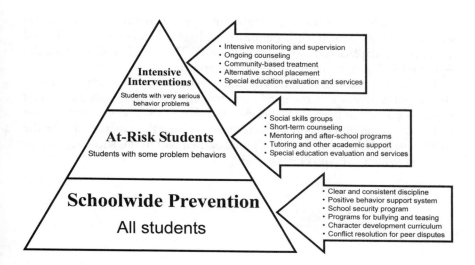

FIGURE 10–1.   Comprehensive model for violence prevention and intervention.

skills so that they can engage in respectful behavior without resorting to aggressive or disobedient actions. PBS represents a growing emphasis on school climates that foster healthy social, emotional and intellectual development in youth (Catalano et al., 2004; Eccles & Gootman, 2002).

All of the recommendations in this book hinge on the provision of adequate financial support for public education. No new program or initiative can succeed if there are not adequate staff and other costly resources to carry it out. Unfortunately, schools are already overburdened by under-funded government mandates, and most prevention programs suffer from fatal deficiencies in funding, staffing, training, or administrative support (Elias, Zins, Graczyk, & Weissberg, 2003). Public education is enormously expensive, but as a popular bumper stick says, "If you think education is expensive, try ignorance." Snyder and Sickmund (1999) estimated that it costs 2 million dollars for every youth who leaves high school for a life of crime and drug abuse. In light of the enormous costs to society of poverty, unemployment, crime, substance abuse, and other social ills, the benefits of an effective educational system are more than cost-effective.

Funding for public education is easily misperceived as excessive by the average taxpayer, because it consumes the lion's share of most local government budgets. The local cost is high, however, largely because the federal contribution (about 7%) is so low—and has never matched the costs imposed by federal requirements (Houston, 2003). The promise of No Child Left Behind cannot be achieved if there is insufficient funding to pay for new require-ments, as many educators, economists, and state legislators have charged (Houston, 2003; Mathis, 2003; Puriefoy, 2003). This, too, is a subject for a dif-ferent book, but one that must be recognized here.

Despite the political rhetoric and controversy over the quality and direc-tion of public education, the good news remains that schools are much safer than the public has been led to believe, and that juvenile violence in schools and in the community has steadily declined—rather than increased—for the past ten years. Educators should be proud of their part in this success, and par-ents and students should be reassured.

References

Achenbach, T. M., McConaughy, S. H., & Howell, C. T. (1987). Child/adolescent behavioral and emotional problems: Implications of cross-informant correlations for situational specificity. *Psychological Bulletin*, 101, 213–232.

Adelman, H. S., & Taylor, L. (2000). Promoting mental health in schools in the midst of school reform. *Journal of School Health*, 70, 171–178.

Advancement Project and The Civil Rights Project. (2000). *Opportunities suspended: The devastating consequences of zero tolerance and school discipline policies.* Boston, MA: Harvard Civil Rights Project. http://www.law.harvard.edu/civilrights/conferences/zero/zt_report2.htm.

Alexander, J. F., & Parsons, B. V. (1982). *Functional family therapy.* Monterey, CA: Brooks/Cole.

Alexander, J., Barton, C., Gordon, D., Grotpeter, J., Hansson, K., Harrison, R., Mears, S., Mihalic, S., Parsons, B., Pugh, C., Schulman, S., Waldron, H., & Sexton, T. (1998). *Blueprints for violence prevention, book three: Functional family therapy.* Boulder, CO: Center for the Study and Prevention of Violence.

American Academy of Child and Adolescent Psychiatry, American Academy of Family Physicians, American Academy of Pediatrics, American Medical Association, American Psychiatric Association, American Psychological Association. (2000). *Joint statement on the impact of entertainment violence on children.* Retrieved March 17, 2006, from http://www.aap.org/advocacy/releases/jstmtevc.htm

American Psychiatric Association. (2000). *Diagnostic and statistical manual of mental disorders* (4th edition, text revision). Washington, DC: Author.

American Psychological Association. (1999). *Warning signs.* Author: Washington, DC.

American School Health Association. (1989). *National adolescent student health survey (NASHS). A report on the health of America's youth.* Oakland, CA: Third Party Publishing Company.

Anderson, C. A., Benjamin, Jr., A. J, & Bartholow, B. D. (1998). Does the gun pull the trigger? Automatic priming effects of weapon pictures and weapon names. *Psychological Science*, 9, 308–314.

Anderson, C. A., Berkowitz, L., Donnerstein, E., Huesmann, L. R., Johnson, J. D., Linz, D., Malamuth, N. M., & Wartella, E. (2003). The influence of media violence on youth. *Psychological science in the public interest*, 4, 81–110.

Anderson, C. A., Carnagey, N. L., & Eubanks, J. (2003). Exposure to violent media: The effects of songs with violent lyrics on aggressive thoughts and feelings. *Journal of Personality and Social Psychology*, 84, 960–971.

Anderson, C. A., Carnagey, N. L., Flanagan, M., Benjamin, A. J., Eubanks, J., & Valentine, J. C. (2004). Violent video games: Specific effects of violent content on aggressive thoughts and behavior. In M. Zanna (Ed.) *Advances in experimental social psychology, Vol. 36* (199–249), NY: Elsevier.

Anderson, C. A., & Dill, K. E. (2000). Video games and aggressive thoughts, feelings, and behavior in the laboratory and in life. *Journal of Personality and Social Psychology, 78,* 772–790.

Anderson, R. N. (2001). Deaths: Leading causes for 1999. *National Vital Statistics Reports, 49,* 1–88.

Associated Press. (2005). *Guards, father charged in alleged "scared straight" abuse in Pennsylvania.* Retrieved April 12, 2005, from http://www.kron4.com/Global/story.asp?S= 3152771

Atkin, C. K., Greenberg, B. S., Korzenny, F., & McDermott, S. (1979). Selective exposure to televised violence. *Journal of Broadcasting, 23*(1), 5–13.

Atkinson, A. J., Deaton, M., Travis, R., & Wessel, T. (1999). *Program planning and evaluation handbook: A guide for safe and drug-free schools and communities act programs.* Harrisonburg, VA: Virginia Effective Practices Project, James Madison University.

Austin, J., Johnson, K. D., & Gregoriou, M. (2000). *Juveniles in adult prisons and jails: A national assessment* (NCJ 182503). Washington, DC: Bureau of Justice Assistance.

Austin, J., Jones, M., & Bolyard, M. (1996). A survey of jail-operated boot camps and guidelines for their implementation. In D. L. MacKenzie & E. E. Heber (Eds.). *National institute of justice report: Correctional boot camps: A tough intermediate sanction* (NCJ 157639). Washington, DC: U.S. Department of Justice. Retrieved July 22, 2005, from http://www.kci.org/publication/bootcamp/docs/nij/Correctional_Boot_Camps/ chpt19.htm.

Bachman, J. G., Johnston, L. D., & O'Malley, P. M. (1999). *Monitoring the future: A continuing study of American youth (12th grade survey), 1996* [Computer file]. Ann Arbor, MI: University of Michigan Survey Research Center.

Ballard, M. E., & Coates, S. (1995). The immediate effects of homicidal, suicidal, and nonviolent heavy metal and rap songs on the moods of college students. *Youth and Society, 27,* 148–168.

Bandura, A., Ross, D., & Ross, S. A. (1961). Transmission of aggression through imitation of aggressive models. *Journal of Abnormal and Social Psychology, 63,* 575–582.

Bandura, A., Ross, D., & Ross, S. A. (1963). Imitation of film-mediated aggressive models. *Journal of Abnormal and Social Psychology, 66,* 3–11.

Barkley, R. A. (1987/1997). *Defiant children: A clinicians manual for assessment and parent training.* New York: Guilford.

Barnett, W. S., & Hustedt, J. T. (2003). Preschool: The most important grade. *Educational Leadership, 60,* 54–7.

Barnett, W. S., & Hustedt, J. T. (2005). Head Start's lasting benefits. *Infants and Young Children, 18,* 16–24.

Barrett, P. M., & Ollendick, T. H. (2004). *Handbook of interventions that work with children and adolescents: Prevention and treatment.* Hoboken, NJ: Wiley & Sons.

Bartholow, B. D., & Anderson, C. A. (2002). Effects of violent video games on aggressive behavior: Potential sex differences. *Journal of Experimental Social Psychology, 38,* 283–290.

Beane, A. (1999). *The bully-free classroom*. Minneapolis, MN: Free Spirit Publishing.

Beck, A. T. (1995). Cognitive therapy: Past, present and future. In M.J. Mahoney (Ed.). *Cognitive and constructive psychotherapies: Theory, research and practice* (pp. 29–41). NY: Springer.

Becker, E., & Pedrick, L. (2001, February 9). As Ex-Theorist on Young 'Superpredators,' Bush Aide Has Regrets. *New York Times*.

Belkin, L. (1999, October 31). Parents blaming parents. *New York Times Magazine*, p. 61.

Belson, W. A. (1978). *Television violence and the adolescent boy*. Westmead, UK: Teakfield.

Berkowitz, L. (1968). Impulse, aggression and the gun. *Psychology Today*, 2 (4), 19–22.

Berkowitz, L. (1993). Aggression: Its causes, consequences, and control. New York: McGraw-Hill.

Berkowitz, L. (1994). Guns and youth. In L. D. Eron, J. H. Gentry, & P. Schlegel (Eds.). *Reason to hope: A psychosocial perspective on violence & youth*. Washington, DC: American Psychological Association.

Berkowitz, L., & Frodi, A. (1977). Stimulus characteristics that can enhance or decrease aggression: Associations with prior positive or negative reinforcements for aggression. *Aggressive Behavior*, 3, 1–15.

Berkowitz, L., & LePage, A. (1967). Weapons as aggressive-eliciting stimuli. *Journal of Personality and Social Psychology*, 7, 202–207.

Bjorkqvist, K., Lagerspetz, K., & Kaukinian, A. (1992). Do girls manipulate and boys fight? Developmental trends in regard to direct and indirect aggression. *Aggressive Behavior*, 18, 117–127.

Blumstein, A., & Wallman, J. (2000). *The crime drop in America*. New York: Cambridge University Press.

Bock, R. (2001). *Bullying widespread in U.S. schools, survey finds*. Press release retrieved March 3, 2005 from http://www.nih.gov/news/pr/apr2001/nichd—24.htm

Bonda, P. (2005). Going From Here to There. What will America look like in 2054? *Green@work Magazine*. Retrieved August 1, 2005, from http://www.greenatwork-mag.com/gwsubaccess/04janfeb/commentary.html

Bonnie, R. (1989). Juvenile homicide: A study in legal ambivalence. In E. Benedek & D. Cornell (Eds.), *Juvenile homicide* (pp. 183–218). Washington, DC: American Psychiatric Press.

Bonnie, R., & O'Connell, M. (Eds.) (2004). *Reducing underage drinking: A collective responsibility*. Washington, DC: National Academies Press.

Borum, R. (1996). Improving the clinical practice of violence risk assessment: Technologies, guidelines and training. *American Psychologist*, 51, 945–956.

Botvin, G. J. (1998). Preventing adolescent drug abuse through Life Skills Training: Theory, methods, and effectiveness. In J. Crane (Ed.) *Social Programs That Work* (pp. 225–257). New York: Russell Sage Foundation.

Botvin, G. J., Baker, E., Dusenbury, L., Botvin, E. M., & Diaz, T. (1995). Long-term follow-up results of a randomized drug abuse prevention trial in a white middle-class population. *Journal of the American Medical Association*, 273, 1106–1112.

Botvin, G. J., Baker, E., Dusenbury, L., Tortu, S., and Botvin, E. M. (1990). Preventing adolescent drug abuse through a multi-modal cognitive-behavioral approach: Results of a 3-year study. *Journal of Consulting and Clinical Psychology*, 58, 437–446.

Boys & Girls Clubs of America (2005). *The facts*. Retrieved May 23, 2005, from http://www.bgca.org/whoweare/facts.asp

Brady Center to Prevent Gun Violence. (2005). *Guns in our nation's schools*. Retrieved August 30, 2005, from http://www.bradycenter.org/stop2/facts/fs5.php

Braga, A. A., Kennedy, D. M., Piehl, A. M., & Waring, E. J. (2001). *Reducing gun violence: The Boston Gun Project's Operation Ceasefire*. Washington, DC: U.S. Department of Justice.

Braga, A. A., Kennedy, D. M., & Tita, G. E. (2002). New approaches to the strategic prevention of gang and group-involved violence. In C. R. Huff (Ed.) *Gangs in America III* (pp 271–285). Thousand Oaks, CA: Sage Publications.

Brener, N. D., Martindale, J., & Weist, M. D. (2001). Mental health and social services: Results from the School Health Policies and Programs Study 2000. *Journal of School Health*, 71, 305–312.

Brener, N. D., Simon, T. R., Krug, E. G., & Lowry, R. (1999). Recent trends in violence-related behaviors among high school students in the United States. *Journal of the American Medical Association*, 282, 440–446.

Brestan, E. V. & Eyberg, S. M. (1998). Effective psychosocial treatments of conduct-disordered children and adolescents: 29 years, 82 studies, and 5272 kids. *Journal of Clinical Child Psychology*, 27, 180–189.

Brooks, K., Schiraldi, V., & Ziedenberg, J. (2000). *School house hype: Two years later.* Washington, D.C.: Justice Policy Institute.

Brown, B., & Merritt, R. (2002). *No easy answers: The truth behind death at Columbine.* New York: Lantern Books.

Browne, J. A., Losen, D. J. & Wald, J. (2001), Zero tolerance: Unfair, with little recourse. *New Directions for Youth Development*, 92:73–99.

Brunsma, D. L. (2002). *School uniforms: A critical review of the literature*. Bloomington, IN: Phi Delta Kappa International.

Brunsma, D. L. (2004). *The school uniform movement and what it tells us about American education: A symbolic crusade.* Lanham, MD: ScarecrowEducation.

Brunsma, D. L., & Rockquemore, K. A. (1998). Effects of student uniforms on attendance, behavior problems, substance use, and academic achievement. *Journal of Educational Research*, 92, 53–62.

Bureau of Alcohol, Tobacco, and Firearms. (1993). *Operation Snapshot*. Washington, DC: Author.

Bureau of Justice Statistics. (2004). *Homicide trends in the U.S.* Washington, DC: Author. Retrieved March 13, 2006, from http://www.ojp.usdoj.gov/bjs/homicide/teens.htm

Burns, B. J., Costello, E. J., Angold, A., Tweed, D., Stangl, D., Farmer, E. M., & Erkanli, A. (1995). Children's mental health service use across service sectors. *Health Affairs (Millwood)*, 14, 147–159.

Bushman, B. J., & Anderson, C. A. (2001). Media violence and the American public: Scientific facts versus media misinformation. *American Psychologist*, 56, 477–489.

Bushman, B. J., & Anderson, C. A. (2002). Violent video games and hostile expectations: A test of the general aggression model. *Personality and Social Psychology Bulletin*, 28, 1679–1686.

Bushman, B. J., & Huesmann, L. R. (2001). Effects of televised violence on aggression. In D. G. Singer & J. L. Singer (Eds.), *Handbook of children and the media* (pp. 223–254). Thousand Oaks, CA: Sage.

Calvert, S. L., & Tan, S. (1994). Impact of virtual reality on young adults' physiological arousal and aggressive thoughts: Interaction versus observation. *Journal of Applied Developmental Psychology*, 15, 125–139.

Caplan, G. (1964). *Principles of preventive psychiatry*. NY: Basic Books.

Catalano, R. F., Berglund, M. L., Ryan, J. A. M., Lonczak, H. S., & Hawkins, J. D. (2004). Positive youth development in the United States: Research findings on evaluations of positive youth development programs. *Annals of the Academy of Political and Social Science*, 591, 98–124.

Cauchon, D. (1999, April 13). Zero-tolerance policies lack flexibility. *USA Today*. Retrieved August 5, 2005, from http://www.usatoday.com/educate/ednews3.htm

Cedar B., & Levant R. (1990). A meta-analysis of the effects of parent effectiveness training. *The American Journal of Family Therapy*, 18, 373384.

Center for Health and Health Care in Schools. (2003). *Caring for kids*. Washington, DC: Author. Retrieved March 17, 2006, from http://www.healthinschools.org/cfk/ment_broch.pdf

Center for the Study and Prevention of Violence. (1998). *CSPV position summary: D.A.R.E. program*. Boulder, CO: Center for the Study and Prevention of Violence, Institute for Behavioral Science, University of Colorado. Retrieved April 17, 2005, from http://www.colorado.edu/cspv/publications/factsheets/positions/pdf/PS—001.pdf

Centers for Disease Control and Prevention. (1991). Weapon-carrying among high school students—United States, 1990. *Morbidity and Mortality Weekly Report*, 40, 681–684.

Centers for Disease Control and Prevention. (1997a). *1997 National school-based Youth Risk Behavior Survey data and documentation manual*. Retrieved August 30, 2005, from http://www.cdc.gov/HealthyYouth/YRBS/data/1997/yrbs1997.pdf

Centers for Disease Control and Prevention. (1997b). Rates of homicide, suicide, and firearm-related death among children—26 industrialized countries. *MMWR Weekly*, 46, 101–105.

Centerwall, B. S. (1989). Exposure to television as a risk factor for violence. *American Journal of Epidemiology*, 129, 643–652.

Centerwall, B. S. (1992). Television and violence: The scale of the problem and where to go from here. *JAMA, The Journal of the American Medical Association*, 267, 3059–3063.

Cline, V. B., Croft, R. G., & Courrier, S. (1973). Desensitization of children to television violence. *Journal of Personality & Social Psychology*, 27, 360–365.

CNN. (1996a, October 3). 'Midol suspension' ends: Honor student returns to class. Retrieved August 5, 2005, from http://www.cnn.com/US/9610/03/midol.suspension/index.html

CNN. (1996b, October 29). *Kindergartner suspended for bringing beeper to school*. Retrieved August 5, 2005, from http://www.cnn.com/US/9610/29/briefs/beeper

CNN. (2002, April 27). *Brave teacher stopped gun rampage*. Retrieved August 30, 2005, from http://archives.cnn.com/2002/WORLD/europe/04/27/germany.shooting

Cole, J., Cornell, D., & Sheras, P. (in press). Identification of school bullies by survey methods. *Professional School Counseling*.

Columbine Review Commission. (2001). *The Report of Governor Bill Owens' Columbine Review Commission*. Retrieved March 16, 2005, from http://www.state.co.us/columbine

Commission on Adolescent Schizophrenia. (2005). Youth suicide. *In* D. L. Evans, E. B. Foa, R. E. Gur, H. Hendin, C. P. O'Brien, M. E. P. Seligman, & B. T. Walsh (Eds.). *Treating and preventing adolescent mental health disorders: What we know and what we don't know* (pp. 77–158). New York: Oxford University Press.

Commission on Adolescent Suicide Prevention. (2005). Youth suicide. In D. L. Evans, E. B. Foa, R. E. Gur, H. Hendin, C. P. O'Brien, M. E. P. Seligman, & B. T. Walsh (Eds.). *Treating and preventing adolescent mental health disorders: What we know and what we don't know* (pp. 433–493). New York: Oxford University Press.

Committee for Children. (2005). *Second Step: A violence prevention curriculum.* Retrieved May 27, 2005 from http://www.cfchildren.org/ssf/ssf/ssindex/

Committee on Juvenile Justice (1997). Report on Governor Pataki's Juvenile Justice Reform Proposals, *The Record of the Association of the Bar of the City of New York, 52,* 445–460.

Conduct Problems Prevention Research Group. (1992). A developmental and clinical mode for the prevention of conduct disorder: The FAST Track Program. *Development and Psychopathology, 4,* 509–527.

Cook, P. J., & Laub, J. H. (1998). The unprecedented epidemic in youth violence. In M. Tonry & M. H. Moore (Eds.). *Youth violence. Crime and Justice: A review of research,* 24, (pp. 27–64). Chicago: University of Chicago Press.

Cook, P. J., & Ludwig, J. (1996). *Guns in America: Results of a comprehensive national survey on firearms ownership and use.* Washington, DC: The Police Foundation.

Cornell, D. (1993). Juvenile homicide: A growing national problem. *Behavioral Sciences and the Law, 11,* 389–396.

Cornell, D. (1999). Child and adolescent homicide. In Vincent B. Van Hasselt & Michel Hersen (Eds.). *Handbook of psychological approaches with violent criminal offenders: Contemporary strategies and issues* (pp. 131–152). New York: Kluwer Academic.

Cornell, D. (2004). Student threat assessment. In E. Gerler (Ed.), *Handbook of school violence* (pp. 115–136). Binghamton, NY: Haworth Press.

Cornell, D. & Sheras, P. (2006). *Guidelines for responding to student threats of violence.* Longmont, CO: Sopris West.

Cornell, D, Sheras, P., & Cole, J. (in press). Assessment of bullying. In S. R. Jimerson & M. J. Furlong (Eds.), *The handbook of school violence and school safety: From research to practice.* Mahwah, NJ: Lawrence Erlbaum and Associates.

Cornell, D. G., & Brockenbrough, K. (2004). Identification of bullies and victims: A comparison of methods. *Journal of School Violence, 3,* 63–87.

Cornell, D. G., & Loper, A. B. (1998). Assessment of violence and other high-risk behaviors with a school survey. *School Psychology Review, 27,* 317–330.

Cornell, D. G., & Sheras, P. L. (2005). *Guidelines for responding to student threats of violence.* New York: Sopris-West Educational Services.

Cornell, D., Sheras, P., Kaplan, S., Levy-Elkon, A., McConville, D. McKnight, L., & Posey, J. (in press). Guidelines for responding to student threats of violence: Field test of a threat assessment approach. In M. J. Furlong, P. M. Kingery, & M. P. Bates (Eds.), *Appraisal and prediction of school violence: Context, issues, and methods.* Binghamton, NY: Haworth.

Cornell, D., Sheras, P. Kaplan, S., McConville, D., Douglass, J., Elkon, A., McKnight, L., Branson, C., & Cole, J. (2004). Guidelines for student threat assessment: Field-test findings. *School Psychology Review, 33,* 527–546.

Cornell, D., Staresina, L., & Benedek, E. (1989). Legal outcome of juveniles charged with homicide. In E. Benedek & D. Cornell (Eds.), *Juvenile homicide* (pp. 164–182). Washington, DC: American Psychiatric Press.

Cornell, D., & Williams, F. (2006). Student threat assessment as a strategy to reduce school violence. In S. R. Jimerson & M. J. Furlong (Eds.), *The handbook of school violence and school safety: From research to practice* (pp. 587–602). Mahwah, NJ: Lawrence Erlbaum and Associates.

Crick, N., & Grotpeter, J. (1995). Relational aggression, gender, and social-psychological adjustment. *Child Development*, 66, 710–722.

Cross, J., & Newman-Gonchar, R. (2004). Data quality in student risk behavior surveys and administrator training. *Journal of School Violence*, 3, 89–108.

Cullen, F., & Gendreau, P. (2001). From nothing works to what works: Changing professional ideology in the 21st century. *Prison Journal*, 81, 313–338.

Cunningham, R. (1994). Editor's deadline changes to D.A.R.E. piece stir trouble. *The Quill*, 82, 12–13.

D. A. R. E. (2005). The official D.A.R.E. Web site. *Drug Abuse Resistance Education*. Retrieved July 21, 2005, from http://www.dare.com/home/default.asp

Davis, A., & Porter, K. (1985). Dispute resolution, the fourth R. *Missouri Journal of Dispute Resolution*, 1, 121–139.

De, S. (2005). School shooter followed video game-like "script." *MSNBC News*. Retrieved July 21, 2005, from http://www.msnbc.msn.com/id/7288381/

Deardorff, N. R. (1958). Richard Clarke Cabot. In R. L. Schulyler & E. T. James (Eds.), *Dictionary of American biography* (Supplement 2, pp. 83–85). NY: Scribner's.

Debarbieux, E., & Blaya, C. (2002). *Violence in schools and public policies*. New York, NY: Elsevier.

DeVoe, J. F., Peter, K., Kaufman, P., Miller, A., Noonan, M., Snyder, T. D., & Baum, K. (2004). *Indicators of School crime and safety: 2004* (NCES 2005–002/NCJ205290). U.S. Departments of Education and Justice. Washington, DC: U.S. Government Printing Office.

Diaz, T. (1999). *Making a killing: The business of guns in America*. New York: The New Press.

Dickinson, T., & Crowe, A. (1997, December). Capacity building for juvenile substance abuse treatment. *Juvenile Justice Bulletin*. Washington, DC: Office of Juvenile Justice and Delinquency Prevention.

DiIulio, J. J. (1996). *Fill churches, not jails: Youth crime and "superpredators."* Testimony before the Senate Judiciary Committee, Subcommittee on Youth Violence. Retrieved August 30, 2005, from http://www.brookings.edu/index/scholarwork.htm?scholar=DiIulio*John*J.*Jr.

DiIulio, J. J. (1996). *How to stop the coming crime wave*. New York: Manhattan Institute.

Dill, K. E., & Dill, J. C. (1998). Video game violence: A review of the empirical literature. *Aggression and Violent Behavior*, 3, 407–428.

Dishion, T. J., McCord, J., & Poulin, F. (1999). When interventions harm: Peer groups and problem behavior. *American Psychologist*, 54, 755–764.

Docurama.com (2005). Arnold Shapiro. Retrieved April 12, 2005, from http://www.docurama.com/filmmakerdetail.html?filmmakerid=48

Dominick, J. R., & Greenberg, B. S. (1972). Attitudes toward violence: The interaction of television exposure, family attitudes, and social class. In G. A. Comstock & E. A.

Rubinstein (Eds.), *Television and social behavior: Television and adolescent aggressiveness: Vol. 3* (pp. 314–335). Washington, DC: Government Printing Office.

Dowdney, L. (2000). Annotation: Childhood bereavement following parental death. *Journal of Child Psychology and Psychiatry, 41,* 819–830.

DuBois D., & Silverthorn, N. (2005). Natural mentoring relationships and adolescent health: Evidence from a national study. *American Journal of Public Health, 95,* 518–524.

DuBois, D., Holloway, B., Valentine, J., & Cooper, H. (2002). Effectiveness of mentoring programs for youth: A meta-analytic review. *American Journal of Community Psychology, 30,* 157–197.

Dwyer, K., Osher, D., & Warger, C. (1998). *Early warning, timely response: A guide to safe schools.* Washington, DC: U.S. Department of Education.

Eccles, J. S., Gootman, J. A., National Research Council, & Institute of Medicine. (2002). *Community programs to promote youth development.* Washington, DC: National Academy Press.

Educational Testing Service. (2000). *The links among school discipline, student delinquency, and academic achievement.* Cited in D. L. Brunsma. *The school uniform movement and what it tells us about American education.* Lanham, MD: ScarecrowEducation.

Elias, M. J., Zins, J. E., Graczyk, P. A., & Weissberg, R. P. (2003). Implementation, sustainability, and scaling up of social-emotional and academic innovations in public schools. *School Psychology Review, 32,* 303–319.

Elliott, D. S. (1997). Editor's Introduction. In D. S. Elliott (Series Ed.), *Blueprints for violence prevention* (pp. xi–xxiii). Boulder, CO: Institute of Behavioral Science, University of Colorado.

Eron, L. (1999, May 18). *Effects of television violence on children.* Testimony before the U.S. Senate Committee on Commerce, Science, and Transportation. Retrieved August 30, 2005, from http://commerce.senate.gov/hearings/0518ero.pdf

Eron, L. D., Huesmann, L. R., Lefkowitz, M. M., & Walder, L. O. (1972). Does television violence cause aggression? *American Psychologist, 27,* 253–263.

Eron, L. D., Walder, L. O., & Lefkowitz, M. M. (1971). *Learning of aggression in children.* Boston: Little, Brown.

Eslea, M., Menesini, E., Morita, Y., O'Moore, M., Mora-Merchan, J., Pereira, B., & Smith, P. (2003). Friendship and loneliness among bullies and victims: Data from seven countries. *Aggressive Behavior, 30,* 71–83.

Espelage, D., & Swearer, S. (Eds.). (2004). *Bullying in American schools: A social-ecological perspective on prevention and intervention.* Mahwah, NJ: Lawrence Erlbaum and Associates.

Evans, D. L., Foa, E. B., Gur, R. E., Hendin, H., O'Brien, C. P., Seligman, M. E. P., Walsh, B. T. (2005). *Treatment and preventing adolescent mental health disorders: What we know and what we don't know.* New York: Oxford University Press.

Family Council on Drug Awareness. (2005). DARE: Good intentions, bad results. Retrieved July 21, 2005, from http://www.fcda.org/dare.html

Family Services Research Center. (1995). *Multisystemic therapy using home-based services: A clinically effective and cost effective strategy for treating serious clinical problems in youth.* Charleston, SC: Author.

Farrell, A. D., & Meyer, A. L. (1997). The effectiveness of a school-based curriculum for reducing violence among urban sixth-grade students. *American Journal of Public Health, 87*, 979–984.

Farrell, A. D., Meyer, A. L. & White, K. (2001). Evaluation of Responding in Peaceful and Positive Ways (RIPP): A school-based prevention program for reducing violence among urban adolescents. *Journal of Clinical Child Psychology, 30*, 451–463.

Federal Bureau of Investigation. (1984–2004). *Uniform crime reports: Crime in the United States.* Washington, DC: U.S. Government Printing Office.

Federal Bureau of Investigation. (1999). *The school shooter: A threat assessment perspective.* Quantico, VA: Author.

Federal Bureau of Investigation. (2004). *Uniform crime reports for the United States 2003.* Washington, DC: U.S. Government Printing Office.

Federal Interagency Forum on Child and Family Statistics. (2005). *America's children: Key national indicators of well-being 2005.* Washington DC: Author. Retrieved August 22, 2005, from http://www.childstats.gov/americaschildren/about.asp

Federal Trade Commission. (2000). *Marketing violent entertainment to children: A review of self-regulation and industry practices in the motion picture, music recording, and electronic game industries* Washington, DC: U.S. Government Printing Office.

Fein, R. A., & Vossekuil, F. (1998). *Protective intelligence and threat assessment investigations: A guide for state and local law enforcement officials.* Washington, DC: U.S. Secret Service.

Fein, R. A., & Vossekuil, F. (1999). Assassination in the United States: An operational study of recent assassins, attackers, and near-lethal approachers. *Journal of Forensic Sciences, 44*, 321–333.

Fein, R. A., Vossekuil, F., & Holden, G. A. (1995). Threat assessment: An approach to prevent targeted violence. *National Institute of Justice: Research in Action*, 1–7 (NCJ 155000), Available http://www.secretservice.gov/ntac.htm

Fein, R. A., Vossekuil, F., Pollack, W. S., Borum, R., Modzeleski, W., & Reddy, M. (2002). *Threat assessment in schools: A guide to managing threatening situations and to creating safe school climates.* Washington, DC: U.S. Secret Service and U.S. Department of Education.

Finckenauer, J. (1982). *Scared Straight! and the panacea phenomenon.* Englewood Cliffs, NJ: Prentice-Hall.

Food Research and Action Center. (2005). *National school lunch program.* Retrieved August 22, 2005, from http://www.frac.org/html/federal_food_programs/programs/nslp.html

Foster, S. E., Vaughan, R. D., Foster, W. H., & Califano, J. A. (2003). Alcohol consumption and expenditures for underage drinking and adult excessive drinking. *Journal of the American Medical Association, 26*, 989–995.

Fox, C., Roth, W. D., & Newman, K. (2003). A deadly partnership: Lethal violence in an Arkansas middle school. In M. H. Moore, C. V. Petrie, A. A. Braga, & B. L. McLaughlin (Eds.) *Deadly lessons: Understanding lethal school violence* (pp. 132–162). Washington, DC: The National Academies Press.

Freedman, J. (1984). Effects of television violence on aggressiveness. *Psychological Bulletin, 96*, 227–246.

Freedman, J. (2002). *Media violence and its effect on aggression: Assessing the scientific evidence.* Toronto: University of Toronto Press.

Freedman, M. (1993). Fervor with infrastructure: Making the most of the mentoring movement. *Equity and Choice*, 9, 21–26.

Furlong, M. J., Bates, M. P., & Smith, D. C. (2001). Predicting school weapon possession: A secondary analysis of the Youth Risk Behavior Surveillance Survey. *Psychology in the Schools*, 38, 127–139.

Gadow, K. & Sprafkin, J. (1987). Effects of viewing high versus low aggressive cartoons on emotionally disturbed children. *Journal of Pediatric Psychology*, 12, 413–427.

Gallup, G., Jr. (1999, May 20). Many teens report copycat-related problems at school in wake of Littleton shooting: Nearly half say their school has violent or violence-prone groups. Retrieved April 2, 2005, from http://www.gallup.com/poll/content/login .aspx?ci=3838

Garrity, C., Jens, K., Porter, W., Sager, N., & Short-Camilli, C. (1994). *Bully-proofing your school.* Longmont, CO: Sopris West.

Gentile, D. A. (Ed.) (2003). *Media violence and children: A complete guide for parents and professionals.* Westport, CT: Praeger.

Gentile, D. A., Lynch, P. J., Linder, J. R., & Walsh, D. A. (2004) The effects of violent video game habits on adolescent hostility, aggressive behaviors, and school performance. *Journal of Adolescence*, 27, 5–22.

Gerbner, G., Gross, L., Morgan, M., Signorielli, N., & Jackson-Beeck, M. (1979). The demonstration of power: Violence Profile No. 10. *Journal of Communication*, 29, 177–195.

Glass, S. (1997, March 3). Don't you DARE. *The New Republic*, 18.

Glass, S. (1998, March 5). Truth and D.A.R.E.: The nation's most prestigious drug prevention program for kids is a failure. Why don't you know this? *Rolling Stone*, 42–43.

Goodlad, J. I., & McMannon, T. J. (Eds.) (1997). *The public purpose of education and schooling.* San Franciso: Jossey-Bass, Inc.

Gottfredson, D. C. (1997). School-based crime prevention. In L. W. Sherman, D. Gottfredson, D. MacKenzie, J. Eck, P. Reuter, & S. Bushway (Eds.) *Preventing crime: What works, what doesn't, what's promising. A report to the United States Congress* (NCJ 171676, pp. 125–182). Washington, DC: National Institute of Justice.

Gottfredson D. C., & Gottfredson, G. D. (2002) Quality of school-based prevention programs: results from a national survey. *Journal of Research in Crime and Delinquency*, 39, 3–35.

Greenberg, D. F. (1977). The correctional effects of corrections: A survey of evaluations. In D. F. Greenberg (Eds.), *Corrections and Punishment* (pp. 111–148). Beverly Hills, CA: Sage.

Greenberg, M. T. (2004). Current and future challenges in school-based prevention: The researcher perspective. *Prevention Science*, 5, 5–13.

Greenberg, M. T., Kusché C. A., Cook, E. T., & Quamma, J. P. (1995). Promoting emotional competence in school-aged children: The effects of the PATHS curriculum. *Development & Psychopathology*, 7, 117–136.

Greenberg, M. T., Kusché C. A., & Mihalic, S. F. (1998). *Blueprints for violence prevention, book ten: Promoting alternative thinking stategies (PATHS).* Boulder, CO: Center for the Study and Prevention of Violence.

Greenberg, M. T., Weissberg, R. P., O'Brien, M. U., Zins, J. E., Fredericks, L., Resnik, H., & Elias, M. J. (2003). Enhancing school-based prevention and youth development through coordinated social, emotional, and academic learning. *American Psychologist*, 58, 466–474.

Greene, J. C. & Caracelli, V. J. (Eds.). (1997). *Advances in mixed-method evaluation: The challenges and benefits of integrating diverse paradigms.* New Directions for Program Evaluation, No. 74, San Francisco: Jossey-Bass.

Grossman, D. C., Neckerman, H. J., Koepsell, T. D., Liu, P. Y., Asher, K. N., Beland, K., Frey, K., and Rivara, F. P. (1997). Effectiveness of a violence prevention curriculum among children in elementary school: A randomized controlled trial. *Journal of the American Medical Association*, 277, 1605–1611.

Grossman, D., & DeGaetano, G. (1999). *Stop teaching our kids to kill: A call to action against TV, movie & video game violence.* New York: Crown Publishers.

Grossman, J. B., & Rhodes, J. E. (2002). The test of time: Predictors and effects of duration in youth mentoring relationships. *American Journal of Community Psychology*, 30, 199–219.

Grossman, J. B., & Tierney, J. P. (1998). Does mentoring work? An impact study of the Big Brothers Big Sisters Program. *Evaluation Review*, 22, 403–426.

Haga, C. (2005, April 12). Relatives: Did meds play a role? *Star Tribune*. Retrieved July 21, 2005, from http://www.startribune.com/stories/462/5312255.html

Hallahan, D., & Kauffman, J. (2003). *Exceptional learners: Introduction to special education.* New York: Allyn and Bacon.

Harding, D., Mehta, J., & Newman, K. (2003). No exit: Mental illness, marginality, and school violence in West Paducah, Kentucky. In M. H. Moore, C. V. Petrie, A. A. Braga, & B. L. McLaughlin (Eds.) *Deadly lessons: Understanding lethal school violence* (pp. 132–162). Washington, DC: The National Academies Press.

Hardy, M. S. (2002). Behavior-oriented approaches to reducing youth gun violence. *Future of Children*, 12, 101–115.

Hardy, M. S., Armstrong, F. D., Martin, B. L., & Strawn, K. N. (1996). A firearm safety program for children: They just can't say no. *Journal of Developmental and Behavioral Pediatrics*, 17, 216–221.

Hart, D. G. (1994). The church's mission: Great commission or great society. Modern Reformation Magazine, 3. Retrieved August 1, 2005, from http://www.modernreformation.org/dgh94greatcom.htm

Hart, H. L. A., & Honoré, T. (1985). *Causation in the law* (2nd edition). Oxford: Clarendon Press.

Hawker, D., & Boulton, M. (2000). Twenty years' research on peer victimization and psychosocial maladjustment: A meta-analytic review of cross-sectional studies. *Journal of Child Psychology & Psychiatry & Allied Disciplines*, 41, 441–455.

Hayeslip, D. W. (1996). Conclusion: The future of boot camps. In D. L. MacKenzie & E. E. Heber (Eds.). *National Institute of Justice Report: Correctional boot camps: A tough intermediate sanction* (NCJ 157639). Washington, DC: U.S. Department of Justice. Retrieved July 22, 2005, from http://www.kci.org/publication/bootcamp/docs/nij/Correctional_Boot_Camps/chpt19.htm

Heath, L., Bresolin, L. B., & Rinaldi, R. C. (1989). Effects of media violence on children. *Archives of General Psychiatry*, 46, 376–379.

Heller, M. S., & Polsky, S. (1976). *Studies in violence and television.* New York: American Broadcasting Companies.

Henggeler, S. W., Melton, G. B., Brondino, M. J., Scherer, D. G., & Hanley, J. H. (1997). Multisystemic therapy with violent and chronic juvenile offenders and their families: The role of treatment fidelity in successful dissemination. *Journal of Consulting and Clinical Psychology, 65,* 821–833.

Henggeler, S. W., Melton, G. B., Smith, L. A., Schoenwald, S. K., & Hanley, J. H. (1993). Family preservation using multisystemic treatment: Long-term follow-up to a clinical trial with serious juvenile offenders. *Journal of Child and Family Studies, 2,* 283–293.

Henggeler, S. W., & Sheidow, A. J. (2003). Conduct disorder and delinquency. *Journal of Marital And Family Therapy, 29,* 505–522.

Henggeler, S. W., & Shoenwald, S. K. (1994). Boot camps for juvenile offenders: Just say no. *Journal of Child and Family Studies, 3,* 243–248.

Henggeler, S. W., Shoenwald, S. K., Borduin, C. M., Rowland, M. D., & Cunningham, P. B. (1998). *Multisystemic treatment of antisocial behavior in children and adolescents.* New York: The Guilford Press.

Honig, A. S. (2002). *Secure relationships: Nurturing infant/toddler attachment in early care settings.* Washington, DC: National Association for the Education of Young Children.

Horne, A. M., Bartolomucci, C. L., Newman-Carlson, D. (2003). *Bully Busters: A teacher's manual for helping bullies, victims, and bystanders* (Grades K–5). Champaign, IL: Research Press.

Houston, P. (2003). AASA offers NCLB facts to counter House Republican leadership fiction. *NCLB News.* Retrieved August 29, 2005, from http://www.susanohanian.org/show_nclb_news.html?id=233

Howard, K. A., Flora, J., & Griffin, M. (1999). Violence-prevention programs in schools: State of the science and implications for future research. *Applied & Preventive Psychology, 8,* 197–215.

Howell, J. C. (Ed.). *Guide for implementing the comprehensive strategy for serious, violent, and chronic juvenile offenders* (NCJ 153681). Washington, DC: U.S. Department of Justice, Office of Justice Programs, Office of Juvenile Justice and Delinquency Prevention.

Huesmann, L. R. (1986). Psychological processes promoting the relation between exposure to media violence and aggressive behavior by the viewer. *Journal of Social Issues, 42,* 15–139.

Huesmann, L. R. (Ed.). (1994). *Aggressive behavior: Current perspectives.* New York: Plenum.

Huesmann, L. R., & Eron, L. D. (2001). Solid facts about media violence. *The Bulletin of the International Society for Research on Aggression, 23,* 5–6.

Huesmann, L. R., & Eron, L.D. (Eds.) (1986). *Television and the aggressive child: A cross-national comparison.* Hillsdale, NJ: Lawrence Erlbaum and Associates.

Huesmann, L. R., Eron, L. D., Klein, R., Brice, P., & Fischer, P. (1983). Mitigating the imitation of aggressive behaviors by children's attitudes about media violence. *Journal of Personality and Social Psychology, 44,* 899–910.

Huesmann, L. R., Moise-Titus, J, Podolski, C., Eron, L. D. (2003). Longitudinal relations between children's exposure to TV violence and their aggressive and violent behavior in young adulthood: 1977–1992. *Developmental Psychology, 39,* 201–221.

Huesmann, L. R., & Taylor, L. D. (2003). The case against the case against media violence. In D. A. Gentile (Ed.), *Media violence and children: A complete guide for parents and professionals* (pp. 107–130). Westport, CT: Praeger.

Huizinga, D., & Elliott, D. (1986). Reassessing the reliability and validity of self-report delinquency measures. *Journal of Quantitative Criminology, 2*, 293–327.

Huston, A. C., Donnerstein, E., Fairchild, H., Feshbach, N. D., Katz, P. A., Murray, J. P., Rubinstein, E. A., Wilcox, B. L., & Zuckerman, D. (1992). *Big world, small screen: The role of television in American society*. Lincoln: University of Nebraska Press.

Institute for Children, Youth, & Families. (2003). *Zero tolerance policies and their impact on students*. East Lansing: Institute for Children, Youth, & Families, Michigan State University.

Institute for Social Research, Monitoring the Future, Ann Arbor: University of Michigan, Survey Research Center, 1997

Irwin, A. R., & Gross, A. M. (1995). Cognitive tempo, violent video games, and aggressive behavior in young boys. *Journal of Family Violence, 10*, 337–350.

Jacob, S., & Hartshorne, T. (2003). Ethics and law for school psychologists (4th edition). Hoboken, NJ: Wiley & Sons.

Johnson, D. W., & Johnson, R. T. (1996). Conflict resolution and peer mediation programs in elementary and secondary schools: A review of the research. *Review of Educational Research, 66*, 459–506.

Johnson, D. W., & Johnson, R. T. (2004). Implementing the "Teaching Students to be Peacemakers Program." *Theory into Practice, 43*, 68–79.

Johnson, J. D., Jackson, L. A., & Gatto, L. (1995). Violent attitudes and deferred academic aspirations: Deleterious effects of exposure to rap music. *Basic and Applied Social Psychology, 16*, 27–41.

Johnson, R. T., & Johnson, D. W. (2002). Teaching students to be peacemakers: A meta-analysis. *Journal of Research in Education. 12*, 25–39.

Johnston, L. D., O'Malley, P. M., & Bachman, J. G. (2003). *Monitoring the Future national results on adolescent drug use: Overview of key findings, 2002*. (NIH Publication No. 03–5374). Bethesda, MD: National Institute on Drug Abuse.

Joint statement on the impact of entertainment violence on children. Congressional Public Health Summit, July 26, 2000. Downloaded 12–4–04 from http://www.aap.org/advocacy/release/jstmtevc.htm

Jones, M. B. & Offord, D. R. (1989). Reduction of anti-social behavior in poor children by nonschool skill development. *Journal of Child Psychology and Psychiatry and Allied Disciplines, 30*, 737–750.

Josephson, W. L. (1987). Television violence and children's aggression: Testing the priming, social script, and disinhibition prediction. *Journal of Personality and Social Psychology, 53*, 882–890.

Juvonen, J., Nishina, A., & Graham, S. (2001). Self-views versus peer perceptions of victim status among early adolescents. In J. Juvonen & S. Graham (Eds.), *Peer harassment in school: A plight of the vulnerable and victimized* (pp. 105–124). New York: Guilford Press.

Kalishman, A. (2003, April). *D.A.R.E. policy fact sheet*. Drug Policy Alliance. Retrieved July 22, 2005, from http://www.drugpolicy.org/library/factsheets/dare/index.cfm

Kam, C., Greenberg, M. T., & Walls, C. T. (2003). Examining the role of implementation quality in school-based prevention using the PATHS curriculum. *Prevention Science*, 4, 55–63.

Kanof, M. E. (2003). *Youth illicit drug use prevention: DARE long-term evaluations and federal efforts to identify effective programs*. Washington, DC: General Accounting Office.

Kao, G., & Thompson, J. S. (2003). Racial and ethnic stratification in educational achievement and attainment. *Annual Review of Sociology*, 29, 417–442.

Karter, M. J. (2004). *Fire loss in the United States during 2003*. Quincy (MA): National Fire Protection Association, Fire Analysis and Research Division.

Kauffman, J., & Hallahan, D. (2005). *Special education: What it is and why we need it*. New York: Pearson.

Kazdin, A. E. (2005). *Parent management training: Treatment for oppositional, aggressive, and antisocial behavior in children and adolescents*. New York: Oxford University Press.

Kazdin, A. E., Siegal, T. C., & Bass, D. (1992). Cognitive problem-solving skills training and parent management training in the treatment of antisocial behavior in children. *Journal of Consulting and Clinical Psychology*, 60, 733–747.

Kennedy, D. M., Braga, A. A., & Piehl, A. M. (2001). Developing and implementing Operation Ceasefire. In Reducing gun violence: The Boston Gun Project's Operation Ceasefire. National Institute of Justice. Washington, DC: U. S. Department of Justice.

Kessler, R. & Walters, E. E. (1998). Epidemiology of DSM-III-R major depression and minor depression among adolescents and young adults in the National Comorbidity Survey. *Depression and Anxiety*, 7, 3–15.

Kim, L. (2002, April 30). Grieving Germany asks: Why? *The Christian Scientist Monitor*. Retrieved August 30, 2005, from http://dorm.tunkeymicket.com/spcom111/controversy/germany_why.html

Kirk, M., Navasky, M., O'Connor, K. (Producers). (2000, January 18). *The killer at Thurstone High*. [Transcript of television broadcast]. New York and Washington, DC: Public Broadcasting Service. Retrieved August 28, 2005, from http://www.pbs.org/wgbh/pages/frontline/shows/kinkel/etc/script.html

Kirsh, S. J. (1998). Seeing the world through Mortal Kombat-colored glasses: Violent video games and the development of a short-term hostile attribution bias. *Childhood*, 5, 177–184.

Klammer, L. (2000). Guns in school: What can you do? *Youth Update*. Retrieved August 11, 2005, from http://www.americancatholic.org/Newsletters/YU/ay0700.asp

Klein, N. C., Alexander, J. F., & Parsons, B. V. (1977). Impact of family systems intervention on recidivism and sibling delinquency: A model of primary prevention and program evaluation. *Journal of Consulting and Clinical Psychology*, 45, 469–474.

Koch Crime Institute. (2000). *Juvenile boot camps and military structured programs*. Topeka, KS: Author. Retrieved April 9, 2005, from http://www.kci.org/publication/bootcamp/prerelease.htm

Komro, K., Perry, C., Munson, K., Stigler, M., & Farbakhsh, K. (2004). Reliability and validity of self-report measures to evaluate drug and violence prevention programs. *Journal of Child & Adolescent Substance Abuse*, 13, 17–51.

Komro, K., Perry, C., Veblen-Mortenson, S., Stigler, M., Bosma, L., Munson, K., & Farbakhsh, K. (2004). Violence-related outcomes of the D.A.R.E. Plus Project. *Health Education & Behavior*, 31, 335–354.

Ksdk.com. (2005). 5 year old handcuffed and arrested at school. Retrieved August 5, 2005, from http://www.ksdk.com/news/news_article.aspx?storyid=76879

Kusché C. A., & Greenberg, M. T. (1994). *The PATHS (Promoting Alternative Thinking Strategies) curriculum.* Seattle, WA: Developmental Research and Programs.

Ladd, G. W., & Kochenderfer-Ladd, B. (2002). Identifying victims of peer aggression from early to middle childhood: Analysis of cross-informant data from concordance, estimation of relational adjustment, prevalence of victimization, and characteristics of identified victims. *Psychological Assessment, 14,* 74–96.

Lally, J. R., Mangione, P. L., & Honig, A. S. (1989). The Syracuse University Family Development Research Program: Long-range impact of an early intervention with low income children and their families. In D. Powell (Ed.), *Parent education as early childhood intervention: Emerging directions in theory, research, and practice* (pp. 79–104). Norwood, NJ: Ablex.

Law Enforcement News. (1999, December 15/31). New twists in the drug debate. Retrieved July 22, 2005, from http://www.lib.jjay.cuny.edu/len/1999/12.30/wrinkles.html

Lawton, M. (1993, August 4). Cabinet heads kick off coordinated effort to curb youth violence. *Education Week, 12* (40), 21.

Leary, W. E. (1990, June 8). Gloomy report on the health of teen-agers. *The New York Times.*

Leff, S., Kupersmidt, J., Patterson, C., & Power, T. (1999). Factors influencing teacher identification of peer bullies and victims. *School Psychology Review, 28,* 505–517.

Leland, J. (1995, December 11). Violence, reel to real. *Newsweek,* 46–48.

Levin, C. (1999, May 13). *Statement of Senator Carl Levin on Juvenile Justice Bill and Youth Access to Firearms.* Press release. Retrieved August 30, 2005, from http://levin.senate .gov/newsroom/release.cfm?id=209429

Levine, F. J., & Rosich, K. J. (1996). *Social causes of violence: Crafting a science agenda.* Washington, DC: American Sociological Association.

Lewin, T. (1997, March 12). School Codes Without Mercy Snare Pupils Without Malice. *New York Times.*

Leyens, J. P., Camino, L., Parke, R. D., & Berkowitz, L. (1975). Effects of movie violence on aggression in a field setting as a function of group dominance and cohesion. *Journal of Personality and Social Psychology, 32,* 346–360.

Leyens, J-P., & Parke, R. D. (1975). Aggressive slides can induce a weapons effect. *European Journal of Social Psychology, 5,* 229–236.

LH Research. (1993). *A survey of experiences, perceptions and apprehensions about guns among young people in America.* New York: Author.

Limber, S., & Small, M. (2003). State laws and policies to address bullying in schools. *School Psychology Review, 32,* 445–455.

Lipsey, M. & Wilson, S. (2001). *Practical meta-analysis.* Thousand Oaks, CA: Sage.

Local6.com News. (2005). Students arrested over 'violent' stick figure drawings. Retrieved August 5, 2005, from http://www.local6.com/news/4130302/detail.html

Lochman, J. D. (2004). Contextual factors in risk and prevention research. Merrill-Palmer Quarterly-Journal of Developmental Psychology, 50, 311–325.

Lochman, J. E. (1992). Cognitive-behavioral intervention with aggressive boys: Three-year follow-up and preventive efforts. *Journal of Consulting and Clinical Psychology, 60,* 426–432.

Los Angeles Unified School District Personnel Commission. (2003). *Update on study of school-site administrative and clerical workload.* Retrieved August 21, 2005, from http://www.lausd.k12.ca.us/lausd/committees/hrc/pdf6/admiworkload.pdf

Louwagie, P., Burcum, J., & Collins, T. (2005, April 13). Guard's family member may have known of Weise's plan. *Star Tribune.*

Ludwig, J., & Cook, P. J. (Eds.) (2003). *Evaluating gun policy: Effects on crime and violence.* Washington, DC: The Brookings Institution.

Lupton-Smith, H. (2004). Peer mediation. In E. R. Gerler, Jr. (Ed.) *Handbook of school violence* (pp. 137–164). Binghamton, NY: Haworth Press.

Lynam, D. R., Milich, R., Zimmerman, R., Novak, S. P., Logan, T. K., Martin, C., Leukefeld, C., & Clayton, R. (1999). Project DARE: No effects at 10-year follow-up. *Journal of Consulting & Clinical Psychology, 67,* 590–593.

Lytton, H. (2000). Toward a model of family-environmental and child-biological influences on development, *Developmental Review, 20.* 150–179

MacKenzie, D. L. (1994). Results of a multisite study of boot camp prisons. *Federal Probation, 58,* 60–66.

MacKenzie, D., & Souryal, C. (1996). Multisite study of correctional boot camps. In D. L. MacKenzie & E. E. Hebert (Eds.) *Correctional boot camps: A tough intermediate sanction.* National Institute of Justice. NCJ 157639

Mager, W., Milich, R., Harris, M. J., & Howard, A. (2005). Intervention groups for adolescents with conduct problems: Is aggregation harmful or helpful? *Journal of Abnormal Child Psychology, 33,* 349–362.

Maginnis, R. (1995). *Violence in the schoolhouse: At ten year update.* Washington, DC: Family Research Council.

Manski, C., Pepper, J, & Petrie, C. (Eds.). (2001). *Informing America's policy on illegal drugs: What we don't know keeps hurting us.* Washington, DC: National Academy Press.

Martinson, R. (1974). What works? Questions and answers about prison reform. *The Public Interest, 35,* 22–54.

Mathis, W. J. (2003, May). No Child Left Behind: Costs and benefits. *Phi Delta Kappan,* 679–686.

May, J. (1999, April 23). Michigan school bombing in 1927 was even more deadly. *Detroit Free Press.* Retrieved March 13, 2005, from http://www.freep.com/news/nw/qbath23.htm

Mayer, G. R. (1995). Preventing antisocial behavior in the schools. *Journal of Applied Behavior Analysis, 28,* 467–478.

McCord, J. (1992). The Cambridge-Somerville Study: A pioneering longitudinal-experimental study of delinquency prevention. In J McCord and R.E. Tremblay (Eds.). *Preventing antisocial behavior: Interventions from birth through adolescence* (pp. 196–208). Guilford Press: NY.

McDonald, L., Billingham, S., Conrad, T., Morgan, A., Nina, O., & Payton, E. (1997). Families and Schools Together (FAST). *Families in Society, 78,* 140–155.

McLearn, K. T., Colasanto, D., & Schoen, C. (1998). Mentoring matters: A national survey of adults mentoring young people. In J. B. Grossman (Ed.). *Contemporary issues in mentoring* (pp. 67–83). Philadelphia, PA: Public/Private Ventures.

McLeod, J. M., Atkin, C. K., & Chaffee, S. H. (1972). Adolescents, parents, and television use: Adolescent self-report measures from Maryland and Wisconsin samples. In G. A.

Comstock & E. A. Rubinstein (Eds.), *Television and social behavior: Television and adolescent aggressiveness: Vol. 3* (pp. 173–239). Washington, DC: Government Printing Office.

McMahon, S. D., Washburn, J., Felix, E. D., Yakin, J., & Childrey, G. (2000). Violence prevention: Program effects on urban preschool and kindergarten children. *Applied and Preventive Psychology*, 9, 271–281.

Medved, M. (1995). Hollywood's 3 big lies. *Reader's Digest*, 147, 155–159.

Melton, G. B., Limber, S. P., Cunningham, P., Osgood, D. W., Chambers, J., Flerx, V., Henggeler, S., & Nation, M. (1998). *Violence among rural youth*. Final report to the Office of Juvenile Justice and Delinquency Prevention.

Merritt, R., & Brown, B. (2002). *No easy answers: The truth behind the murders at Columbine*. New York: Lantern Books.

Meyer, A., L., Farrell, A. D., Northup, W., Kung, E., & Plybon, L. (2000). *Promoting nonviolence in early adolescence*. New York: Kluwer Academic/Plenum Press.

Milavski, J. R., Kessler, R., Stipp, H., Rubens, W. S. (1982). Television and aggression: Results of a panel study. In D. Pearl, L. Bouthilet, & J. Lazar (Eds.) *Television and behavior: Ten years of scientific progress and implications for the eighties, Vol. 2* (pp. 138–157). Washington, DC: U.S. Government Printing Office.

Miller, D. (2001, October 19). DARE reinvents itself—with help from its social-scientist critics. *Chronicle of Higher Education*.

Million, J. (1996). Do the clothes make the student? School uniforms may be coming your way. *Communicator, PR Primer*, pp. 5–6. Retrieved June 2, 2005, from http://www.naesp.org/ContentLoad.do?contentId=266

Moeller, T. G. (2001). *Youth aggression and violence: A psychological approach*. Mahwah, New Jersey: Lawrence Erlbaum Associates.

Molgaard, V. M., & Spoth, R. (2001). Strengthening Families Program for young adolescents: Overview and outcomes. In S. Pfeiffer & L. Reddy (Eds.) *Innovative mental health programs for children* (pp. 15–29). Binghamtom, NY: The Haworth Press.

Molgaard, V. M., Spoth, R., & Redmond, C. (2000). Competency training: The Strengthening Families Program for Parents and Youth 10–14. *Juvenile Justice Bulletin* (NCJ 182208). Washington, DC: U.S. Department of Justice, Office of Juvenile Justice and Delinquency Prevention.

Moore, M. H. Petrie, C. V., Braga, A. A., & McLaughlin, B. L. (2003). *Deadly lessons: Understanding lethal school violence*. Washington, DC: The National Academies Press.

Morrow, K. V., & Styles, M. B. (1995). Building relationships with youth in program settings: A study of Big Brothers/Big Sisters. Philadelphia: Public/Private Ventures.

Mothers Against Drunk Driving. (2005). *Stats and resources*. Retrieved July 22, 2005, from http://www.madd.org/stats

Mulvey, E., Steinberg, L., Fagan, J., Cauffman, E., Piquero, A., Chassin, L., Knight, G., Brame, R., Schubert, C., Hecker, T., Losoya, S. (2004). Theory and research on desistance from antisocial activity among serious adolescent offenders. *Youth Violence and Juvenile Justice*, 2, 213–236.

Mulvey, E. P., & Cauffman, E. (2001). The inherent limits of predicting school violence. *American Psychologist*, 56, 797–802.

Mumola, C. J. (2000). *Incarcerated parents and their children. (NCJ 182335). Bureau of Justice Statistics Special Report*. Washington, DC: U.S. Dept. of Justice.

Munoz, R. F., Mrazek, P. J., & Haggerty, R. J. (1996). Institute of Medicine Report on Prevention of Mental Disorders: Summary and commentary. *American Psychologist*, 51, 1116–1122.

Munthe, E. (1989). Bullying in Scandinavia. In E. Roland & E. Munthe (Eds). *Bullying an international perspective*. London: David Fulton Publishers.

Nabuzoka, D. (2003). Teacher ratings and peer nominations of bullying and other behaviour of children with and without learning difficulties. *Educational Psychology*, 23, 307–321.

Nagy, J., & Danitz, T. (2000). *Parental fears heightened by Columbine, poll shows*. Retrieved March 19, 2005, from http://www.stateline.org/live/ViewPage.action?siteNodeId=136&languageId=1&contentId=13994

Nansel, T., Overpeck, M., Pilla, R., Ruan, W., Simons-Morton, B., & Scheidt, P. (2001). Bullying behaviors among US youth: Prevalence and association with psychosocial adjustment. *American Medical Association*, 285, 2094–2100.

Nathanson, A. I. (1999). Identifying and explaining the relationship between parental mediation and children's aggression. *Communication Research*, 26, 124–143.

National Association of Elementary School Principals. (2005). *NAESP fact sheet on the principal shortage*. Retrieved August 21, 2005, from http://www.naesp.org/Content Load.do?contentId=1097&pageNum=2

National Center for Education Statistics. (1995). *The condition of education 1995* (NCES 95273). Washington, DC: U.S. Department of Education, Office of Educational Research and Improvement.

National Center for Education Statistics. (2000). *Digest of education statistics 2000*. Washington, DC: U.S. Department of Education, Office of Educational Research and Improvement.

National Center for Education Statistics. (2002). Table 99. Public secondary schools, by grade span and average school size, by state: 2001–01. *Digest of education statistics tables and figures*. Retrieved August 26, 2005, from http://nces.ed.gov/programs/digest/d02/dt099.asp

National Center for Health Statistics. (2004). *Health, United States, 2004*. Washington, DC: U.S. Government Printing Office. Retrieved August 6, 2005, from http://www.cdc.gov/nchs/data/hus/hus04trend.pdf#pref

National Center for Injury Prevention and Control. (2005). *Child passenger safety: Fact sheet*. Retrieved August 23, 2005, from http://www.cdc.gov/ncipc/factsheets/childpas.htm

National Center for Injury Prevention and Control. (2005). *WISQARS leading causes of death reports 1999–2002*. Retrieved August 6, 2005, from http://webappa.cdc.gov/sasweb/ncipc/leadcaus10.html

National Clearinghouse on Child Abuse and Neglect Information. (2005). Child maltreatment 2003: Summary of key findings. Retrieved August 23, 2005, from http://nccanch.acf.hhs.gov/pubs/factsheets/canstats.cfm

National Crime Prevention Council. (1995). *Strategy: Gun-Free School Zones*. http://www.ncpc.org/ncpc/ncpc/?pg=2088–10796

National Highway Traffic Safety Administration. (2002). *Traffic safety facts 2002. Young drivers*. Retrieved July 22, 2005, from http://www-nrd.nhtsa.dot.gov/pdf/nrd—30/NCSA/TSF2002/2002ydrfacts.pdf

National Institute of Mental Health (1982). *Television and behaviour: Ten years of scientific progress and implications for the eighties (Vol. 1), Summary report*. Washington, DC: United States Government Printing Office.

National Institutes of Health. (1998). Diagnosis and treatment of attention deficit hyper-activity disorder. *NIH Consensus Statement*, 16.

National Research Council. (2005). *Firearms and violence: A critical review*. Washington, DC: The National Academies Press.

National Rifle Association (n.d.). *What is the Eddie Eagle Gunsafe Program?* Fairfax, VA: National Rifle Association. Retrieved February 5, 2005 from http://www.nrahq.org/safety/eddie

National School Boards Association (1993). *Violence in the schools: How America's school boards are safeguarding your children*. Alexandria, VA: Author.

National School Safety Center (1998). *Checklist of characteristics of youths who have caused school-associated violent deaths*. Westlake Village, CA. Retrieved March 1, 2005 from http://www.nssc1.org

National School Safety Center (2005). *School associated violent deaths*. Westlake Village, CA. Retrieved March 1, 2005 from http://www.nssc1.org

National Television Violence Study, Vol. 3 (1998). Thousand Oaks, CA: Sage Publications.

New Freedom Commission on Mental Health. (2003). *Achieving the promise: Transforming mental health care in America*. Rockville, MD: Author.

Noll, K., & Carter, J. (1998). *Taking the bully by the horns*. Unicorn Press.

Oatis, P. J., Fenn Buderer, N. M., Cummings, P., & Fleitz, R. (1999). Pediatric practice based evaluation of the Steps to Prevention Firearm Injury program. *Injury Prevention*, 5, 48–52.

Oetting, E., Beauvais, F., Edwards, R., & Waters, M. (1984). *The drug and alcohol assessment system. Book II: Instrument development, reliability, and validity*. Rocky Mountain Behavioral Sciences Institute. Fort Collins, CO.

Olweus, D. (1991). Bully/victim problems among schoolchildren: Basic facts and effects of a school based intervention program. In D. Pepler & K. Rubin (Eds.), *The development and treatment of childhood aggression* (pp. 411–448). Hillsdale, NJ: Lawrence Erlbaum and Associates.

Olweus, D. (1993). *Bullying in schools: What we know and what we can do*. Oxford: Blackwell Publishers.

Olweus, D. (1996). *The Revised Olweus Bully/Victim Questionnaire*. Bergen, Norway: Mimeo, Research Center for Health Promotion (HEMIL), University of Bergen.

Olweus, D. (1999). Norway. In P. K. Smith, Y. Morita, J. Junger-Tas, D. Olweus, R. Catalano, & P. Slee (Eds.), *The nature of school bullying: A cross-national perspective* (pp. 28–48). New York: Routledge.

Olweus, D. (2002). *General information about the Revised Olweus Bully/Victim Questionnaire, PC program and teacher handbook* (pp. 1–12). Bergen, Norway: Mimeo, Research Center for Health Promotion (HEMIL), University of Bergen.

Olweus, D., Limber, S., & Mihalic, S. F. (1999). *Blueprints for violence prevention, book nine: Bullying Prevention Program*. Boulder, CO: Center for the Study and Prevention of Violence.

O'Neill, B. (1994b). The invention of the school discipline lists. *School Administrator*, 51, 8–11.

O'Neill, B. (1994a). The history of a hoax. *The New York Times Magazine*, March 6, 1994, pp. 46–49.

Osher, D., Dwyer, K., & Jackson, S. (2004). *Safe, supportive and successful schools: Step by step*. Longmont, CO: Sopris West.

O'Toole, M. E. (2000). *The school shooter: A threat assessment perspective*. Quantico, VA: Federal Bureau of Investigation.

Page, D., & O'Neal, E. (1977). "Weapons effect" without demand characteristics. *Psychological Reports*, 41, 29–30.

Paik, H., & Comstock, G. (1994). The effects of television violence on antisocial behavior: A meta-analysis. *Communication research*, 21, 516–546.

Patterson, G. R., Reid, J. B., & Dishion, T. J. (1992). *Antisocial boys: A social interactional approach*. Eugene, OR: Castalia.

Pawlak, D. (n.d.). *Just another summer day: The Bath school disaster*. Retrieved March 13, 2005, from http://www.themediadrome.com/content/articles/history_articles/disaster_in_bath.htm

Pellegrini, A. D., Bartini, M., & Brooks, F. (1999). School bullies, victims, and aggressive victims: Factors relating to group affiliation and victimization in early adolescence. *Journal of Educational Psychology*, 91, 216–224.

Pepler, D. J., Craig, W. M., Ziegler, S., & Charach, A. (1994). An evaluation of an anti-bullying intervention in Toronto schools. *Canadian Journal of Community Mental Health*, 13, 95–110.

Perry, C., Komro, K., Veblen-Mortenson, S., Bosma, L., Farbakhsh, K., Munson, K., Stigler, M., & Lytle, L. (2003). A randomized controlled trial of the middle and junior high school D.A.R.E. and D.A.R.E. Plus programs. *Archives of Pediatric and Adolescent Medicine*, 157, 178–184.

Perry, D., Kusel, S., & Perry, L. (1988). Victims of peer aggression. *Developmental Psychology*, 24, 807–814.

Peters, M., Thomas, D., and Zamberlan, C. (1997). *Boot camps for juvenile offenders*. Washington, DC: U.S. Office of Juvenile Justice and Delinquency Prevention.

Peterson, D. L., & Pfost, K. S. (1989). Influence of rock videos on attitudes of violence against women. *Psychological Reports*, 64, 319–322.

Petrosino, A. (2005). From Martinson to meta-analysis: Research reviews and the U.S. offender treatment debate. *Evidence & Policy: A Journal of Research, Debate and Practice*, 1, 149–172.

Petrosino, A., Turpin-Petrosino, C., & Buehler, J. (2003). "Scared Straight" and other juvenile awareness programs for preventing juvenile delinquency (Updated C2 Review). *The Campbell Collaboration Reviews of Intervention and Policy Reviews (C2 RIPE)*. Philadelphia: Campbell Collaboration.

Pew Research Center for the People and the Press. (2000, April 19). *A year after Columbine public looks to parents more than schools to prevent violence*. Retrieved August 30, 2005, from http://people-press.org/reports/display.php3?ReportID=40

Phillips, D. P. (1979). Suicide, motor vehicle fatalities, and the mass media: Evidence toward a theory of suggestion. *American Journal of Sociology*, 84, 1150–1174.

Phillips, D. P. (1982). The impact of fictional television stories on U.S. adult fatalities: New evidence on the effect of the mass media on violence. *American Journal of Sociology*, 87, 1340–1359.

Phillips, D. P. (1983). The impact of mass media violence on U.S. homicides. *American Sociological Review*, 48, 560–568.

Pingree, S., & Hawkins, R. (1981). U.S. programs on Australian television: The cultivation effect. *Journal of Communication*, 21, 97–105.

Pipher, M. (1994). *Reviving Ophelia: Saving the selves of adolescent girls.* New York: Ballantine Books.

Piquero, A., Macintosh, R., & Hickman, M. (2002). The validity of a self-reported delinquency scale: Comparisons across gender, age, race, and place of residence. *Sociological Methods & Research, 30,* 492–529.

Pluymert, K. (2002). Best practices in developing exemplary mental health programs in schools. In A. Thomas & J. Grimes (Eds.). *Best Practices in School Psychology IV* (Vol. 2, pp. 963–975). Bethesda, MD: National Association of School Psychologists.

Pugh, T. (1999, August 8). DARE course loses backing in some cities. *San Jose Mercury News.*

Puriefoy, L. (2003). Paying the price of public education. *Connections,* Public Education Network. Retrieved August 29, 2005, from http://www.publiceducation.org/pdf/Publications/Connections/Fall2003_10_1.pdf

Rave, J. (2005, July 10). Family of Red Lake killer still trying to understand. *LaCrosse Tribune.* Retrieved July 21, 2005, from http://www.lacrossetribune.com/articles/2005/07/10/news/red_lake.txt

Redding, R. E. (2001). Sociopolitical diversity in psychology: The case for pluralism. *American Psychologist, 56,* 205.

Redding, R. E., Goldstein, N. E., & Heilbrun, K. (2005). Juvenile delinquency: Past and present. In K. Heilbrun, N. E. Goldstein, & R. E. Redding (Eds.) *Juvenile delinquency: Prevention, assessment, and intervention* (pp. 3–18). New York: Oxford University Press.

Redding, R. E., & Mrozoski, B. (2005). Adjudicatory and dispositional decision making in juvenile justice. In K. Heilbrun, N. E. S. Goldstein, & R. E. Redding (Eds.) *Juvenile delinquency: Prevention, assessment, and intervention* (pp. 232–256). New York: Oxford University Press.

Redding, R. E., & Shalf, S. M. (2001). The legal context of school violence: The effectiveness of federal, state, and local law enforcement efforts to reduce gun violence in schools. *Law & Policy, 23,* 297–343.

Reddy, M., Borum, R., Berglund, Vossekuil, Fein, & Modzeleski, W. (2001). Evaluating risk for targeted violence in schools: Comparing risk assessment, threat assessment, and other approaches. *Psychology in the Schools, 38,* 157–172.

Reiss, A. J., & Roth, J. A. (Eds.) (1993). *Understanding and preventing violence.* Washington, DC: National Academy Press.

Rhodes, J. (2002). *Stand by me: The risks and rewards of mentoring today's youth.* Cambridge, MA: Harvard University Press.

Rhodes, R. (2000, September 17). Hollow claims about fantasy violence. *New York Times,* Section 4, p. 19.

Riggs, N. R., & Greenberg, M. T. (2004). After-school youth development programs: A developmental-ecological model of current research. *Clinical Child and Family Psychology Review, 7,* 177–190.

Ringwalt, C., Greene, J., Ennett, S., Iachan, R., Clayton, R. R., & Leukefeld, C. G. (1994). *Past and future directions of the DARE program: An evaluation review: Draft final report.* Washington, DC: National Institute of Justice.

Robinson, J. P., & Bachman, J. G. (1972). Television viewing habits and aggression. In G. A. Comstock & E. A. Rubinstein (Eds.), *Television and social behavior: Television and adolescent aggressiveness: Vol. 3* (pp. 372–383). Washington, DC: Government Printing Office.

Rogers, R. (Ed.) (1997). *Clinical assessment of malingering and deception* (2nd ed.). New York: Guilford.

Roland, E. (2000). Bullying in school: Three national innovations in Norwegian schools in 15 years. *Aggressive Behavior, 26,* 135–143.

Roland, E., & Munthe, E. (1997). The 1996 Norwegian program for preventing and managing bullying in schools. *Irish Journal of Psychology, 18,* 233–247.

Romer, D., & McIntosh, M. (2005). The roles and perspectives of school mental health professionals in promoting adolescent mental health. *In* E. L. Evans, E. B. Foa, R. E. Gur, H. Hendin, C. P. O'Brien, M. E. P. Seligman, & B. T. Walsh (Eds.). *Treating and preventing adolescent mental health disorders: What we know and what we don't know.* (pp. 597–615). New York: Oxford University Press.

Rosenbaum, D., & Hanson, G. (1998). Assessing the effects of school-based drug education: A six-year multi-level analysis of project D.A.R.E. *Journal of Research in Crime and Delinquency, 35,* 381–412.

Rosenkoetter, L. I., Rosenkoetter, S., Ozretich, R. A., Acock, A. C. (2004). Mitigating the harmful effects of violent television. *Applied Developmental Psychology, 25,* 25–47.

Rosenthal, R. (1990). How are we doing in soft psychology? *American Psychologist, 45,* 775–777.

Rutherford Institute. (2003). *Tracking and fighting zero tolerance. 10/27/2003.* Retrieved July 4, 2005, from http://www.rutherford.org/articles_db/legal_features.asp?article_id=71

Saad, L. (1999, April 23). *Public views Littleton tragedy as sign of deeper problems in country.* Retrieved April 2, 2005, from http://www.gallup.com/poll/content/login.aspx?ci=3898

SAMHSA (n.d.). *The Olweus bullying prevention program.* Retrieved March 5, 2005, from http://modelprograms.samhsa.gov

Sarre, R. (2001). Beyond 'what works?'—A 25-year jubilee retrospective of Robert Martinson's famous article. *Australian and New Zealand Journal of Criminology, 34,* 38–46.

Schinke, S. P., Orlandi, M. A. & Cole, K. C. (1992). Boys & Girls Clubs in public housing developments: Prevention services for youth at risk. *Journal of Community Psychology: OSAP Special Issue,* 118–128.

Sewell, K. W., & Mendelsohn, M. (2000). Profiling potentially violent youth: Statistical and conceptual problems. *Children's services: Social policy, research, and practice, 3,* 147–169.

Shaffer, D., Gould, M. S., Fisher, P., Trautment, P., Moreau, D., Kleinman, M., & Flory, M. (1996). Psychiatric diagnosis in child and adolescent suicide. *Archives of General Psychiatry, 53,* 339–348.

Sheehan, P. W. (1983). Age trends and the correlates of children's television viewing. *Australian Journal of Psychology, 35,* 417–431.

Sheley, J. F., & Wright, J. D. (1993). *Gun acquisition and possession in selected juvenile samples.* NCJ—145326. Washington, DC: Office of Juvenile Justice and Delinquency Prevention.

Sherman, L. W., Gottfredson, D., MacKenzie, D., Eck, J., Reuter, P., & Bushway, S., (1997). *Preventing crime: What works, what doesn't, what's promising: A report to the United States Congress.* Washington, DC: National Institute of Justice. (Download at http://www.ncjrs.org/works/)

Sickmund, M, Snyder, H. N., & Poe-Yamagata, E. (1997). *Juvenile offenders and victims: 1997 update on violence.* Washington, DC: Office of Juvenile Justice and Delinquency Prevention.

Silvia, S., Thorne, J. T., & Tashjian, C. (1997). *School-based drug prevention programs: A longitudinal study in selected school districts, final report.* Research Triangle Park, NC: Research Triangle Institute.

Simons, L. S., & Turner, C. W. (1974). A further investigation of the weapons effect. *Personality and Social Psychology Bulletin,* 1, 186–188.

Simons, L. S., & Turner, C. W. (1976). Evaluation apprehension, hypothesis awareness, and the weapons effect. *Aggressive Behavior,* 2, 77–87.

Simmons, R. (2002). *Odd girl out: The hidden culture of aggression in girls.* Orlando, FL: Harcourt.

Sinclair, B., Hamilton, J., Gutman, B. Daft, J., Bolcki, D. (1998). *Report on state implementation of the Gun-Free Schools Act—School year 1996–97. Final Report.* Washington, DC: U.S. Department of Education.

Singer, J. L., & Singer, D. G. (1986). Television viewing and family communication style as predictors of children's imagination, restlessness, and aggression. *Journal of Social Issues,* 42, 107–124.

Singer, J. L., Singer, D. G., & Rapaczynski, W. S. (1984). Family patterns and television viewing as predictors of children's beliefs and aggression. *Journal of Communication,* 34, 73–89.

Skiba, R. J., & Knesting, K. (2001). Zero Tolerance, zero evidence: An analysis of school disciplinary practice. *New Directions for Youth Development: Theory, Practice, and Research,* 92, 17–43.

Skiba, R., & Noam, G. G. (Eds.) (2001). Zero tolerance: Can suspension and expulsion keep schools safe? In G. G. Noam (Ed.) *New directions for youth development,* No 92. San Francisco, CA: Jossey-Bass.

Skiba, R., & Peterson, R. (1999, March). The dark side of zero tolerance: Can punishment lead to safe schools? *Phi Delta Kappan.*

Skinner, B.F. (1971). *Beyond freedom and dignity.* New York: Bantam Books.

Smith, P. (1997). Bullying in schools: The UK experience and the Sheffield Anti-Bullying project. *The Irish Journal of Psychology,* 18, 191–201.

Smith, J. D., Schneider, B. H., Smith, P. K., & Ananiadou, K. (2004). The effectiveness of whole-school antibullying programs: A synthesis of evaluation research. *School Psychology Review,* 33, 547–560.

Smith, P. K., Ananiadou, K. & Cowie, H. (2003). *Canadian Journal of Psychiatry,* 48, 591–599.

Smith, P. K., Cowie, H. Olafsson, R. F., & Liefooghe, A. P. D. (2002). Definitions of bullying: A comparison of terms used, and age and gender differences, in a fourteen-country international comparison. *Child Development,* 73, 1119–1133.

Smith, P. K., Madsen, K. C. & Moody, J. C. (1999). What causes age decline in reports of being bullied at school? Towards a developmental analysis of risks of being bullied. *Educational Research,* 41, 267–285.

Smith, T. W. (2000). *1999 National gun policy survey of the National Opinion Research Center: Research findings.* Chicago: University of Chicago.

Snyder, H., Finnegan, T., Wan, Y., & Kang, W. (2002). *Easy access to the FBI's supplementary homicide reports: 1980–2000."* Online. Accessed January 10, 2005 at http://ojjdp.ncjrs.org/ojstatbb/ezashr

Snyder, H., & Sickmund, M. (1999). *Juvenile Offenders and Victims: 1999 National Report.* Washington, DC: U.S. Department of Justice, Office of Juvenile Justice and Delinquency Prevention.

Snyder, H. N., Sickmund, M., & Poe-Yamagata, E. (1997). Juvenile offenders and victims: 1997 update on violence. Washington, DC: Office of Juvenile Justice and Delinquency Prevention.

Solberg, M., & Olweus, D. (2003). Prevalence estimation of school bullying with the Olweus Bully/Victim Questionnaire. *Aggressive Behavior, 29,* 239–268.

Sommerfeld, M. (1993, August 4). About 10 percent of youths say they have fired a gun or been shot at, new survey finds. *Education Week, 12,* 20.

Southwest Educational Development Laboratory. (2003). *26 Scientifically based programs.* Retrieved June 7, 2005, from http://www.sedl.org/secac/sdfsc.html

Spiess, M. (2003). *Juveniles and drugs.* White House Office of National Drug Control Policy Fact Sheet. Rockville, MD: Drug Policy Information Clearinghouse. Retrieved August 24, 2005, from http://www.whitehousedrugpolicy.gov/publications/factsht/juvenile

Sprague, J., & Walker, H. (2000). Early identification and intervention for youth with anti-social and violent behavior. *Exceptional Children, 66,* 367–379.

St. Pierre, T. L., Mark, M. M., Kaltreider, D. L., & Aikin, K. J. (1997). Involving parents of high-risk youth in drug prevention: A three-year longitudinal study in Boys & Girls Clubs. *Journal of Early Adolescence, 17,* 21–50.

Stack, B. (2005, March 30). 'Scared straight' bid goes awry. *Pittsburgh Post Gazette.* Retrieved April 12, from http://www.post-gazette.com/pg/05089/479758.stm

Stanley, M. S. (1996). School uniforms and safety. *Education and Urban Society, 28,* 424–435.

Steinberg, J. (1999, January 3). "Storm warning: The coming crime wave is washed up." *The New York Times.*

Substance Abuse and Mental Health Services Administration. (2005). *SAMHSA effective programs.* Washington, DC: Author. Retrieved August 28, 2005, from http://model-programs.samhsa.gov/template_cf.cfm?page=effective_list

Sugai, G., Horner, R. H., Dunlap, G., Hieneman, M., Lewis, T. J., Nelson, C. M.,Scott, T., Liaupsin, C., Sailor, W., Turnbull, A. P., Turnbull, H. R. III, Wickham, D., Reuf, M., & Wilcox, B. (2000). Applying positive behavior support and functional behavioral assessment in schools. *Journal of Positive Behavior Interventions, 2,* 131–143.

Sugarmann, J., & Rand, K. (1992). *More gun dealers than gas stations: A study of federally licensed firearms dealers in America.* Washington, DC: Violence Policy Center.

Tebo, M. G. (2000, April). Zero tolerance, zero sense. *American Bar Association Journal.* www.abanet.org/journal/apr00/04FZERO.html

TheSanDiegoChannel.com (2002). *Survivors Remember '79 Cleveland Elementary Shooting.* Retrieved March 27, 2005, from http://www.10news.com/news/528926/detail.html

Thomas, M. H., & Drabman, R. S. (1975). Toleration of real life aggression as a function of exposure to televised violence and age of subject. *Merrill-Palmer Quarterly, 21,* 227–232.

Thornton, T. N., Craft, C. A., Dahlberg, L. L., Lynch, B. S., & Baer, K. (2000). *Best practices of youth violence prevention: A sourcebook for community action.* Atlanta, GA: Centers for Disease Control and Prevention, National Center for Injury Prevention and Control.

Trump, K. S. (1998). *Practical school security. Basic guidelines for safe and secure schools.* Thousand Oaks, CA: Corwin Press.

Trump, K. S. (2000). *Classroom killers? Hallway hostages? How schools can prevent and manage school crises.* Thousand Oaks, CA: Corwin Press.

Turn Off the Violence. (2005). *Facts & Quotes.* Retrieved August 1, 2005, from http://www.turnofftheviolence.org/facts&quotes.htm

Turner, C. W., Hesse, B. W., & Peterson-Lewis, S. (1986). Naturalistic studies of the long-term effects of television violence. *Journal of Social Issues, 42,* 51–73.

Turner, C. W., & Simons, L. S. (1974). Effects of subject sophistication and evaluation apprehension on aggressive responses to weapons. *Journal of Personality and Social Psychology, 30,* 341–348.

Turner, C. W., Simons, L. S., Berkowitz, L., & Frodi, A. (1977). The stimulating and inhibiting effects of weapons on aggressive behavior. *Aggressive Behavior, 3,* 355–378.

Underwood, M. K. (2003). Social aggression among girls. New York: Guilford Press.

U.S. Department of Justice. (2004). *The nation's two crime measures.* Retrieved August 6, 2005, from http://www.ojp.usdoj.gov/bjs/pub/pdf/ntcm.pdf

U.S. Department of Justice. (2005). *Criminal victimization in the United States, 2003 statistical tables.* Retrieved August 6, 2005, from http://www.ojp.usdoj.gov/bjs/abstract/cvusst .htm#full

U.S. Census Bureau. (2004). *Educational attainment in the United States: 2003.* Retrieved August 21, 2005, from http://usgovinfo.about.com/gi/dynamic/offsite.htm?zi=1/XJ &sdn=usgovinfo&zu=http%3A%2F%2Fwww.census.gov%2Fprod%2F2004pubs%2 Fp20-550.pdf

U.S. Department of Education. (1998). *Non-regulatory guidance for implementing the SDFS-CA principles of effectiveness.* Washington, DC: Author.

U.S. Department of Education. (2001). *2001 Exemplary and promising school-based programs that promote safe, disciplined and drug-free schools.* Retrieved June 2, 2005, from http:// www.ed.gov/admins/lead/safety/exemplary01/panel.html

U.S. Department of Education. (2002). *Exemplary and promising, safe disciplined, and drug-free schools 2001.* Jessup, MD: Author. Retrieved June 7, 2005, from http://www.ed .gov/admins/lead/safety/exemplary01/exemplary01.pdf

U.S. Department of Education. (2003). *When schools stay open late: The national evaluation of the 21st century community learning centers program.* (Publication No. ED—99-CO— 0134). Jessup, MD: Author.

U.S. Department of Education. (2004). *Report on the implementation of the gun-free schools act in the states and outlying areas for school year 2001–2002,* Washington, DC: Author.

U.S. Department of Health and Human Services (2001). *Youth violence: A report of the Surgeon General.* Rockville, MD: Author.

U.S. Department of Health and Human Services. (1999). *Mental health: A report of the Surgeon General.* Rockville, MD: Author.

U.S. Department of Health and Human Services. (2000). *Federal activities addressing violence in schools.* Retrieved August 13, 2005, from http://www.cdc.gov/HealthyYouth/ injury/pdf/violenceactivities.pdf

U.S. Department of Justice (2000). Challenging the myths. *1999 National report series. Juvenile Justice Bulletin.* Washington, DC: Author.

U.S. House Judiciary Committee (1999, May 13). *Hearing: Youth Violence and Culture.* Serial No. 20. GPO Stock No. 552–070–25232–1. Retrieved August 30, 2005, from http://commdocs.house.gov/committees/judiciary/hju62441.000/hju62441_0f.htm

U.S. Public Health Service. (2000). *Report of the Surgeon General's Conference on Children's Mental Health: A National Action Agenda.* Washington, DC: Department of Health and Human Services.

U.S. Senate Committee on the Judiciary. (1999). Children, violence, and the media: A report for parents and policymakers. Retrieved March 17, 2006 from http://judiciary.senate.gov/mediavio.htm

U.S. Surgeon General's Scientific Advisory Committee on Television and Social Behavior (1972). *Television and growing up: The impact of televised violence.* (DHEW Publication No. HSM 72–9086). Washington, DC: U.S. Government Printing Office.

Unnever, J. & Cornell, D. (2003). The culture of bullying in middle school. *Journal of School Violence, 2,* 5–27.

Unnever, J. & Cornell, D. (2004). Middle school victims of bullying: Who reports being bullied? *Aggressive Behavior, 30,* 373–388.

Upton, J. (2000, February 27). D.A.R.E.: Failing our kids. *Detroit News.* www.cerd.org/press/press09.html

USA Today. (2005, July 14). *Clinton seeks 'Grand Theft Auto' probe.* Retrieved July 21, 2005, from http://www.usatoday.com/news/washington/2005–07–14-clinton-game_x.htm?csp=15

Virginia Department of Education. (1995). *Report on acts of violence and substance abuse: 1993–94 School year.* Richmond, VA: Author.

Virginia Department of Education. (2004). *Annual report on Discipline, Crime, and Violence: School year 2002–2003.* Richmond, VA: Author.

Virginia State Police (2005). *Crime in Virginia 2004.* Richmond, VA: Author.

Volokh, A. with Snell, L. (n.d.). *School Violence Prevention: Strategies to Keep Schools Safe (Unabridged).* Policy Study 234, Reason Public Policy Institute. Retrieved August 1, 2005, from http://www.rppi.org/ps234.html

Vossekuil, B., Fein, R. A., Reddy, M., Borum, R., & Modzeleski, W. (2002). *The final report and findings of the Safe School Initiative: Implications for the prevention of school attacks in the United States.* Washington, DC: U.S. Secret Service and U.S. Department of Education.

Wagner, E. F., Tubman, J. G., & Gil, A. G. (2004). Implementing school-based substance abuse interventions: Methodological dilemmas and recommended solutions. *Addiction, 99,* 106–119.

Waite, B. M., Hillbrand, M., & Foster, H. G. (1992). Reduction of aggressive behavior after removal of Music Television. *Hospital and Community Psychiatry, 43,* 173–175.

Webster-Stratton, C. (1999). *How to promote social and emotional competence in young children.* London: Sage Publishers.

Webster-Stratton, C. & Hammond, M. (1997). Treating children with early-onset conduct problems: A comparison of child and parent training interventions. *Journal of Consulting and Clinical Psychology, 65,* 93–109.

Webster-Stratton, C., Mihalic, S., Fagan, A., Arnold, D., Taylor, T, & Tingley, C. (2001). The incredible years series. In D. S. Elliott (Series Ed.), *Blueprints for violence preven-*

tion. Boulder, CO: Center for the Study and Prevention of Violence, Institute of Behavioral Science, University of Colorado at Boulder.

Wegner, D. (2002). *The illusion of free will.* Cambridge, MA: Bradford Books.

Weinstein, R. S., Gregory, A., & Stambler, M. J. (2004). Intractable self-fulfilling prophecies: Fifty years after Brown v. Board of Education. *American Psychologist, 59,* 511–520.

Weisberg, H., Krosnick, J. A., & Bowen, B. (1996). *Introduction to survey research, polling, and data analysis.* Thousand Oaks, CA: Sage.

Weisbrot, D. M., & Ettinger, A. B. (2002). Aggression and violence in mood disorders. *Child & Adolescent Psychiatric Clinics of North America, 11,* 649–672.

Weiss, B., Harris, V., & Catron, T. (2004). Development and initial validation of the peer-report measure of internalizing and externalizing behavior. *Journal of Abnormal Child Psychology, 30,* 285–294.

West, S. L., & O'Neal, K. K. (2004). Project D.A.R.E. outcome effectiveness revisited. *American Journal of Public Health, 94,* 1027–1029.

Wester, S. R., Crown, C. L., Quatman, G. L., & Heesacker, M. (1997). The influence of sexually violent rap music on attitudes of men with little prior exposure. *Psychology of Women Quarterly, 21,* 497–508.

Whitaker D. J., Rosenbluth, B., Valle, L.A., & Sanchez, E. (2004). Expect Respect: A School-based intervention to promote awareness and effective responses to bullying and sexual harassment. *In* D. L., Espelage & S. M. Swearer (Eds.). *Bullying in American Schools: A Social-Ecological Perspective on Prevention and Intervention* (pp. 327–350). Hillsdale, NJ: Lawrence Erlbaum and Associates.

Wilkinson, D. L., & Fagan, J. (2001). What we know about gun use among adolescents. *Clinical Child and Family Psychology Review, 4,* 109–132.

Williams, F., & Cornell, D. (2005, August). *Student willingness to seek help for threats of violence.* Poster presented at the American Psychological Association Annual Convention. Washington, DC.

Williams, S. S., Mulhall, P. F., Reis, J. S., & DeVille, J. O. (2002). Adolescents carrying handguns and taking them to school: Psychosocial correlates among public school students in Illinois. *Journal of Adolescence, 25,* 551–567.

Williams, T. M. (1986). *The impact of television: A natural experiment in three communities.* NY: Praeger.

Wilson, J. Q. (1995). Crime and public policy. In. J. Q. Wilson & J. Petersilia (Eds.) *Crime* (pp. 489–510). San Francisco: Institute for Contemporary Studies Press.

Wilson, J., & Herrnstein, R. (1985). *Crime & human nature.* New York: Simon and Schuster.

Wilson, S. J., & Lipsey, M. W. (2000). Wilderness challenge programs for delinquent youth: A meta-analysis of outcome evaluations. *Evaluation and Program Planning, 23,* 1–12.

Wilson, S. J., Lipsey, M. W., & Derzon, J. H. (2003). The effects of school-based intervention programs on aggressive behavior: A meta-analysis. *Journal of Consulting and Clinical Psychology, 71,* 136–149.

Wintemute, G. (2000). Guns and gun violence. In A. Blumstein and J. Wallman (Eds.) *The crime drop in America* (pp. 45–96). New York: Cambridge University Press.

Wiseman, R. (2002). *Queen bees and wannabes: Helping your daughter survive cliques, gossip, boyfriends, and other realities of adolescence.* New York: Three Rivers Press.

Witkin, G. (1991, April 8). Kids who kill; disputes once settled with fists are now settled with guns. *U.S. News & World Report.* 110, 26 (7).

Wolfgang, M., Figlio, R., & Sellin, T. (1972). *Delinquency in a birth cohort*. Chicago: University of Chicago Press.

Woodard, IV, E. H., & Gridina, N. (2000). *Media in the home 2000: The fifth annual survey of parents and children*. Annenberg Public Policy Center of the University of Pennsylvania. Accessed 1–2–05 from http://www.annenbergpublicpolicycenter.org

Zenere, III, F. J. (2005). Tragedy at Red Lake: Epilogue. *Communiqué*, 34, 6.

Zernike, K. (2001, May 17). Crackdown on threats in schools fails a test. *The New York Times*, p. A21.

Zimring, F. (1998). *American youth violence*. New York: Oxford University Press.

Zuzul, M. (1989). *The weapons effect and child aggression: A field experiment*. Unpublished doctoral dissertation. Croatia: University of Zagreb.

Author Index

Achenbach, T. M., 94, 213, 225
Acock, A.C., 118, 234
Adelman, H. S., 198, 213
Advancement Project and The Civil
    Rights Project, 7, 170, 210, 213
Aikin, K. J., 138, 236
Alexander, J., 140, 213
Alexander, J. F., 140, 213, 226
American Academy of Child Adolescent
    Psychiatry, 213
American Academy of Family Physicians,
    213
American Academy of Pediatrics, 213
American Medical Association, 213
American Psychiatric Association, 78, 193,
    213
American Psychological Association, 15,
    174, 213
American School Health Association, 59,
    61, 213
Ananiadou, K., 4, 90, 92, 95, 96, 235
Anderson, C. A., 5, 75, 108, 110, 111,
    114, 116, 117, 118, 213, 214, 216
Anderson, R. N., 21, 22, 214
Angold, A., 216
Armstrong, F. D., 70, 223
Arnold, D., 139, 237
Asher, K. N., 222
Associated Press, 32, 214
Atkin, C. K., 102, 103, 214, 228
Atkinson, A. J., 142, 201, 214
Austin, J., 12, 149, 214

Bachman, J. G., 102, 146, 214, 233
Baer, K., 237

Baker, E., 215, 155
Ballard, M. E., 110, 214
Bandura, A., 101, 214
Barkley, R. A., 139, 214
Barnett, W. S., 209, 214
Barrett, P. M., 131, 214
Bartholow, B. D., 75, 111, 213, 214
Bartini, M., 94, 232
Bartolomucci, C. L., 79, 224
Barton, C., 140, 213
Bass, D., 131, 226
Bates, M. P., 62, 222
Baum, K., 219
Beane, A., 79, 215
Beauvais, F., 231
Beck, A. T., 131, 215
Becker, E., 15, 16, 215
Beland, K., 223
Belkin, L., 39, 215
Belson, W. A., 102, 215
Benedek, E., 49, 219
Benjamin, Jr., A. J., 75, 213, 214
Berglund, M. L., 217, 233
Berkowitz, L., 5, 53, 74, 75, 76, 102, 213,
    215, 227, 237
Billingham, S., 139, 228
Bjorkqvist, K., 80, 215
Blaya, C., 219
Blumstein, A., 11, 74, 215
Bock, R., 83, 215
Bolcki, D., 7, 64, 235
Bolyard, M., 149, 214
Bonda, P., 18, 215
Bonnie, R., 49, 145, 195, 215
Borduin, C. M., 224

Subject Index

DATE DUE

DEC 15 '07			
2010			
JAN 0 4 2011			
MAR 0 6 2012			